Furthering Interfaith Biblical Scholarship

Furthering Interfaith Biblical Scholarship

A Festschrift in Memory of
André LaCocque

Edited by
DOREEN M. McFARLANE

☙PICKWICK *Publications* · Eugene, Oregon

FURTHERING INTERFAITH BIBLICAL SCHOLARSHIP
A Festschrift in Memory of André LaCocque

Copyright © 2024 Wipf and Stock Publishers. All rights reserved. Except for brief quotations in critical publications or reviews, no part of this book may be reproduced in any manner without prior written permission from the publisher. Write: Permissions, Wipf and Stock Publishers, 199 W. 8th Ave., Suite 3, Eugene, OR 97401.

Pickwick Publications
An Imprint of Wipf and Stock Publishers
199 W. 8th Ave., Suite 3
Eugene, OR 97401

www.wipfandstock.com

PAPERBACK ISBN: 978-1-6667-7681-2
HARDCOVER ISBN: 978-1-6667-7682-9
EBOOK ISBN: 978-1-6667-7683-6

Cataloguing-in-Publication data:

Names: McFarlane, Doreen M., editor.

Title: Furthering interfaith biblical scholarship : a festschrift in memory of André LaCocque / Doreen M. McFarlane.

Description: Eugene, OR: Pickwick Publications, 2024. | Includes bibliographical references.

Identifiers: ISBN 978-1-6667-7681-2 (paperback). | ISBN 978-1-6667-7682-9 (hardcover). | ISBN 978-1-6667-7683-6 (ebook).

Subjects: LCSH: LaCocque, André. | Bible. OT—Theology. | Bible. OT—Criticism, interpretation, etc. | Dialogue—Religious aspects.

Classification: BS1192.6 F91 2024 (print) | BS1192.6 (ebook)

06/10/24

Unless otherwise noted, Scripture quotations are from the New Revised Standard Version Bible, copyright © 1989 National Council of the Churches of Christ in the United States of America. Used by permission. All rights reserved worldwide.

Scripture quotations marked (NKJV) are taken from the New King James Version®. Copyright © 1982 by Thomas Nelson. Used by permission. All rights reserved.

This volume is dedicated to Dr. LaCocque's beloved family of whom he was so proud: his sons Pierre-Emmanuel and Michel, his daughter Elizabeth, their spouses and children, and to the memory of his beloved wife, Claire (née Tournay) (1928–2011), who brought him a lifetime of joy, wisdom, and companionship.

Contents

Preface		ix
List of Abbreviations		xiii
Contributors		xv
1	In Honor of André LaCocque, Our Teacher W. Dow Edgerton	1
2	Jewish and Christian Views of the Messiah John J. Collins	3
3	Two Resurrected Pharisees: Saul of Tarsus and Yoḥanan ben Zakkai and the Beginnings of Christianity and Rabbinic Judaism Laurence L. Edwards	17
4	"A Question That Is Left Hanging" André LaCocque and Paul Ricoeur: A Dialogue for Our Time Joseph Edelheit and James Moore	36
5	Imagine I Am Sitting There: An Interreligious Perspective on Matthew 23 Rachel S. Mikva	45
6	Isaiah 52:13—53:12: The Suffering Servant in Judaism, Christianity, and Modern Thought Brian Britt	58
7	Gender, Animality, and Ecology in Genesis 2–3: Reflections on the Hermeneutics of Subversion Ken Stone	75

CONTENTS

8 The Dialectic of Praxis and the Theology of Work 93
   Bo-Myung Seo

9 Creative and Destructive Work: Greek and Slavic Distributaries
   of Hebrew Biblical Lifeblood 108
   Isaiah (Yeshayahu) Gruber

10 Wedded to Power: Two Biblical Women Married to Kings 130
   Doreen M. McFarlane

11 Nonrefoulement: Responding to Asylum-seekers through the Prism
   of Subversive Stories: A Study of Three Trials of Innocence 139
   Craig B. Mousin

Books of André LaCocque 177

Preface

IF YOU ACQUIRED THIS Festschrift written in honor of the late Dr. André LaCocque because you had the privilege of knowing him in person, you will enjoy reading these chapters as you recall all that beloved André meant to you personally as a friend or family member, or what his words have brought to your own scholarly or ministerial work. Every chapter herein is written by a well-known scholar (Jewish or Christian) who knew or was connected with him through scholarship. And each chapter, in some substantial way, forwards André's own scholarship. If you did not know him and are not familiar with his work, then you are in for an eye-opening treat! These chapters are filled with his quotations, as well as his advanced and life-giving answers, ideas, and suggestions! These will provide a real glimpse into his profound thinking, deep biblical understanding, and delightful personality. In reading this book, you will also have the opportunity to see how his friends and former students are moving his scholarship forward in such exciting areas as Jewish-Christian dialogue and female-male relations, as well as intertestamental and interdisciplinary studies.

A long and fruitful life describes that of André LaCocque. Predeceased by his beloved wife, Claire, who passed away in 2011, his passing in 2022 at the age of 94 marked a great loss to all who knew and loved him and who greatly appreciated his insights. These include his children: Michel (Jeannie Roziak), Pierre-Emmanuel (Victoria Quero), and daughter Elizabeth (Andrew Brunner), and grandchildren, David, Rebecca, Jeremy, Jonathan, Natalie, Daniel, and Anne. He is also fondly remembered by the countless scholars, former students, and followers who so greatly treasured his words and his friendship. André had a profound understanding of the biblical texts and was enormously gifted in teaching and writing about them.

PREFACE

André's calling began when, as a young man, his father, a Christian pastor, chose in solidarity with the Jews, in the midst of the Second World War, to convert to Judaism and move to Israel. André chose to remain Christian because of "the person of Jesus." Deeply moved, however, by his father's action, André chose to dedicate his life to advancing Jewish and Christian understanding. Right up till the time of his passing, he continued to grow, teach, and write; expanding his understanding of all things theological and relational and especially leading the way in Jewish-Christian understanding.[1]

During a sabbatical from the Faculté Universitaire Théologie Protestante de Bruxelles to which he returned during 1967–68, he taught at Chicago Theological Seminary to which he was permanently appointed in 1968, and where he served until his retirement in 1996. While at CTS, he met Otto Betz and, together, they established a Center of Jewish–Christian Studies, as a part of the CTS Doctorate of Religion program, with the participation of scholars from the Oriental Institute (University of Chicago) and Spertus College of Judaica. This later, in 2010, broadened to become the present Center for Jewish, Christian, and Islamic Studies.

André's list of publications is lengthy. His landmark book, *Thinking Biblically: Exegetical and Hermeneutical Studies*, co-written with philosopher Paul Ricoeur, brought together the genres of philosophical hermeneutics and biblical studies. This book won the prestigious University of Chicago Press Gordon J. Laing Award. Within André's publication legacy, are a number of volumes that address the lives and work of biblical women. These include *Feminine Unconventional: Four Subversive Figures in Israel's Tradition* (1990), *Romance, She Wrote: a Hermeneutical Essay on the Song of Songs* (1998), *Ruth: A Continental Commentary* (2004) translated by K. C. Hanson, and *Esther Regina: a Bakhtinian Reading* (2008). He also wrote many books on biblical themes including Genesis, Daniel, and Jonah. His final volume, written in his 90s, was, in many ways, his crowning achievement. *Work and Creativity: A Philosophical Study from Creation to Postmodernity* (2019), offers a model for future interdisciplinary scholarship—in this case, biblical studies interacting with philosophy.

Each chapter in this Festschrift is written by a scholar who was profoundly influenced by André LaCocque. Some were his colleagues, some

---

1. Daniel Patte, obituary for André LaCocque, published by Society of Biblical Literature (2022). Deepest thanks go to Daniel Patte for writing such an accurate and thoughtful obituary of Dr. LaCocque.

his students, and many his friends. All were deeply influenced by his writings. Every chapter is intended to engage with his work and his words and, in doing so, to forward the scholarly discourse. André, we trust, would have been pleased to know that scholarship is moving along in ways that enhance human relationships and human understanding.

DOREEN M MCFARLANE

Abbreviations

AB	Anchor Bible
b.	Babylonian Talmud (Babli)
BAGD	Walter Bauer, W. F. Arndt, F. W. Gingrich, and Fredrick W. Danker, *Greek–English Lexicon of the New Testament and Other Early Christian Literature,* 2nd ed. Chicago: University of Chicago Press, 1979 (Bauer-Arndt-Gingrich-Danker)
BH	Biblia Hebraica
BibInt	Biblical Interpretation Series
BIA	Board of Immigration Appeals
CP	Constantinople Pentateuch
DJD	Discoveries in the Judean Desert
ErJb	*Eranos-Jahrbuch*
ESJ	*European Scientific Journal*
IRFA	International Religious Freedom Act of 1998—passed to promote religious freedom as a foreign policy of the United States, to promote religious freedom in countries which engage in or tolerate violations of religious freedom, and to advocate on the behalf of individuals persecuted for their religious beliefs and activities in foreign countries
JBQ	*Jewish Bible Quarterly*
JES	*Journal of Ecumenical Studies*
JBL	*Journal of Biblical Literature*

ABBREVIATIONS

JJS	*Journal of Jewish Studies*
JR	*Journal of Religion*
JSIJ	*Jewish Studies: An Internet Journal*
JSNT	*Journal for the Study of the New Testament*
JSOT	*Journal for the Study of the Old Testament*
JSOTSup	Journal for the Study of the Old Testament Supplement Series
LSJ	Henry George Liddell, Robert Scott, and Henry Stuart Jones. *A Greek-English Lexicon.* 9th ed. With revised supplement. Oxford: Clarendon, 1996
LXX	Septuagint—Greek Old Testament/Prime Testament
NIJC	The National Justice Center (legal services to low-income immigrants)
OED	*Oxford English Dictionary*
OTL	Old Testament Library
RB	*Revue biblique*
RÉJ	*Revue d'étudie Juive*
SPCK	Society for Promoting Christian Knowledge
STDJ	Studies on the Texts of the Desert of Judah
t.	Tosefta
TDNT	*Theological Dictionary of the New Testament.* Edited by Gerhard Kittel and Gerhard Friedrich. Translated by Geoffrey W. Bromily. 10 vols. Grand Rapids: Eerdmans, 1964–1976
TDOT	*Theological Dictionary of the Old Testament.* Edited by G. Johannes Botterweck and Helmer Ringgren. Translated by John T. Willis et al. 8 vols. Grand Rapids: Eerdmans, 1974–2006
TRAC	An open-source, web-based project management and bug tracking system
UNHCR	United Nations High Commissioner for Refugees
WUNT	Wissenschaftliche Untersuchungen zum Neuen Testament

Contributors

BRIAN BRITT. PhD University of Chicago, Professor of Religion and Culture at Virginia Tech

JOHN J. COLLINS. PhD Harvard University, Holmes Professor of Old Testament Criticism and Interpretation Emeritus, Yale University

LAURENCE L. EDWARDS. PhD Chicago Theological Seminary, Rabbi, recently retired lecturer in Religious Studies at DePaul University, University of Illinois at Chicago, and Hebrew Seminary (Skokie)

JOSEPH A. EDELHEIT. DMin University of Chicago Divinity School, 2021 Alumnus of the Year, Rabbi, Emeritus Professor of Religious and Jewish Studies at St Cloud University

W. DOW EDGERTON. PhD Chicago Theological Seminary, Ordained UCC minister, Professor of Ministry Emeritus of Chicago Theological Seminary

YESHAYA (ISAIAH) GRUBER. PhD Georgetown University, Professor of Jewish History and Culture at the Israel Bible Center

DOREEN M MCFARLANE. PhD Chicago Theological Seminary, Ordained Lutheran pastor (ELCIC), retired Professor Bible and Biblical Languages Nanjing Seminary, Shanghai University. Former Core Faculty South Florida Center for Theological Studies, Miami and Orlando; adjunct St. Thomas University, Miami

RACHEL S. MIKVA. PhD Jewish Theological Seminary, Rabbi, Herman E. Schaalman Professor of Jewish Studies and Senior Faculty Fellow of the Interreligious Institute, Chicago Theological Seminary

CONTRIBUTORS

JAMES MOORE. Ordained Lutheran Clergy (ELCA), Senior Research Professor of Theology at Valparaiso University

CRAIG B. MOUSIN. Ordained UCC minister, lawyer—JD University of Illinois, adjunct faculty DePaul University's College of Law, Grace School of Applied Diplomacy, and its Refugee and Forced Migration Studies program

BO MYUNG SEO. PhD Chicago Theological Seminary, Professor of Theology and Cultural Criticism, Chicago Theological Seminary

KEN STONE. PhD Vanderbilt, Distinguished Service Professor and Professor of Bible, Culture and Hermeneutics at Chicago Theological Seminary

1

In Honor of André LaCocque, Our Teacher

W. DOW EDGERTON

"Ho, everyone who thirsts, come to the waters; and those who have no money, come, buy and eat! Come, buy wine and milk without money and without price..."

(Isa 55:1 NKJV)

> An ordinary classroom, on an ordinary day:
> A ring of tables, students, a teacher.
> In front of each student a book, waiting;
> In front of the teacher the same book.
> He opens the book, lightly touches the page
>   and withdraws his hand.
> Although he knows the words by heart
> He will read them aloud, because reading matters.
> Although we could read for ourselves we will listen,
>   because listening matters.
> Everyone is listening, even the teacher who reads.

Furthering Interfaith Biblical Scholarship

Who knows what word will pronounce itself?
And if we listen, perhaps we will actually hear,
There, in an ordinary classroom, on an ordinary day.

There, in an ordinary classroom, on an ordinary day
Through the page a door opens, and beyond the door,
The Word swirling and falling, thirsty earth
    quenched by rain and snow.
Beyond the door, wine and milk,
Seed for the sower, bread for the eater,
More than enough, and even more:
Hills and mountains singing, trees of the field
Clapping their hands in joy, in peace.
There, there, through the page, beyond the open door,
The beginning of the world, and the world to come.

There, there.

Here.

2

Jewish and Christian Views of the Messiah

JOHN J. COLLINS

"Any discussion of the problems relating to Messianism is a delicate matter," wrote Gershom Scholem, "for it is here that the essential conflict between Judaism and Christianity has developed and continues to exist."[1] For Scholem the essential difference was that "Judaism . . . has always maintained a concept of redemption as an event which takes place publicly, on the stage of history" while "Christianity conceives of redemption as an event in the spiritual and unseen realm, an event which reflected in the soul, in the private world of each individual, and which effects an inner transformation which need not correspond to anything outside."[2] Other scholars have articulated the difference in different ways.[3] Key issues in the debate concern the divinity of the messiah, the use of violence, the role of suffering, and more generally the goals and objectives that a messiah should pursue.

---

1. Scholem, *The Messianic Idea*, 1.
2. Scholem, *The Messianic Idea*, 1.
3. For an overview see Novenson, *The Grammar of Messianism*, 187–216.

While the contrast articulated by Scholem has enjoyed broad acceptance, it has also been subjected to criticism. Especially since the discovery of the Dead Sea Scrolls it has been widely recognized that a variety of messianic figures were expected around the turn of the era.[4] The Community Rule famously speaks of "the coming of a prophet and the messiahs of Aaron and Israel" (1QS 9:11). The Damascus Document (CD) refers to "the messiah of Aaron and Israel" (CD 12:23; 14:10; 19:10. Compare "a messiah from Aaron and from Israel" in CD 20:1). This phrase, too, must be understood to refer to two messiahs, one of whom was a priest.[5] As F. M. Cross argued cogently, the mention of both Aaron and Israel would be redundant if only one messiah was in question.[6] It has long been known that the "one like a son of man" in Dan 7:13 was interpreted as a messiah in the first century CE, in Jewish apocalyptic texts as well as in the Gospels.[7] Prophets could also be called "anointed ones" or "messiahs" (CD 2:12; 1QM 11:7).

In light of this diversity, some scholars conclude that Scholem's contrast of two messianic ideas is overdrawn. So, Loren Stuckenbruck writes: "If we allow for such diversity in both early Christian and Jewish communities, there is no reason to suppose that, beyond the reconciliation of 'Messiah' by Christians to the experiences of Jesus, Jewish and Christian ideas were necessarily very distinct from one another."[8]

A more fundamental critique has been offered by Matthew Novenson, who disputes the characterization of messianism as an idea.[9] For Novenson, messianism should be viewed in terms of linguistic usage:

> By 'messiah language,' I simply mean discourse that uses the Hebrew word משיח (transliterated 'messiah,' translated 'anointed one') and its translation equivalencies (Aramaic משיחא, Greek μεσσιας, χριστος, Latin *Christus* and *unctus* and so on).[10]

Jewish and Christian usage, then is part of a continuum, all of which relies on allusion to older scriptural texts. Novenson recognizes that "many

---

4. Collins, *The Scepter and the Star*. Zimmermann, *Messianische Texte*.

5. See Collins, *The Scepter and the Star*, 79–83.

6. Cross, "Some Notes," 14.

7. Collins, *Daniel*, 79–105. Note the essay of LaCocque, "The Vision of the Eagle in 4 Esdras," 237–58.

8. Stuckenbruck, "Messianic Ideas," 90–113.

9. Novenson, *The Grammar of Messianism*, 1–33. Compare Novenson, *Christ Among the Messiahs*.

10. Novenson, *The Grammar of Messianism*, 29–30.

figures called *messiah* go by other names as well in their respective texts, and that these wider contexts are relevant to the study of messiah language per se."[11] But this concession complicates his linguistic approach, if it does not undercut it entirely. It is further complicated by the fact that the older usage of the term משיה in the Hebrew Bible does not have the eschatological overtones that the term acquired in postbiblical usage. When the king in Psalm 2 is called a משיח he is not thereby designated as a "messiah" in the later sense of the term. Novenson rightly recognizes that messianic discourse is closely tied to specific scriptural texts, but the repertoire of messianic prophecies in the New Testament departs in some cases from that of pre-Christian Judaism and it makes a difference which texts are invoked.

In fairness to Scholem, when he wrote of "the messiah" he meant the Davidic, royal messiah who has always enjoyed primary importance in Jewish tradition. As is clear from the Dead Sea Scrolls, the Davidic messiah, or messiah of Israel, had a very distinct profile in Jewish texts from the Hasmonean and early Roman periods.[12] He was conceived as a warrior, who would kill the wicked with the breath of his lips (Isa 11:2), drive out the Gentiles, and restore the kingdom of Israel. This profile is quite different from that of Christ in the Gospels. In that respect, Scholem was correct. But there were other profiles of messiah on offer in Second Temple Judaism, so a contrast between the standard view of the Davidic messiah and the New Testament is not necessarily a contrast between Jewish and Christian views *tout courte*. The followers of Jesus were also Jewish, and they attempted to make sense of their leader by drawing on Jewish tradition. To appreciate how they did this, however, we must attend not only to the language they used but to the functions expressed in that language and the social realities to which it referred.

THE DIVINITY OF THE MESSIAH

The Christian claim that Christ was divine was controversial already in antiquity. In Justin's *Dialogue with Trypho*, the Jewish interlocutor insists that "we all expect that Christ will be a man [born] of men."[13] On the Christian

---

11. Novenson, *The Grammar of Messianism*, 30, in acknowledgement of the argument of Collins, *The Scepter and the Star*, 16–17. Fitzmyer, *The One Who is to Come*, is unwilling to make that concession and clings more rigidly to the use of specific terms.

12. See Collins, *The Scepter and the Star*, 77–78.

13. Justin, *Dial* 49. Trans. Coxe, *The Apostolic Fathers*, 219.

side, the *Epistle of Barnabas* declares that Christ is "not son of man, but son of God, manifested in a type in the flesh."[14] But while Christianity eventually proclaimed Christ "one in being with the Father" in the Nicene Creed, the New Testament references to Jesus as Son of God did not transgress the bounds of Jewish tradition.[15] The expression "son of God" was used in various ways in Judaism. It could refer to Israel, collectively, as in Exod 4:22–23 and Hos 11:1, or to a righteous person, as in Wis 2:13, 16, 18. But it was also virtually a messianic title.

The basis of the messianic usage is clear in Psalm 2, where God says to his anointed king: "you are my son; today I have begotten you." It is also reflected in the promise to David in 2 Sam 7:14: "I will be a father to him and he will be a son to me." The latter passage is cited in 4Q174, the Florilegium, where it is referred to "the shoot of David" who will arise in Zion in the latter days. Other occurrences in the Dead Sea Scrolls are controversial, but unnecessarily so. In 1QSa 2:11–12 there is now consensus that the text reads "when God begets (יוליד)." Many scholars emend the text to יוליך, "brings," but "begets" is a clear allusion to Psalm 2.[16] The so-called "Aramaic Apocalypse," 4Q246 speaks of a figure of whom it is said: "Son of God he shall be called and they will name him Son of the Most High." It goes on to speak of an everlasting kingdom. By far the closest parallel to this language is found in the story of the annunciation in Luke 1:30–35, where Mary is told that her son "will be great and will be called the Son of the Most High, and the Lord God will give to him the throne of his ancestor David . . . he will be called the Son of God." Despite numerous attempts to evade the messianic reading of 4Q246, it is overwhelmingly probable that there too the reference is to the Davidic messiah.[17] The Davidic messiah is also called God's son in 4 Ezra 7:28–9. While it is sometimes argued that the Latin *filius* may reflect the Greek *pais*, which can mean "servant" as well as "son," it should be noted that in 4 Ezra 13 the "man from the sea" who takes his stand on a mountain to do battle with the nations is clearly modeled on the king/messiah of Psalm 2.[18]

14. *Barn* 12.10–11.

15. Yarbro Collins and Collins, *King and Messiah as Son of God*. Hurtado, *Ancient Jewish Monotheism*.

16. See Bloch, Ben Dov and Stökl Ben Ezra, "The Rule of the Congregation," 19. They favor emendation. The emendation was originally proposed by J. T. Milik.

17. For full discussion see Yarbro Collins and Collins, *King and Messiah as Son of God*, 48–74.

18. See further Collins, "The Interpretation of Psalm 2," 97–99.

To say that the messiah is Son of God, in a Jewish context, is not necessarily to deny that he is a man born of men, or indeed to say anything about the manner of his birth. The point is that he stands in a special relationship with God, one that is expressed in Psalm 2 as being begotten rather than adopted by God. It certainly does not imply parity with the Most High. But Judaism was heir to a long tradition that imputed divinity to the king in some sense. The claims made for Jesus in the New Testament in this respect are not incompatible with traditional Jewish claims for the king messiah.

The question of the divinity of the messiah is further complicated by the Son of Man tradition. In Daniel 7, the one like a son of man who comes on the clouds is most plausibly identified as the archangel Michael.[19] Daniel has no place for a messianic king from the line of David. By the first century CE, however, this figure is reinterpreted as a messiah in several sources.[20]

In the Similitudes of Enoch, which most probably date from the early first century CE, the Lord of Spirits is accompanied by a figure called "that Son of Man" who clearly corresponds to the figure in Daniel's vision.[21] This figure is heavenly, and never appears on earth.[22] He is, however, associated with the Davidic messiah, although there is no hint of Davidic lineage. The spirit of wisdom and insight that dwells in him recalls the messianic oracle in Isaiah 11. In 48:10 the kings of the earth are condemned for having denied "the Lord of Spirits and his Anointed One" in language reminiscent of Psalm 2. Again in 52:4 Enoch is told that all he has seen "will serve the authority of his Anointed One." It is not suggested that the Son of Man is descended from David, but he sits on the throne of glory, like the king in Psalm 110 and he serves as eschatological judge. Here again he functions in a manner reminiscent of the traditional messiah: "the spirit of righteousness was poured out on him and the word of his mouth will slay all the sinners" (62:2).

---

19. Collins, *Daniel*, 304-10; LaCocque, *The Book of Daniel*, 133-34; Newsom and Breed, *Daniel*, 235-36.

20. Collins, *Daniel*, 79-84; Newsom and Breed, *Daniel*, 245-7.

21. On the date of the Similitudes see Nickelsburg and VanderKam, *1 Enoch 2*, 58-64. See also Boccaccini, ed., *Enoch and the Messiah Son of Man*.

22. On the question whether he is identified with Enoch in 71:14 see Collins, *The Scepter and the Star*, 196-205. The apparent identification occurs in a second epilogue to the Similitudes and appears to be a secondary addition. There is no hint of such an identification in the body of the Similitudes.

The Danielic "one like a son of man" is also evoked in 4 Ezra 13.[23] Here a figure like a man rises on a cloud from the sea and takes his stand on a mountain to withstand the onslaught of the nations, like the king/messiah in Psalm 2. He defeats his adversaries by a stream of fire that issues from his mouth, the traditional messianic "breath of his lips." Although the messiah is said in 4 Ezra 12 to arise from the line of David and is symbolized as a lion, in chapter 13 he rises from the sea and it is not clear whether he is begotten by man. He is in any case a heavenly being who appears on earth. Here again the Gospels had good precedents and parallels in late Second Temple Judaism.

MESSIANIC VIOLENCE

The relation between Jewish and Christian conceptions of the messiah in the matter of violence is also ambivalent. The standard expectation of the Davidic messiah was that he would be a warrior who would drive out the Gentiles.[24] The prayer for the Prince of the Congregation in the Scroll of Blessings from Qumran (1QSb) says: "With your scepter may you lay waste the earth. With the breath of your lips may you kill the wicked . . . May he make your horns of iron and your hoofs of bronze. May you gore like a bu[ll . . . and may you trample the nation]s like mud of the streets."[25] In a fragment related to the eschatological war the Prince of the Congregation/Branch of David is said to kill someone, most probably the king of the Kittim.[26] The fact that he kills the wicked by the breath of his lips does not lessen the violence of the action.

Despite occasional attempts in modern scholarship to depict Jesus as a violent revolutionary,[27] it seems clear that he was not.[28] Indeed, it is far from clear that Jesus cast himself in the role of the Davidic messiah.

---

23. Stone, *Fourth Ezra*, 381–409; Collins, *The Scepter and the Star*, 205–10.

24. Collins, *The Scepter and the Star*, 77. Elgvin, *Warrior, King, Servant, Savior*, 241.

25. 1QSb 5:25, 27.

26. 4Q285, frag. 5.5. The Kittim was a name given to Gentiles from the west and could refer to either Greeks or Romans. On the fragment see Vermes, "The Oxford Forum," 85–90. The fragment does not overlap with 1QM and may belong to a different text.

27. E.g., the classic attempt of Brandon, *Jesus and the Zealots*; and the more recent attempts of Aslan, *Zealot*; and Martin, "Jesus in Jerusalem."

28. Joseph, *The Nonviolent Messiah*, 23–50; Meggitt, "Putting the Apocalyptic Jesus to the Sword," 371–404.

His reticence on that subject gives rise to the so-called Messianic Secret, whereby he forbids his disciples to proclaim his messianic identity (Mark 8:30).[29] The most explicitly messianic action attributed to him is his entry into Jerusalem to shouts of "Hosanna to the Son of David" on Palm Sunday (Matt 21:1–11; Mark 11:1–11; Luke 19:28–38). But that action can be understood as analogous to the actions of the sign prophets in Josephus, who evoked Biblical precedents, such as the crossing of the sea (Theudas, *Ant* 20. 97–98) or the collapse of the walls of Jericho (the Egyptian, *Ant.* 20. 169–71), to signify imminent divine deliverance.[30] The Romans did not greatly concern themselves as to whether such people posed a realistic threat; they took no chances.

In Mark, when Jesus tells his disciples not to tell anyone that he is the messiah, he proceeds to speak of "the Son of Man" (Mark 8:31). The claim that Jesus is the Davidic messiah is fused with his identification with the "one like a son of man" in Daniel's vision. As we have seen the Son of Man is interpreted as messiah also in non-Christian Jewish texts from the first century CE, in the Similitudes of Enoch and in 4 Ezra. (The messiah is explicitly Davidic in 4 Ezra 12). The identification of Jesus with the Son of Man circumvents the problem that he did not restore the kingdom of Israel or drive the Gentiles out of Jerusalem. It also circumvents his failure to take violent action against the Romans. The violence, however, is not repudiated, but deferred. The violence of the Second Coming is spelled out most vividly in Revelation 19, where Jesus comes from heaven on a white horse:

> From his mouth comes a sharp sword with which to strike down the nations, and he will rule them with a rod of iron; he will tread the wine press of the fury of the wrath of God the Almighty. (Rev 19:15).

Here Jesus conforms entirely to the violent messianic paradigm, despite the non-violent nature of his earthly career and its inglorious conclusion on the cross.

On the matter of violence, then, Jesus does not conform to the traditional expectations about the Davidic messiah, but he is aligned with a different understanding of the messiah, as the "Son of Man" foretold by Daniel, whose messianic kingdom is deferred to the future. The violent

---

29. The expression "Messianic Secret" was coined by Wrede, *Das Messiasgeheimnis in den Evangelien*, English translation: *The Messianic Secret*. See Raisänen, *The 'Messianic Secret'*; Yarbro Collins, *Mark*, 170–72.

30. On the sign prophets see Johnson, "Early Jewish Sign Prophets."

action traditionally associated with the messiah is not repudiated but postponed to the end of history.

A SUFFERING MESSIAH

Jesus departs, however, from traditional Jewish expectations in Mark 8:31: "the Son of Man must undergo great suffering and be rejected by the elders, the chief priests and the scribes, and be killed; and after three days rise again." No such expectations are associated with the "one like a son of man" in Daniel. In the Similitudes of Enoch, the Son of Man does not appear on earth at all and in 4 Ezra 13 the man from the sea is a mighty warrior who annihilates his enemies.

The view that Jesus, as messiah and Son of Man, must suffer and die is associated in the New Testament especially with the suffering servant of Isaiah 53. Older scholarship tended to assume that Jesus identified with the servant, and that tendency can still be found in more recent work, but it was debunked to a great degree by the work of Morna Hooker.[31] But regardless of what Jesus may have thought, the analogy with the servant played a key role for his followers in interpreting his death. When Philip meets the Ethiopian eunuch in Acts 8:26–40, Isa 53:7–8 provides the key to "the good news about Jesus." Several New Testament texts speak of Jesus being handed over, using language derived from the LXX of Isa 53:12. So Rom 4:25 says that Jesus "was handed over to death for our trespasses and raised for our justification."[32] Heb 9:28 says that Jesus was offered once to bear the sins of many.[33] First Peter 2:22–25 invokes Isaiah 53 explicitly with reference to the death of Jesus. The idea that Jesus had poured out his blood for many seems to have entailed a combination of the terminology of sacrifice with the language of Isaiah 53.[34]

Some scholars, notably Joachim Jeremias[35] and Peter Stuhlmacher[36] have argued that the messianic interpretation of Isaiah 53 was current in early Judaism, but the evidence is far from clear. Justin's *Dialogue with*

---

31. Hooker, *Jesus and the Servant*; "Did the Use of Isaiah 53?," 88–103.

32. Compare Mark 9:31. The verb to hand over, *paradidōmi*, is used ten times in Mark 14–15. See Yarbro Collins, *Mark*, 441.

33. Attridge, *The Epistle to the Hebrews*, 266.

34. See Yarbro Collins, "Finding Meaning in the Death of Jesus," 222–23.

35. Jeremias, "παις θεου," 674–717. See Yarbro Collins, *Mark*, 441.

36. Stuhlmacher, "Isaiah 53 in the Gospels and Acts," 149.

Trypho 90:1 has the Jewish interlocutor concede that the messiah must suffer and be led as a sheep, but the concession is authored by the Christian apologist. It is important to remember that the so-called "servant songs"[37] were not grouped together in antiquity or thought to refer to a single figure. Consequently, allusions to the other "servant songs" do not necessarily imply the kind of suffering implied. In Isaiah 53. The Son of Man in the Similitudes of Enoch is said to be the light of the nations (1 Enoch 48:4; compare Isa 42:6; 49:6) and is also said to be hidden (1 Enoch 48:6; compare Isa 49:2). But the Son of Man is not a suffering figure and does not atone for sin in the manner of the servant. Again, the messiah is said to die in 4 Ezra 7:29–30, but his death does not entail suffering and has no atoning significance.[38] The Targum of Isaiah, which is of uncertain date, takes Isaiah 53 to refer to the messiah, but the statements about the suffering of the servant are generally not related to him.[39] Jeremias argued that the Targum had undergone an anti-Christian polemic,[40] but this is at best dubious evidence for a pre-Christian messianic interpretation.

More recently, some scholars have tried to find a suffering messiah in the Dead. Sea Scrolls.[41] A manuscript of Isaiah from Qumran (1QIsaᵃ) has a variant at Isa 52:14. The traditional Hebrew text reads מִשְׁחַת מֵאִישׁ מַרְאֵיהוּ ("his appearance was marred beyond that of a man"). The Qumran manuscript reads מָשַׁחְתִּי, "I anointed his appearance beyond that of man." Martin Hengel argued that "the Servant's unique exaltation and his anointing by God correspond to one another," and concluded that "this interesting variant in 1QIsaᵃ could be based on a conscious interpretation of Isa 52:14 in Qumran."[42] He also noted that the prophet claimed to be anointed in Isa

---

37. Isa 42:1–7; 49:1–7; 50:4–9 and 52:13—53:12.

38. This is also true of the later tradition of the messiah son of Joseph, who dies in battle with Gog before the final victory of the messiah son of David. See Novenson, *The Grammar of Messianism*, 201–7. For a Jewish messiah who atones for sin by his suffering we have to wait until the medieval Pesiqta Rabbati. See Schäfer, *The Jewish Jesus*, 236–71; Elgvin, *Warrior, King, Servant, Savior*, 311–15.

39. Jeremias, "παις θεου," 694–5. The exceptions are the statements that "he will be despised" (Isa 53:3) and "he gave up his soul to death" (53:12).

40. Jeremias, "παις θεου," 695.

41. See especially Knohl, *The Messiah Before Jesus*; Wise, *The First Messiah*, offers extensive evidence that the Teacher of Righteousness known from the Dead Sea Scrolls identified himself with the Servant and assumes that the Servant was regarded as a messiah, on the basis of the textual variant at Isa 52:14 in 1QIsaa (see below).

42. Hengel, "The Effective History of Isaiah 53," 103–5.

61:1. The addition of a single *yod*, however, could be simply a scribal error.[43] Even scribal errors could affect how a text was read, but this particular variant is never cited in any other passage in the Scrolls.

Two other texts are sometimes adduced in support of the messianic interpretation of the Servant in the Scrolls.

A fragmentary Aramaic text, 4Q541, speaks of a figure who "will atone for all the children of his generation." His light will be kindled in all the corners of the earth. People will speak evil against him, but the text does not say that he will be put to death. Already in 1963 Jean Starcky claimed to find here "a suffering messiah, in the perspective opened up by the Servant poems,"[44] and this view was endorsed by the eventual editor Émile Puech.[45] It seems clear that this text is referring to an eschatological priest, the figure elsewhere called the messiah of Aaron. He will atone for the sin of his people, but he will presumably do so by offering the prescribed sacrifices, not by his own death.[46]

The other text that is sometimes adduced as evidence for a suffering messiah is the so-called "self-glorification hymn."[47] This is a fascinating but enigmatic text in which the speaker claims to be reckoned with the gods and to have a throne in heaven. He also claims to bear sorrows and endure evil. There is no consensus as to the identity of the speaker. Possibilities include the messianic High Priest and the Teacher after his death. The Hebrew word משיח does not occur in the surviving fragments. While there is some general similarity to the Servant insofar as a figure who endures abuse is finally exalted, there is no suggestion of redemptive suffering or atoning death.

In fact there is no clear evidence for a messiah who atones for sin by his death in pre-Christian Judaism. The variant in 1QIsa^a could be read that

---

43. Abegg, Flint, and Ulrich, *The Dead Sea Scrolls Bible*, 359, suggest that the variant be translated as "my marring," but this seems very implausible.

44. Starcky, "Les quatres étapes," 492.

45. Puech, "Fragments d'un apocryphe de Lévi," 492-99. Compare Elgvin, *Warrior, King, Servant, Savior*, 244.

46. This was recognized by Starcky and Puech. Puech, "4Q540.Apocryphe de Lévi," 213-4. Knohl, in contrast argues that he atones by his suffering. See Knohl, *The Messiah Confrontation*, 119-21.

47. 4Q491c, 4Q471b; 4Q427 7 and 1QHa 25:35-26:10; 4Q431. Collins, *The Scepter and the Star*, 149-70. See Knohl, *The Messiah before Jesus*, 75-86; *The Messiah Confrontation*, 121-23; Wise, *The First Messiah*, 220-24; Hengel, *The Effective History of Isaiah 53*, 140-45.

way, but it may well be a scribal error, and there is no clear evidence that anyone inferred from it that the Servant was a messiah.

The need for atonement emerged as a major consideration in Second Temple Judaism, in the wake of the disaster of the Babylonian conquest. Atonement was normally achieved by priests performing the rituals prescribed in the book of Leviticus. Isaiah 53 is exceptional in suggesting that the suffering of the servant atoned for the sin of the people.[48] The identification of the servant in the prophetic context is unclear.[49] The fact that a messiah could be said to atone for sin by any means was an important development in Jewish messianic expectation, and an important presupposition of early Christian understanding. Nonetheless, the idea that the atonement would be achieved by the death of the messiah was strikingly novel. It arose from the need to find meaning in the death of Jesus.[50] This was not the only case in which the idea of the messiah was modified in light of historical developments. Many scholars think that the idea of the Messiah son of Joseph, who is killed in battle, reflects the fate of Bar Kochba, who died in battle with the Romans.[51] But the idea of the death of the messiah as an atoning sacrifice was distinctive to the followers of Jesus and became one of the factors that distinguished the Jesus movement from its parent religion.

CONCLUSION

For most Jews in the time of Jesus, the Davidic messiah was supposed to be a warrior who would drive out the Romans and restore the kingdom of Israel. Jesus of Nazareth did not meet that expectation. There were, however, other messianic paradigms by which he could be understood, notably that of the Son of Man who would come on the clouds of heaven. Atonement for sin was also associated with the messianic age but was usually assigned to a non-Davidic priestly figure. The followers of Jesus interpreted his death in

---

48. See Spiekermann, "The Conception and Prehistory of the Idea of Vicarious Suffering," 1–14.

49. North, *The Suffering Servant*, surveys the options. Opinion is divided as to whether the servant is a collective figure or an individual. Blenkinsopp, *Isaiah 40–55*, 356, opts for the prophet who wrote the poem, but any individual interpretation requires us to posit biographical events that are otherwise unattested. Accordingly, I lean to the view that the servant is the righteous remnant of Israel.

50. See Yarbro Collins, "Finding Meaning in the Death of Jesus."

51. See Skarsaune, "Jews and Christians in the Holy Land, 135–325 C. E.," 161.

light of the Jewish traditions available to them, but they used some of those traditions in novel ways. The idea that the Davidic messiah would atone for sin by his own suffering and death was a striking innovation, even though it was based on an interpretation of traditional sources.

Scholem's statement that "Judaism has always maintained a concept of redemption as an event which takes place publicly," remains true as a generalization. Redemption would also have its spiritual aspect, but it remains a political and historical ideal. Christianity also retained the ideal of public transformation of the world as an ultimate goal but shifted its primary concern to atonement for sin in the spiritual realm. The contrast is not absolute, but the difference in emphasis remains a persistent source of tension between the two traditions.[52]

BIBLIOGRAPHY

Abegg, Martin, et al. *The Dead Sea Scrolls Bible*. San Francisco: HarperSanFrancisco, 1999.
Aslan, Reza. *The Life and Times of Jesus of Nazareth*. New York: Random House, 2013.
Attridge, Harold W. *The Epistle to the Hebrews*. Hermeneia. Minneapolis: Fortress, 1989.
Blenkinsopp, Joseph. *Isaiah 40–55*. AB 19A. New York: Doubleday, 2000.
Bloch, Yigal, et al. "The Rule of the Congregation from Cave 1 of Qumran. A New Annotated Edition." *RÉJ* 178 (2019) 1–46.
Boccaccini, Gabriele, ed. *Enoch and the Messiah Son of Man. Revisiting the Book of Parables*. Grand Rapids: Eerdmans, 2007.
Brandon, S. G. F. *Jesus and the Zealots. A Study of the Political Factor in Primitive Christianity*. New York: Scribner, 1967.
Coxe, A. Cleveland. *The Apostolic Fathers with Justin Martyr and Irenaeus*. Grand Rapids: Eerdmans, 1985.
Collins, John J. *Daniel. A Commentary on the Book of Daniel, with an essay "The Influence of Daniel on the New Testament," by Adela Yarbro Collins*. Hermeneia. Minneapolis: Fortress, 1993.
———. "The Interpretation of Psalm 2." In *Scriptures and Sectarianism: Essays on the Dead Sea Scrolls*, 87–91. WUNT 332. Tübingen: Mohr Siebeck, 2014.
———. *The Scepter and the Star. Messianism in Light of the Dead Sea Scrolls*. 2nd ed. Grand Rapids: Eerdmans, 2010.
Cross, Frank Moore. "Some Notes on a Generation of Qumran Studies." In *The Madrid Qumran Congress*, edited by Julio Trebolle Barrera and Luis Vegas Montaner, 1–14. STDJ 11. Leiden: Brill, 1992.
Elgvin, Torleif. *Warrior, King, Servant, Savior: Messianism in the Hebrew Bible and Early Jewish Texts*. Grand Rapids: Eerdmans, 2022.
Fitzmyer, Joseph A. *The One Who Is to Come*. Grand Rapids: Eerdmans, 2007.

---

52. It is a pleasure to dedicate this essay to the memory of André LaCocque, scholar and gentleman, who was deeply concerned for Jewish-Christian relations.

Hengel, Martin, with Daniel P. Bailey. "The Effective History of Isaiah 53 in the Pre-Christian Period." In *The Suffering Servant: Isaiah 53 in Jewish and Christian Sources*, ed. Bernd Janowski and Peter Stuhlmacher, 75–147. Grand Rapids: Eerdmans, 2004.

Hooker, Morna. "Did the Use of Isaiah 53 to Interpret His Mission Begin with Jesus?" In *Jesus and the Suffering Servant*, edited by William H. Bellinger and William R. Farmer, 88–103. Harrisburg, PA: Trinity, 1999.

———. *Jesus and the Servant. The Influence of the Servant concept of Deutero-Isaiah in the New Testament*. London: SPCK, 1959.

Hurtado, Larry W. *Ancient Jewish Monotheism and Early Christian Jesus-Devotion: The Context and Character of Christological Faith*. Library of Early Christology Series. Waco, TX: Baylor, 2017.

Jeremias, Joachim. "παις θεου." In *TDNT* 5 (1967) 674–717.

Johnson, Nathan C. "Early Jewish Sign Prophets." In *Critical Dictionary of Apocalyptic and Millenarian Movements*, edited by James Crossley and Alastair Lockhart. https://www.cdamm.org/articles/ (Dec. 8, 2021).

Joseph, Simon J. *The Nonviolent Messiah: Jesus, Q, and the Enochic Tradition*. Grand Rapids: Eerdmans, 2014.

Knohl, Israel. *The Messiah before Jesus: The Suffering Servant of the Dead Sea Scrolls*. Berkeley: University of California Press, 2000.

Knohl, Israel. *The Messiah Confrontation: Pharisees versus Sadducees and the Death of Jesus*. Philadelphia: Jewish Publication Society, 2019.

LaCocque, André. *The Book of Daniel*. Atlanta: John Knox, 1979.

———. "The Vision of the Eagle in 4 Esdras. A Rereading of Daniel 7 in the First Century CE." In *Society of Biblical Literature Seminar Papers*, edited by Kent H. Richards, 237–58. Chico, CA: Scholars, 1981.

Martin, Dale B. "Jesus in Jerusalem. Armed and Not Dangerous." *JSNT* 37 (2014) 3–24.

Meggitt, Justin. "Putting the Apocalyptic Jesus to the Sword: Why Were Jesus's Disciples Armed?" *JSNT* 45(2023) 371–404.

Newsom, Carol A. *Daniel. A Commentary*, with Brennan W. Breed. OTL. Louisville: Westminster John Knox, 2014.

Nickelsburg, George W. E. and James C. VanderKam. *1 Enoch 2. A Commentary on the Book of 1 Enoch Chapters 37–82*. Hermeneia. Minneapolis: Fortress, 2012.

North, C. R. *The Suffering Servant in Deutero-Isaiah*. 2nd ed. Oxford: Oxford University Press, 1956.

Novenson, Matthew. *Christ among the Messiahs: Christ Language in Paul and Messiah Language in Ancient Judaism*. New York: Oxford, 2012.

———. *The Grammar of Messianism: An Ancient Jewish Political Idiom and Its Users*. New York: Oxford University Press, 2017.

Puech, Émile. "4Q540. 4QApocryphe de Lévi[a]? ar and 4Q541. 4QApocryphe de Lévi[b] ar." *DJD* 31, 217–56.

———. "Fragments d'un apocryphe de Lévi et la personage eschatologique. 4Q Test Lévi c–d (?) et 4Q Aja." In *The Madrid Qumran Congress*, edited by Julio Trebolle Barrera and Luis Vegas Montaner, 2:449–501. STDJ 11. Leiden: Brill, 1992.

Raisänen, Heikki. *The 'Messianic Secret' in Mark*. Edinburgh: T. & T. Clark, 1990.

Schäfer, Peter. *The Jewish Jesus: How Judaism and Christianity Shaped Each Other* Princeton: Princeton University Press, 2012.

Scholem, Gershom, *The Messianic Idea in Judaism and Other Essays on Jewish Spirituality.* New York: Schocken, 1971, 1. German original: "Zum Verständnis der messianischen Idee im Judentum," *ErJb* 28(1959) 173–239.

Skarsaune, Oskar. "Jews and Christians in the Holy Land, 135–325 C.E." In *Redemption and Resistance: The Messianic Hopes of Jews and Christians in Antiquity*, edited by Markus Bokmuehl and James Carleton Paget, 158–70. London: T. & T. Clark, 2007.

Starcky, Jean. "Les quatres étapes du messianisme à Qumrân," *RB* 70 (1965) 481–505.

Stone, Michael E. *Fourth Ezra*. Hermeneia. Minneapolis: Fortress, 1990.

Stuckenbruck, Loren T. "Messianic Ideas in the Apocalyptic and Related Literature of Early Judaism," in *The Messiah in the Old and New Testaments,* edited by Stanley E. Porter, 90–113. Grand Rapids: Eerdmans, 2007.

Stuhlmacher, Peter. "Isaiah 53 in the Gospels and Acts," in *The Suffering Servant. Isaiah 53 in Jewish and Christian Sources,* edited by Bernd Janowski and Peter Stuhlmacher, 147–62. Grand Rapids: Eerdmans, 2004.

Spiekermann, Hermann. "The Conception and Prehistory of the Idea of Vicarious Suffering in the Old Testament," in *The Suffering Servant*, edited by Berndt Janowski and Peter Stuhlmacher, 1–14. Grand Rapids: Eerdmans, 2004.

Vermes, Geza. "The Oxford Forum for Qumran Research Seminar on the Rule of War from Cave 4(4Q285)." *JJS* 43(1992) 85–90.

Wise, Michael O. *The First Messiah. Investigating the Savior Before Christ.* San Francisco: HarperSanFrancisco, 1999.

Wrede, William. *Das Messiasgeheimnis in den Evangelien: Zugleich ein Beitrag zum Verständnis des Markusevangeliums.* Göttingen: Vandenhoeck & Ruprecht, 1901. English translation: *The Messianic Secret.* Cambridge: James Clarke, 1971.

Yarbro Collins, Adela. "Finding Meaning in the Death of Jesus." In *Collected Essays on the Gospel according to Mark*, 221–41. WUNT 497. Tübingen: Mohr Siebeck, 2022.

———. *Mark. A Commentary*. Hermeneia. Minneapolis: Fortress, 2007.

Yarbro Collins, Adela, and John J. Collins, *King and Messiah as Son of God. Divine, Human, and Angelic Messianic Figures in Biblical and Related Literature.* Grand Rapids: Eerdmans, 2008.

Zimmermann, Johannes. *Messianische Texte aus Qumran*. WUNT 2/104 Tübingen: Mohr Siebeck, 1998.

3

Two Resurrected Pharisees
Saul of Tarsus and Yoḥanan ben Zakkai and the Beginnings of Christianity and Rabbinic Judaism

LAURENCE L. EDWARDS

THE MAIN PURPOSE OF *this paper is to explore a common trope—that of resurrection—in two stories that relate to the origins of Rabbinic Judaism and of Christianity. One in the Book of Acts describes the experience of Saul of Tarsus (Paul) on the road to Damascus. The second, included in several rabbinic collections, is the story of Rabban Yoḥanan ben Zakkai being smuggled out of besieged Jerusalem in a coffin. These two narratives are not contemporary with the events they describe, so no claim is made here about their historicity. However, the fact that they appear, re-shaped and re-told by later writers, and are well-known to members of their respective communities, confirms the significance of these "legends" for each tradition. I do not argue that one influenced the other, nor that they have a common origin. The more modest intention is to offer close readings of the two narratives, note several parallels, and suggest that the idea of resurrection is expressed, albeit indirectly, in these foundational texts. Both emerge out of a common context of pharisaic ideology which, in a broad sense, is the religious matrix out of which the sibling traditions of Rabbinic Judaism and Christianity are birthed.*

The Pharisees of history are a disembodied presence. They left no writings of their own, no original documents that proclaim their ideology or describe their way of life. Rather, they are represented in later narratives—both Jewish and Christian—figuratively "resurrected" and re-imagined by those who came after them and who projected upon them the conflicting agendas of later eras. They loom large in the Gospels and in Acts, often as opponents of Jesus (Matt 12:14; Matt 23; Mark. 3:6; John. 7:32–52; 11:45–57; 18:3), sometimes as his interlocutors (Matt 16:1; 19:3–9; ch. 22; Mark. 2:18 [compared there with the disciples of John the Baptizer]; 2:23–28; 7:1–23), and sometimes even as Jesus' followers (John 3 of Nicodemus [the only named Pharisee in the Gospels]; Acts 15:5; and, of course, Paul).

In Josephus they emerge as forerunners of the Rabbis, prime candidates for Jewish leadership under Roman sponsorship.[1] In the tannaitic layers of the rabbinic literature they do not often appear under the name "Pharisee," but they are brought back in the later amoraic layers as individual teachers—by then the stuff of legend—who in their lifetimes are presumed to have been affiliated with the pharisaic party. For many Jews the Pharisees come to be seen as the Jewish liberals, interpreters of Torah who prepare the way for post-Temple Judaism. Among their multiple roles in these literatures, they mark a point of common origin and a site of contention between the emerging communities of Christians and rabbinic Jews.

---

1. The author wishes to thank Susan Boone, Tat-Siong Benny Liew, Michael Fishbane, Laura Dingeldein, and anonymous journal readers for helpful comments on earlier drafts. This is suggested, for example, by this description of their administrative experience:

> Alexander bequeathed the kingdom to his wife Alexandra . . . Beside Alexandra, and growing as she grew, arose the Pharisees, a body of Jews with the reputation of excelling the rest of their nation in the observances of religion, and as exact exponents of the laws. To them, being herself intensely religious, she listened with too great deference; while they, gradually taking advantage of an ingenuous woman, became at length *the real administrators of the state*, at liberty to banish and to recall, to loose and to bind, whom they would. In short, the enjoyments of royal authority were theirs . . . But if she ruled the nation, the Pharisees ruled her.

See Josephus, *Wars* 1:110–12 (italics added). Loeb: *Josephus* Vol. II, 52–55. Elsewhere Josephus describes them as influential and popular:

> Because of these views they are, as a matter of fact, extremely influential among the townsfolk; and all prayers and sacred rites of divine worship are performed according to their exposition. This is the great tribute that the inhabitants of the cities, by practising the highest ideals both in their way of living and in their discourse, have paid to the excellence of the Pharisees.

See Josephus, *Antiquities* 18.15. Loeb: *Josephus* Vol. IX, 13.

There is little doubt that there really was such a group, part of the broad spectrum of "Judaisms"[2] that existed in the last century or two before the destruction of the Temple. Josephus (who will not be closely examined in the present work) identifies himself as a follower of pharisaic practice,[3] and the Paul of Acts insists on his own pharisaic credentials as a student of the great Rabbi Gamaliel the Elder (Acts 22:3). But, other than these two claimants of pharisaic pedigree, we have no first-hand writings describing the movement, or directly presenting pharisaic teachings. A fair and careful picture is offered by Jacob Neusner:

> The Pharisees formed a social entity, of indeterminate classification (sect? church? political party? philosophical order? cult?), in the Jewish nation in the Land of Israel in the century or so before A.D. 70. They are of special interest for two reasons. First, they are mentioned in the synoptic Gospels [also in John] as contemporaries of Jesus, represented sometimes as hostile, sometimes as neutral, and sometimes as friendly to the early Christians represented by Jesus. Second, they are commonly supposed to stand behind the authorities who, in the second century, made up the materials that come to us in the Mishnah, the first important document, after Scripture, of Judaism in its classical or normative form. Hence the Mishnah and some related writings are alleged to rest upon traditions going back to the Pharisees before A.D. 70. These views impute to the Pharisees greater importance than, in their own day, they are likely to have enjoyed . . . No writings survive that were produced by them; all we do know is what later writers said about them.[4]

Scholars have no doubt that there *were* Pharisees, but since we possess no descriptions in their own words, it is difficult to know how to classify them.

---

2. We have become accustomed to this plural usage, a warning against seeing late Second Temple Judaism as a unified phenomenon recognizable on the basis of rabbinic texts set down three or more generations after the destruction of the Temple. See Morton Smith's brief but richly suggestive article "A Comparison of Early Christian and Early Rabbinic Tradition," and also his now classic statement, "Palestinian Judaism in the First Century."

3. His formal affiliation (was there such a thing?) has been questioned by Steve Mason, "Was Josephus a Pharisee?"

4. Neusner, "Mr. Sanders' Pharisees—and Mine," 277.

RESURRECTION IN PHARISAIC THOUGHT

One marker of pharisaic belief is the doctrine of the resurrection of the dead. It is associated with the Pharisees in several New Testament passages,[5] and is one of the pharisaic doctrines that Paul inherited and understood anew in connection with his experience of the risen Christ. Josephus lists resurrection as a major pharisaic teaching, one that (as in Acts) distinguished the Pharisees from their chief rivals, the Sadducees.[6] Insofar as the corpus of the Mishnah may be taken to reflect pharisaic traditions, Sanhedrin 10:1 is a clear statement of belief in resurrection as a biblical teaching.[7] It is thus possible to view the Pharisees, and their doctrine of resurrection, as a bridge (construed positively), or a site of contention (construed negatively), but in any case a point of overlap between Judaism and Christianity. Indeed, the Pharisees have themselves been periodically "resurrected" in the overlapping discourses of Judaism and Christianity.

As a trope, resurrection is alluded to significantly in the portraits of two pivotal pharisaic figures, Saul of Tarsus and Yoḥanan ben Zakkai. Saul of Tarsus (later known as Paul) and Yoḥanan ben Zakkai (later known by the title Rabban) were contemporaries, students—perhaps of the same teachers—in first-century CE Jerusalem. Yoḥanan ben Zakkai is the key

---

5. See, for example, Matt 22:23; Mark 12:18; Luke 20:27, which impute belief in resurrection to the Pharisees by identifying the Sadducees as the ones who do *not* believe in resurrection. The belief is stated most explicitly in Paul's speech in Acts 23:8.

6. "The Pharisees . . . believe that souls have power to survive death and that there are rewards and punishments under the earth for those who have led lives of virtue or vice: eternal imprisonment is the lot of evil souls, while the good souls receive an easy passage to a new life . . . The Sadducees hold that the soul perishes along with the body." Josephus, *Antiquities* 18:15–16. It has been questioned whether Josephus is actually describing here the doctrine of (bodily) resurrection, as opposed to the immortality of the soul—related but distinct ideas. It is clear, however, from other sources that pharisaic and (later) rabbinic teaching about resurrection referred to resurrection of the body. See, for example, the discussion in Davies, *Paul and Rabbinic Judaism*, 299–300. More simply, Paula Fredriksen, in discussing Paul, refers to resurrection as "characteristically Pharisaic." See Fredriksen, "What Does It Mean to See Paul 'within Judaism'?," 377.

7. "These are the ones who have no portion in the world to come: one who says that that the [doctrine of the] resurrection of the dead is not from the Torah, or that the Torah is not from heaven, and an *apikoros*," m. Sanh. 10:1. (There are versions that omit the words, "from the Torah," and simply refer to "those who say there is no resurrection.") The gemara that follows (chap. 11 in the Babylonian Talmud) contains an extensive discussion, with various prooftexts. It is unusual for the Talmud to articulate points of doctrinal belief, done here by marking dissenting views as denying their adherents a "portion in the world to come." On rabbinic heresiology, see Boyarin, *Border Lines*, esp. chap. 2.

transitional figure in the traditional Jewish narratives of the shift from late Second Temple "Pharisaic" Judaism to post-Temple "Rabbinic" Judaism.[8] A remarkable parallel is found in the story of Saul of Tarsus, the figure who, more than any other, embodies the transition from Pharisaic Judaism to what would come to be known as Christianity.

The striking narratives of Paul's Damascus Road experience (as described in the Book of Acts, not by Paul himself but by a later writer) and Rabban Yoḥanan ben Zakkai's escape from Jerusalem (also the work of later writers) open a narrative window into the origins of the two traditions that, of the many forms of first-century Judaisms, were the ones that survived the destruction of the Temple, namely Rabbinic Judaism and Christianity. Both stories incorporate powerful elements of a resurrection motif. No claim is made here of influence of one writer upon another, nor that either of these stories is intended as an argument for belief in resurrection. Rather, the point here is to propose that the trope of resurrection plays a significant role in the constructed narratives of these two transitional/foundational figures.

SAUL OF TARSUS

The ninth chapter of Acts (vv. 1–31) narrates the turning point in Paul's career:

> Meanwhile Saul, still breathing threats and murder against the disciples of the Lord, went to the high priest [2]and asked him for letters to the synagogues at Damascus, so that if he found any who belonged to the Way, men or women, he might bring them bound to Jerusalem. [3]Now as he was going along and approaching Damascus, suddenly a light from heaven flashed around him. [4]He fell to the ground and heard a voice saying to him, "Saul, Saul, why do you persecute me?" [5]He asked, "Who are you, Lord?" The reply came, "I am Jesus, whom you are persecuting. [6]But get up and enter the city, and you will be told what you are to do." [7]The men who were traveling with him stood speechless because they heard the voice but saw no one. [8]Saul got up from the ground, and though his eyes were open, he could see nothing; so they led him by the hand and brought him into Damascus. [9]For three days he was without sight, and neither ate nor drank.

---

8. The most ambitious effort to reconstruct the known facts of Yoḥanan's life is the early work of Jacob Neusner, *A Life of Rabban Yohanan ben Zakkai*, and its companion volume, *Development of a Legend*.

¹⁰Now there was a disciple in Damascus named Ananias. The Lord said to him in a vision, "Ananias." He answered, "Here I am, Lord." ¹¹The Lord said to him, "Get up and go to the street called Straight, and at the house of Judas look for a man of Tarsus named Saul. At this moment he is praying, ¹²and he has seen in a vision a man named Ananias come in and lay his hands on him so that he might regain his sight." ¹³But Ananias answered, "Lord, I have heard from many about this man, how much evil he has done to your saints in Jerusalem; ¹⁴and here he has authority from the chief priests to bind all who invoke your name." ¹⁵But the Lord said to him, "Go, for he is an instrument whom I have chosen to bring my name before Gentiles and kings and before the people of Israel; ¹⁶I myself will show him how much he must suffer for the sake of my name." ¹⁷So Ananias went and entered the house. He laid his hands on Saul and said, "Brother Saul, the Lord Jesus, who appeared to you on your way here, has sent me so that you may regain your sight and be filled with the Holy Spirit." ¹⁸And immediately something like scales fell from his eyes, and his sight was restored. Then he got up and was baptized, ¹⁹and after taking some food, he regained his strength.

For several days he was with the disciples in Damascus, ²⁰and immediately he began to proclaim Jesus in the synagogues, saying, "He is the Son of God." ²¹All who heard him were amazed and said, "Is not this the man who made havoc in Jerusalem among those who invoked this name? And has he not come here for the purpose of bringing them bound before the chief priests?" ²²Saul became increasingly more powerful and confounded the Jews who lived in Damascus by proving that Jesus was the Messiah.

²³After some time had passed, the Jews plotted to kill him, ²⁴but their plot became known to Saul. They were watching the gates day and night so that they might kill him; ²⁵but his disciples took him by night and let him down through an opening in the wall, lowering him in a basket. ²⁶When he had come to Jerusalem, he attempted to join the disciples; and they were all afraid of him, for they did not believe that he was a disciple. ²⁷But Barnabas took him, brought him to the apostles, and described for them how on the road he had seen the Lord, who had spoken to him, and how in Damascus he had spoken boldly in the name of Jesus. ²⁸So he went in and out among them in Jerusalem, speaking boldly in the name of the Lord. ²⁹He spoke and argued with the Hellenists; but they were attempting to kill him. ³⁰When the believers learned of it, they brought him down to Caesarea and sent him off to Tarsus.

³¹Meanwhile the church throughout Judea, Galilee, and Samaria had peace and was built up. Living in the fear of the Lord and in the comfort of the Holy Spirit, it increased in numbers. (NRSV)

Whether one refers to the event here described as a conversion, a prophetic call, a commissioning,[9] or a resurrection (see section below on "Saul's Death and Resurrection"), it is clear that Paul's direction and self-understanding (i.e., the figure of Paul as described in Acts) take a 180-degree turn. It is told in the third person, presented as an objective account by an omniscient narrator. In analyzing this passage, one must also take into consideration the parallel versions that appear in chapters 22 and 26. In these the narrative is placed in Paul's own mouth, as he speaks first to a crowd in Jerusalem, and later (in chains) before Festus, the new Roman governor, and Agrippa, the Jewish King.

The latter two tellings, presented as first-person narratives, at first give the appearance of being Paul's own words. One must remember, of course, that all three versions are re-tellings, fashioned and contextualized by the author of Acts ("Luke").[10] As such, they are not reliable as direct historical accounts, but they are "facts" in the sense that they have shaped much of the traditional Christian understanding of Paul and his role in the early years of the Church. In chapter 22 Paul speaks to the crowd in Jerusalem in defense of himself. He recounts the story, and in this version he is not "commissioned" until the end of the narrative, verse 21, with its pregnant statement: "Then he said to me, 'Go, for I will send you far away to the Gentiles.'"

In chapter 26 he is in Caesarea, again defending himself, this time before King Agrippa and Festus. The account of the Damascus Road experience is given in vv. 12–18. This time the "commission" is elaborated in greater detail than in the other two accounts:

> I have appeared to you for this purpose, to appoint you to serve and testify to the things in which you have seen me and to those in

---

9. See the classic discussion of "Call Rather Than Conversion," in Stendahl, *Paul among Jews and Gentiles*, 7–23. In a more recent and quite thorough study of Acts, Daniel Marguerat falls back into the older language of "Saul's conversion." See Marguerat, *The First Christian Historian*, Chap. 9. Marguerat does sometimes try out other terminology, e.g., "the overturning of his identity" (p. 185), or "the reversal of Saul's identity" (p. 191). "Conversion" has a stubborn hold: see Levine and Brettler, eds., *The Jewish Annotated New Testament*, 216, refers to the "Conversion of Saul/Paul."

10. For a review of recent literature on Luke and Paul, including the tradition that Luke is the author of Acts, see Adams, "Paul and Luke: What's Their Relationship?"

which I will appear to you. I will rescue you from your people and from the Gentiles—to whom I am sending you to open their eyes so that they may turn from darkness to light and from the power of Satan to God, so that they may receive forgiveness of sins and a place among those who are sanctified by faith in me.

In addition to the three accounts in Acts,[11] commentators also make reference to Paul's own allusions to the "event" in his letters, including 1 Cor 9:1 ("Have I not seen Jesus our Lord?"); 15:8 ("Last of all, as to one untimely born, he appeared also to me."); Gal 1:15–16 ("But when God, who had set me apart before I was born and called me through his grace, was pleased to reveal his Son to me, so that I might proclaim him among the Gentiles . . ."[12]) We shall concentrate here on the narrative of events in Acts 9, the most highly developed of the accounts.[13]

The narrative begins with Saul "still breathing threats and murder"—emphasizing his determination to put a stop to the "Way."[14] The source of the persecution is clearly identified as the high priest, though it is Saul himself who takes the initiative and asks for letters of authorization. He is passionate about this mission; in dramatic terms, it also adds to the power of his reversal. Saul's personality, and his commitment to this cause, are in stark contrast to the portrayal of his teacher, Gamaliel, who in Acts (5:34–39) counsels restraint.[15] The contrast between the two characters may serve

---

11. Marguerat offers a thorough and suggestive analysis of this "thrice-told tale" in *The First Christian Historian*, chap. 9.

12. Here his language recalls Jer 1:5–6, with its references to "womb"—*kolías / koilía* (LXX) and nations/Gentiles—*ethnesin / ethne* (LXX)]); and Phil 3:8 ("More than that, I regard everything as loss because of the surpassing value of knowing Christ Jesus my Lord . . .").

13. Our purpose here is not to recover the original "event," but to consider the force of the account as it has developed over time. Acts 9 also represents a version whose composition is closer in time to (though still earlier than) the developed accounts of Yoḥanan ben Zakkai's escape from Jerusalem, with which we shall be comparing it.

14. David W. Pao suggests that the term "Way"—*hodos*—functions in Acts as an "identity marker," occurring "always in the context where the Christians are trying to establish their identity in relation to the Jewish community . . ." Pao, *Acts and the Isaianic New Exodus*, 65–66. It is equivalent, Pao shows, to the Hebrew term *derekh* which appears often in Isaiah 40–55, "a term that evoked the Exodus tradition and signaled the presence of the new salvific act of God."

15. The novelist Sholem Asch constructs a moving scene of the final meeting between the two, after Gamaliel receives word of Saul's involvement in the lynching of Stephen. Gamaliel reproves his pupil in the strongest terms, accusing him of murder, then:

"I am afraid for thee, Saul of Tarshish. The path which thou hast chosen for thyself

as a reminder that no group or movement is monolithic—here two very different personalities (Saul and Gamaliel) both claim (or have claimed for them) the label "Pharisee."

SAUL'S "DEATH AND RESURRECTION" (ACTS 26:3-9)

Key to what I am claiming is the narrative's resurrection motif are the two verbs used in connection with Saul's rising from the ground. Jesus says to him *hanástethi*—"rise" (Acts 9:6). Two verses later Saul gets up from the ground: *hegérthe de Saulos hapò tes ges*. These two verbs—*hanistemi* and *hegeiro* (it is not clear why two different verbs are used)—both carry strong overtones of resurrection. *Hanistemi* is a verb often (though not exclusively) related to resurrection (e.g., 2 Macc 7:9; John 6:39; Acts 2:24 in connection with the resurrection of Jesus).[16] It is also used in the LXX of Hos 6:2 to translate the Hebrew *yaqimenu*—will raise us up—a verse understood in the New Testament as a prophecy of resurrection on the third day.

Hegeiro is also connected in many instances with resurrection. In Acts 9:8 it appears in the aorist passive intransitive form *hegérthe*, for which BAGD again offers a number of examples that refer to resurrection, especially the resurrection of Jesus (e.g., Acts 3:15; 4:10; 13:30; Gal 1:1).[17] Again, it is not clear why, other than stylistic reasons, two different verbs are used in this passage, but it seems quite clear from the use of both words that Saul's experience is being given overtones of resurrection, whether literal or symbolic. It is relevant to this motif that he remains blind and neither eats nor drinks for three days (as if dead), a parallel to Jesus' resurrection.[18] Saul's traveling companions hear the voice but see no one. (In the retelling of 22:9, they

---

is narrow and perilous; the abyss lies on either side of it. Know that those who fall into it are never lifted . . . There is but one thread for thee to hold on to: 'Thou shalt love thy neighbor as thyself' . . ."

This is a modern "midrashic" construction by a Yiddish writer seeking, among other things, the Jewish context of New Testament narratives. In modern literature, as in scholarship, the details of a pharisaic conversation must be filled in by the imagination. See Asch, *The Apostle*, 128–29. It is worth noting that Asch anticipates the so-called "new approach" to Paul, or "Paul within Judaism," by setting him squarely in the context of his Jewish/Pharisaic background.

16. BAGD, 83: *anastasis*. (*Anastethi* is the imperative form of a second aorist intransitive verb.) See also LSJ, 144.

17. BAGD, 271, *hegeiro*. See esp. def. 6. See also LSJ, 469.

18. Among the gospel writers, Luke, the likely author of Acts, makes the most explicit reference to "the third day" when discussing the resurrection of Jesus (Luke 24:21).

see the light but do not hear the voice. In the third version, all fall to the ground, and Saul hears the voice speaking in Hebrew [26:14]).

In the various commentaries on Acts that I have surveyed, I have not found any comments on what seems to me an intentional linguistic hint at an analogy between Saul's "resurrection" experience and that of Jesus. Beverly Gaventa, for example, observes that, "'Get up and enter' reflects the language of the Septuagint, where *anistemi* frequently introduces divine commissions (e.g., Gen 21:18; 31:13; 1 Kgs 17:9; Jonah 1:2)."[19] Hans Conzelmann apparently disagrees with my reading, though without direct reference to the vocabulary that I am claiming suggests a resurrection-like experience: "It is important to note that Luke has not assimilated this event to the Easter experience of Jesus. He distinguishes this vision fundamentally from those appearances—contrary to what Paul himself does."[20] In contrast to Conzelmann, Luke Timothy Johnson claims that "the identification . . . between Saul and Jesus is established in this encounter,"[21] but without reference to the specific language that I am suggesting would actually support his argument.

An element of the Paul narrative that will also be seen in the story of Yoḥanan ben Zakkai is that of "escape from a city." Luke claims a plot on the part of "the Jews" in Damascus to kill Saul. It does not seem as if he has been hiding out, for he has been preaching publicly in the synagogues. Yet, the Jews are said to keep watch at the gates, day and night, in an apparent effort to prevent his escape. His disciples lower him over the wall by night, in a basket, and he makes his getaway. As Jack Sanders points out, this is quite different from the way Paul himself tells the story. In 2 Cor 11:32–33, Paul tells the story of the basket-over-the-wall escape from Damascus thus: "At Damascus, the governor under King Aretas guarded the city of Damascus in order to seize me, but I was let down in a basket through a window in the wall and escaped from his hands."

Unless there were two separate escapes from Damascus (in a basket), one must assume that Paul's version of the story is closer to the truth. Sanders notes "that Luke's retelling of the event shows enough verbal similarities to Paul's account to warrant our thinking that Luke had read Paul's account (or had heard it and remembered it) and had rewritten it

---

19. Gaventa, *Acts*, 149.
20. Conzelmann, *Acts of the Apostles*, 73.
21. Johnson, *The Acts of the Apostles*, 168.

to his own satisfaction."²² Luke reshapes the account to hold "the Jews" responsible, though "it did not occur to Paul that 'the Jews' were after him in Damascus."²³ Johannes Munck also acknowledges as much: "As Paul does not mention the Jews and as his account of his own life is usually preferred to that of Acts, there is every reason to believe him when he said that it was the ethnarch and not the Jews who had on that occasion persecuted him, but it is impossible to explain what exactly occurred."²⁴ Such a reshaping of the incident seems to fit with the overall arc of Acts, portraying Jews as a group more and more opposed to Paul's mission, which becomes increasingly focused on the Gentiles.²⁵ Paul, the self-proclaimed pharisaic Jew, "dies" and is "resurrected" as the apostle to the Gentiles, in a very real sense a father of Christianity.²⁶

RABBAN YOḤANAN BEN ZAKKAI

Rabban Yoḥanan is often presented as the youngest, or least, disciple of Hillel the Elder (despite some problems in chronology).²⁷ The legend of his

---

22. Sanders, *The Jews in Luke–Acts*, 254. Sanders notes the verbal similarity of the phrase *diá tou teíxous* (lit., "through the wall," Acts 9:25) and the use of the verb *xaláo* (lower). On the other hand, the word used for "basket" is different in the two accounts (*sturídi* and *sargáne*). Still, they seem to be referring to the same incident. Fitzmyer and others state that "the Lucan and Pauline accounts describe the same situation from different perspectives," and cites Barrett: "it is too much to suppose that Paul twice left Damascus in a basket." Fitzmyer, *The Acts of the Apostles*, 434. He refers to Barrett, *Acts*, 466.

23. Sanders, 255.

24. Munck, *The Acts of the Apostles*, 85.

25. For further discussion, see Edwards, "Luke's Pharisees," esp. 133.

26. Though he has been seen by some as "the" father of Christianity, I am careful to avoid that claim. See a cautionary discussion in Gager, *The Jewish Lives of the Apostle Paul*, esp. 12–15.

27. As Paul refers to himself as "the least of the apostles" (1 Cor 15:9), so Yoḥanan ben Zakkai is referred to as *qatan*, the least (or "youngest," though the context suggests "least") of the disciples of Hillel the Elder (b. Sukkah 28a). The chronology would work better if we imagined both Yoḥanan and Saul as students of Gamaliel the Elder, the son of Hillel. Some have suggested that Yoḥanan may not even have been a Pharisee, based on the statement attributed to him in m. Yadayim 4.6, where he responds to a complaint of the Sadducees by saying, "Have we nothing on the Pharisees except only this?" I think that this retort can more sensibly be read as mocking the Saduceean opinion (rather than identifying with it). Alternatively, it might also be read as Yoḥanan distancing himself from both parties, in a sense anticipating the rabbinic emergence from Pharisaic Judaism, or Late Second Temple Judaism in general.

escape from Jerusalem just before its destruction by the Romans is narrated in four sources: two versions of Avot d'Rabbi Natan (ARNa and ARNb), Babylonian Talmud, and the midrash collection Lamentations Rabbah. The story appears in its most basic form in the ARNa version:

> Now, when Vespasian came to destroy Jerusalem he said to the inhabitants: "Fools, why do you seek to destroy this city and why do you seek to burn the Temple? For what do I ask of you but to send me one bow or one arrow, and I shall go off from you?"
> They said to him: "Even as we went forth against the first two who were here before thee and slew them, so shall we go forth against thee and slay thee."
> When Rabban Johanan ben Zakkai heard this, he sent for the men of Jerusalem and said to them: "My children, why do you destroy this city and why do you seek to burn the Temple? For what is it that he asks of you? Verily he asks nought of you save one bow or one arrow, and he will go off from you."
> They said to him: "Even as we went forth against the two before him and slew them, so shall we go forth against him and slay him."
> Vespasian had men stationed inside the walls of Jerusalem. Every word which they overheard they would write down, attach (the message) to an arrow, and shoot it over the wall, saying that Rabban Johanan ben Zakkai was one of the Emperor's friends.
> Now, after Rabban Johanan ben Zakkai had spoken to them one day, two and three days, and they still would not attend to him, he sent for his disciples, for Rabbi Eliezer and Rabbi Joshua.
> "My sons," he said to them, "arise and take me out of here. Make a coffin that I might lie in it."
> Rabbi Eliezer took hold of the head end of it, Rabbi Joshua took hold of the foot; and they began carrying him as the sun set, until they reached the gates of Jerusalem.
> "Who is this?" the gatekeepers demanded.
> "It's a dead man," they replied. "Do you not know that the dead may not be held overnight in Jerusalem?"
> "If it's a dead man," the gatekeepers said to them, "take him out."
> So they took him out and continued carrying him until they reached Vespasian. They opened the coffin and Rabban Johanan stood up before him.
> "Art thou Rabban Johanan ben Zakkai?" Vespasian inquired; "tell me, what may I give thee?"

"I ask naught of thee," Rabban Johanan replied, "save Jamnia, where I might go and teach my disciples and there establish a prayer [house] and perform all the commandments.

"Go," Vespasian said to him, "and whatever thou wishest to do, do."

Said Rabban Johanan to him: "By thy leave, may I say something to thee?"

"Speak," Vespasian said to him.

Said Rabban Johanan to him: "Lo, thou art about to be appointed king." [There is a parallel in Josephus; see below.]

"How dost thou know this?" Vespasian asked.

Rabban Johanan replied: "This has been handed down to us, that the Temple will not be surrendered to a commoner, but to a king; as it is said, *And he shall cut down the thickets of the forest with iron, and Lebanon shall fall by a mighty one*" [Isa. 10:34; Lebanon is often taken in rabbinic literature as a reference to the Temple].

It was said: No more than a day, or two or three days, passed before messengers reached him from his city (announcing) that the emperor was dead and that he had been elected to succeed as king.

A catapult was brought to him, drawn up against the wall of Jerusalem. Boards of cedar were brought to him which he set into the catapult, and with these he struck against the wall until he made a breach in it. A swine's head was brought and set into the catapult, and this he hurled toward the (sacrificial) lambs which were on the altar.

It was then that Jerusalem was captured.

Meanwhile Rabban Johanan ben Zakkai sat and waited trembling, the way Eli had sat and waited; as it is said, *Lo, Eli sat upon his seat by the wayside watching; for his heart trembled for the ark of God* (I Sam. 4:13). When Rabban Johanan ben Zakkai heard that Jerusalem was destroyed and the Temple was up in flames, he tore his clothing, and his disciples tore their clothing, and they wept, crying aloud and mourning.[28]

The versions in the Talmud and in Lamentations Rabbah contain additional details, which are not directly relevant to the present study.[29]

28. Goldin, ed., *The Fathers according to Rabbi Nathan* 4.5, 35–37.

29. Lamentations Rabbah I.5.31 and Babylonian Talmud Gittin 56a. The later versions attempt to account for some of the questions implicit in this earliest version: How did Yoḥanan conclude that the defense of Jerusalem was a lost cause? How did he outwit the Jewish zealots (the "gatekeepers")? Why did he not plead with Vespasian to spare the

Jacob Neusner has made a careful comparison of the versions,[30] and concludes that ARNa is the earliest, but even the earliest version of this legend appears long after the event it purports to describe:

> None [of the versions] can possibly date from before ca. A.D. 200. In Tannaitic traditions, attributed to authorities before A.D. 200, we find not the slightest reference to an escape. Indeed, we should not know how Yoḥanan reached Yavneh if we had to rely on [these sources] . . . We may only imagine that at some point after 200, it became important to tell escape stories; no single account was ever widely accepted.[31]

As the subtitle of Neusner's study (*The Peripatetic Saying: The Problem of the Thrice-Told Tale in Talmudic Literature*) implies, it is common to find retellings of legendary material in three different layers of rabbinic texts. This certainly bears comparison with the three tellings of Saul's "conversion" in the Book of Acts. Although these all appear in the same layer of New Testament literature (indeed, within the same book), there is something about the appearance of a "thrice-told tale" which emphasizes its importance at the same time that it undercuts its claim of historical veracity. It is important enough to be told and re-told and told again. Yet insofar as each version differs in its details, the accuracy of any one version is called into question by the others.[32]

The legend of Rabban Yoḥanan's escape also plays on the motif of resurrection, here even more obvious than in the Acts accounts of Paul's

---

city? There are also elements of other versions that hint at Yoḥanan's powers of prophecy (see below, note 35). Underlying most of these questions is some tension around issues of patriotism versus collaboration. The comparison with Jeremiah is apt (see below).

30. Neusner, *Peripatetic Saying*, 151–58. For a detailed analysis of the version in BT Gittin, see Rubenstein, *Talmudic Stories*, 139–75. Rubenstein discusses the ARNa version and compares the three versions of the story on pp. 169–73. It is worth noting that Yoḥanan is clearly the hero of the ARN version, whereas the more extended version in Gittin is critical of him.

31. Neusner, *Peripatetic Saying*, 151–52. In this dating, Neusner follows Judah Goldin, who argues that, although the date of compilation may have been sometime between the seventh and ninth centuries, "the language and the teachings and the idiom are typical of what we find in Tannaite sources [and therefore] the composition of the contents of ARN cannot be much later than the third or following century. . ." Goldin, *The Fathers*, xxi. The textual history of ARN is beyond the scope of this paper, but for those interested in a brief summary, including the recent work of Menahem Kister, see the review by Zellentin of *Avot De-Rabbi Natan*, 363–66.

32. For *Acts*, see again Maguerat, chap. 9.

experience. Yoḥanan actually performs his own death: he climbs into a coffin, is proclaimed dead by his disciples, and is carried outside the walls of Jerusalem, ostensibly for burial. (Note also the reference to "three days.") Once outside he emerges from the coffin and requests an audience with the Roman general. Nowhere does the text refer to this as a resurrection, nor is any special language required in order to make the connection—the action of the story is clear enough. The teacher leaves the doomed city, the Temple is destroyed, and Judaism is reborn at Yavneh (Jabneh, Jamnia).

Any number of familiar accounts of Jewish history make clear that this story is commonly understood as a turning point, one that marks the end of Temple-, priest-, and sacrifice-centered Judaism. It is the beginning of Judaism as the religion of the book, centered on prayer and the study of the sacred text. As a popular work by Jonathan Rosen puts it:

> In a sense, ben Zakkai's journey in his coffin is the symbolic enactment of the transformation Judaism made when it went from being a religion of embodiment to being a religion of the mind and of the book. Jews died as a people of the body, of the land, of the Temple service of fire and blood, and, in one of the greatest acts of translation in human history, they were reborn as the people of the book.[33]

Rosen's interpretation of this legend, though not the work of a historian, is typical of the way in which it has resonated in the popular Jewish imagination. It is not only Yoḥanan who is "resurrected," but Judaism and the Jewish people as well.

Rabban ben Zakkai is one of the heroes of Jewish history. Yet there is every reason to assume that, in the minds of the Zealots, and perhaps of other Jews as well, there was some question of Yoḥanan's loyalty to the group. The prophet Jeremiah faced a similar situation at the time of the destruction of the first Temple, and Amram Tropper has shown that Jeremiah echoes within all four versions of the Yoḥanan ben Zakkai legend.[34] Of the polemi-

---

33. Rosen, *Talmud and the Internet*, 15.

34. Tropper, "Rabban Yoḥanan ben Zakkai, Jeremiah, and the Sack of Jerusalem." Among the parallels between Jeremiah and Yoḥanan ben Zakkai: both are suspected of betrayal (Jer 37; 38); Nebuchadnezzar commands that Jeremiah be looked after by the Babylonian general, and "grant whatever he asks of you" (Jer 39:12), as Vespasian grants Yoḥanan permission to go to Yavneh; Yoḥanan in a coffin might be compared to Jeremiah in the pit (Jer 38:6); both foresaw the destruction of Jerusalem. For expanded treatment see Tropper's article, "Yohanan ben Zakkai, *Amicus Caesaris*" in JSIJ. For the Jeremiah parallels, see esp. pp. 143–49. The article also treats the comparison with

cal purposes served by the legend of his escape, Neusner places first the fact that

> it counters the accusations that Yohanan was a traitor with the opposite claim, that the zealots were over-confident fools, whose only accomplishment was to cause the destruction of the Temple. It was not Yohanan's "treason" that was responsible for the disaster. And the zealots were not only foolish, but also incompetent, for the master succeeded in outwitting them.[35]

If the story was meant on some level to refute accusations against Yohanan, then there must have been such accusations circulating, even at the relatively late date of the legend's appearance.

Indeed, a somewhat less traditional reading of the language suggests that such accusations still lurk, even in this pro-Yohanan text. For the words with which Yohanan initially reproves the zealous defenders of the city echo almost verbatim the words of the Roman general ("Why do you seek to destroy this city and why do you seek to burn the Temple? For what do I ask of you but to send me one bow or one arrow, and I shall go off from you?"). The Roman spies identify Yohanan as "one of the Emperor's friends." Nor, in this version (though the issue comes up in a later version), does he plead with Vespasian to spare the city. He has given up on Jerusalem, and although he bewails its destruction, an anti- Yohanan interpreter could read his mourning as mere formality. In other words, this version of the legend alone does not fully defend (from a "patriotic" Jewish point of view) Yohanan's role. Despite the implied criticism in the Gittin version,[36] Yohanan stands out as the pivotal figure who saved Judaism after the destruction of the Second Temple.

In these legends of Paul and of Yohanan, we see two Pharisees as transitional figures—between the Judaisms of the late Second Temple period and the new forms of Judaism beginning to emerge in Christianity and Rabbinic Judaism. Each narrative depicts a kind of resurrection—itself a marker of pharisaic identity—which functions as a central trope: an old form of Judaism dies and new ones are coming into view.[37]

Josephus (see below).

35. Neusner, *Development of a Legend*, 117.

36. See the reference to Rubenstein's analysis above, n. 31.

37. On the theme of transition, we might also note that the death of Nero, during the siege of Jerusalem, brought an end to the Julio-Claudian house, and the accession of Vespasian marks the beginning of the Flavian dynasty.

Alongside this pair we might briefly mention two more incidents. Josephus, who also claims to be a follower of pharisaic practices, narrates his own narrow escape from a suicide pact, followed by an interview with Vespasian. This too might be read as a trope of resurrection, leading to Josephus' second career as historian, his writings a major source of information about first-century Judaism.[38] The "escape from Jerusalem" motif is also seen in the Christian tradition of the flight to Pella in Transjordan.[39] Galit Hasan-Rokem suggests that both the Yoḥanan and the Pella narratives "take on the meaning of legitimation and authorization for the founding of a religious center outside of Jerusalem after the destruction of the city."[40]

There is no intention here to suggest exact parallels between these various legends, nor that they were composed in any sort of direct "competition" with one another. We are noting a discourse around the theme of resurrection that characterizes the accounts of both Paul and Yoḥanan ben Zakkai. It marks the identities of these two pivotal Pharisees, and the emergence of Christianity and Rabbinic Judaism out of common biblical and pharisaic tropes—and hopes.

BIBLIOGRAPHY

Adams, Sean A. "Paul and Luke: What's Their Relationship?" In *Paul and His Social Relations*, edited by Stanley E. Porter and Christopher D. Land, 125–42. Pauline Studies 7. Leiden: Brill, 2013.
Asch, Sholem. *The Apostle*. Translated by Maurice Samuel. New York: Putnam, 1943.
Barrett, C.K. *Acts*. International Critical Commentary. London: T. & T. Clark, 2004.
Bauer, Walter, et al., *A Greek-English Lexicon of the New Testament and Other Early Christian Literature*. 3rd ed. Chicago: University of Chicago Press, 2000.

---

38. Josephus, *War* III.viii.3–9. He portrays himself as prophesying to Vespasian the latter's future ascendancy to Emperor. This motif is found in the other rabbinic versions of Yoḥanan's interview with Vespasian (LamR. I.5.31 and b. Git. 56a). Josephus adds some details of his own negotiations with Titus in *The Life* 75. One wonders whether the Josephus and Yoḥanan accounts might somehow share a common origin. Jacob Neusner has suggested that the Pharisees received Roman favor at least in part due to Josephus' advocacy: "Josephus himself was probably instrumental in obtaining the recognition of Pharisaic hegemony." See Neusner, *From Politics to Piety*, 149. "Hegemony," such as it was under Roman imperial sponsorship: the Pharisees managed to form the rabbinic coalition. See Cohen, "Significance of Yavneh" and his claim that "The tannaim refused to see themselves as Pharisees . . ." 29.

39. Eusebius, *Ecclesiastical History*, Book 3, Chapter 5.

40. Hasan-Rokem, *Web of Life-Folklore*, 201. Cited in Boyarin, *Border Lines*, 91, and see Boyarin's discussion there.

Boyarin, Daniel. *Border Lines: The Partition of Judaeo-Christianity*. Philadelphia: University of Pennsylvania Press, 2004.

Cohen, Shaye J.D. "The Significance of Yavneh: Pharisees, Rabbis, and the End of Jewish Sectarianism," *Hebrew Union College Annual* 55 (1984) 27–53.

Conzelmann, Hans. *Acts of the Apostles*. Translated by James Limburg, et al. Hermeneia. Philadelphia: Fortress, 1987.

Davies, W. D. *Paul and Rabbinic Judaism*. 4th ed. Philadelphia: Fortress, 1980.

Edwards, Laurence L. "Luke's Pharisees: Emerging Communities." In *Contesting Texts: Jews and Christians in Conversation about the Bible*, edited by Melody D. Knowles et al., 119–35. Minneapolis: Fortress, 2007.

Eusebius. *Ecclesiastical History*. Translated by Kirsopp Lake. Loeb Classical Library. Cambridge: Harvard University Press, 1926.

Fitzmyer, Joseph A. *The Acts of the Apostles*. AB. New York: Doubleday, 1998.

Fredriksen, Paula. "What Does It Mean to See Paul 'within Judaism'?" *JBL* 141 (2022) 359–80. https://doi.org/10.15699/jbl.1412.2022.9

Gager, John G. *The Jewish Lives of the Apostle Paul*. New York: Columbia University Press, 2015.

Gaventa, Beverly Roberts. *Acts*. Abingdon New Testament Commentaries. Nashville: Abingdon, 2003.

Goldin, Judah, ed. *The Fathers According to Rabbi Nathan*. Yale Judaica Series 10. New Haven: Yale University Press, 1955.

Hasan-Rokem, Galit. *The Web of Life-Folklore in Rabbinic Literature: The Palestinian Aggadic Midrash Eikha Rabba* (Hebrew) Tel Aviv: Am Oved, 1996.

Johnson, Luke Timothy. *The Acts of the Apostles*. Sacra Pagina. Collegeville, MN: Liturgical, 1992.

Josephus. *Wars*. Translated by H. St. J. Thackeray. Loeb Classical Library. Cambridge: Harvard University Press, 1956.

Josephus. *Antiquities*. Translated by Louis H. Feldman. Loeb Classical Library. Cambridge, MA: Harvard University Press, 1965.

Levine, Amy-Jill and Marc Zvi Brettler, eds. *The Jewish Annotated New Testament*. Oxford University Press, 2011.

Liddell, H. G. and Robert Scott. *A Greek-English Lexicon*. Revised ed. [L-S] Oxford: Clarendon Press, 1996.

Marguerat, Daniel. *The First Christian Historian: Writing the 'Acts of the Apostles.'* Society for New Testament Studies Monograph Series 121. Cambridge University Press, 2002.

Mason, Steve. "Was Josephus a Pharisee? A Re-examination of Life 10–12" *JJS* 40 (1989) 31–45.

Munck, Johannes. *The Acts of the Apostles*. AB 31. Garden City, NY: Doubleday, 1967.

Neusner, Jacob. *Development of a Legend: Studies on the Traditions concerning Yohanan ben Zakkai*. Studia Post-Biblica 16. Leiden: Brill, 1970.

———. *From Politics to Piety: The Emergence of Pharisaic Judaism*. 1973. Reprint, Eugene, OR: Wipf & Stock, 2003.

———. *A Life of Rabban Yohanan ben Zakkai, Ca. 1–80 C.E.* Studia Post-Biblica 6. Leiden: Brill, 1962.

———. "Mr. Sanders' Pharisees—and Mine." In *The Twentieth Century Construction of "Judaism": Essays on the Religion of Torah in the History of Religion*, 275–79. South Florida Studies in the History of Judaism 32. Atlanta: Scholars, 1991.

———. *The Peripatetic Saying: The Problem of the Thrice-Told Tale in Talmudic Literature.* Brown Judaic Studies 89. Chico, CA: Scholars, 1985.

Pao, David W. *Acts and the Isaianic New Exodus.* 2000. Reprint, Grand Rapids: Baker Academic, 2002.

Rosen, Jonathan. *The Talmud and the Internet: A Journey between Worlds.* New York: Farrar, Straus & Giroux, 2000.

Rubenstein, Jeffrey L. *Talmudic Stories: Narrative Art, Composition and Culture.* Baltimore: Johns Hopkins University Press, 1999.

Sanders, Jack T. *The Jews in Luke–Acts.* Philadelphia: Fortress, 1987.

Smith, Morton. "A Comparison of Early Christian and Early Rabbinic Tradition." *JBL* 82 (1963) 169–76.

———. "Palestinian Judaism in the First Century." In *Israel: Its Role in Civilization,* edited by Moshe Davis, 67–81. New York: Harper, 1965.

Stendahl, Krister. *Paul among Jews and Gentiles.* Philadelphia: Fortress, 1976.

Tropper, Amram. "Rabban Yohanan ben Zakkai, Jeremiah, and the Sack of Jerusalem." Paper presented at the 36th Association for Jewish Studies Conference, Chicago, December 21, 2004.

———. "Yohanan ben Zakkai, *Amicus Caesaris.*" JSIJ (Jewish Studies, an Internet Journal, Bar Ilan University) https://www.academia.edu/44674594/_Yohanan_ben_Zakkai_Amicus_Caesaris_A_Jewish_Hero_in_Rabbinic_Eyes_

Zellentin, Holger. Review of Hans-Jürgen Becker and Christoph Berner, *Avot de-Rabbi Natan: Synoptische Edition Beider Versionen. Hebrew Studies* 49 (2008) 363–66.

4

"A Question That Is Left Hanging"
André LaCocque and Paul Ricoeur:
A Dialogue for Our Time

JOSEPH EDELHEIT AND JAMES MOORE

WE OFFER THIS INTERFAITH essay in memory and honor of two persons who remain our personal and professional role models. We have each worked with André LaCocque in several Jewish Christian dialogues in Chicago and we studied with Paul Ricoeur at the Divinity School of the University of Chicago. When asked to write something for this volume we decided to use the textual dialogue between LaCocque and Ricoeur in *Thinking Biblically: Exegetical and Hermeneutical Studies*. We have chosen their work on Psalm 22, a lamentation, a classic scriptural text appropriate for this unique volume of memorial reflections.

LaCocque describes his friend of decades, his relationship with Paul Ricoeur in his *homage*, "Reading Scripture with Paul Ricoeur":

> "[h]e was exposed from tender age to the Biblical conception of reality, thus to "thinking biblically." To say that he liked it is an understatement. Paul remained faithful to this first love till his last breath. He not only cultivated the formidable Biblical message but felt thoroughly fed by it. In parallel, he developed a strong respect for the Jewish people, old and contemporary. This intrinsic association of the two, People and Scripture, was to him decisive,

the Biblical world being a combination of the People and Faith of Israel."[1] ..." The text is endowed with a life of its own that demands a *'lecture infinie'* (an endless interpretation in light of an infinite revelation of history). The text implies a trajectory of meaning from alpha to omega, from promise to fulfillment; its bearing is teleological."[2]

André LaCocque's Protestant background in Belgium, a dominant Catholic country and culture, made his link to Scripture similar to that of Ricoeur. LaCocque's pastor father saved Jews; an experience so profound that he would later convert to Judaism and make *Aliyah*; immigrate to Israel. This obviously influenced André who studied in a rabbinic academy and used his entire career to teach and interpret Jewish scripture as a Christian professor at Chicago Theological Seminary. He became one of the most active leaders in Chicago's Jewish-Christian dialogues. This engaged him with Paul Ricoeur who had begun to teach *at* the Divinity School of the University of Chicago. The two men and their families became very close and shared their lives.

THINKING BIBLICALLY ABOUT THE UNTHINKABLE (PSALM 22)—JOSEPH A. EDELHEIT

The two European Protestant religious thinkers transformed by the Shoah ultimately produced a paradigm of dialogue and theological reflections; *Thinking Biblically: Exegetical and Hermeneutical Studies*. This is an extraordinary book in which they emphasize the distinctiveness of their respective disciplines (historical-critical biblical scholarship and philosophical hermeneutic) only to underscore the extent to which Ricoeur carefully based his hermeneutical interpretation on a careful critical exegesis of the biblical text and the extent to which LaCocque was not satisfied with his critical exegetical interpretation of the biblical text as long as it did not account for its relationship with the hermeneutical readings in the Jewish tradition in all of its forms. This overlapping of their concerns led to a remarkable dialogue and an extraordinary contribution to the study of key texts of the Hebrew Bible.

Psalm 22 is known among Christians for its opening words of anguish: "My God, My God, why have you abandoned me; why so far from

1. LaCocque, "Reading Scripture with Paul Ricoeur: Homage," 15.
2. LaCocque and Ricoeur, *Reading Scripture*, 16.

delivering me and from my anguished roaring?" (Ps 22:2). These words are repeated by Jesus on the Cross. "Already—not yet: the whole 'Christian' faith is fully present in Psalm 22. Because of the absence of hiatus between the two poles, the Psalm is said by Christ on the cross as if it were for the very first time."[3]

LaCocque pushes the reader to experience the Lament as an essential religious experience of being human. He notes the shift from anguish to praise for God, noting that the biblical voice of lament is one we fully understand. "Life is lived between the two poles of lament and praise. The tension is brilliantly expressed by bringing the two together in the same psalm . . . God is hidden, yet he made himself known through his acts of deliverance to the psalmist's ancestors. Were it not for the divine past self-revelation, there would be no psalm at all, no lament, no asking why, only the silence of nothingness."[4]

The Psalmist illuminates the suffering of being in relationship with God. "Trust in *YHWH* is grounded in memory. There is between yesterday and today the bridge of remembrance. This is how God is also the God of history. The lament roots itself in history, in the history of salvation . . . God is with those who suffer . . . being himself a 'suffering God,'" . . .[5]

LaCocque understands this suffering as refracted through his experience of the Shoah, using Psalm 22 to illuminate the shared Jewish-Christian questions after Auschwitz: "God is my God, not just our God or the God of the Ancestors. Conversely, it is not just our God who has forsaken me, but my God, the one whom I used to trust and who all the same remains in all circumstances my God . . . The one who says 'my God' wonders how it is possible to live on a collective level within the covenantal communion with God, while on an individual level feeling abandoned by God" . . .[6]

There is a midrash, rabbinic interpretation, of 'Lament' using the Hebrew word *Eikha*, which is the Hebrew title of the Book of Lamentations: Rabbi Neḥemya says: The term *eikha* is nothing other than an expression of lamentation. That is what is written: "The Lord God called to the man, and said to him: Where are you [*ayeka*]?" (Gen 3:9), woe are you [*oy lekha*]. (Midrash Rabbah/Eikha) The point of the midrash is that the very first question asked to Adam/Eve was "Where are you?" a question of relationship

---

3. LaCocque, "My God, My God, Why Have You Forsaken Me?," 209.
4. LaCocque and Ricoeur, *Thinking Biblically*, 189.
5. LaCocque and Ricoeur, *Thinking Biblically*, 191.
6. LaCocque and Ricoeur, *Thinking Biblically*, 199.

not spatial placement; this question was an exclamation of "Woe/Alas/Lament!" over the behavior of these first humans. Both LaCocque and Ricoeur seem to be aware that Psalm 22 offers this deeper and possibly much darker reading of the relationship between God and humans.

> What the Psalms of Lamentation preserve, in the first place, is the specificity of individual suffering, which no theology of history seems able to account for. The distinction between individual lamentation and that of the people finds a new legitimation here . . . The Psalms of Lamentation are there to recall that the individual is fragile, exposed to illness and death, vulnerable to the attacks of others. In the final analysis, up to and including the disasters of history, it is the individual who suffers . . . Suffering requires a place for the first person that the anonymity of history cannot grant.[7]

Ricoeur's reading is stimulated by his friend's textual analysis; rereading LaCocque, Ricoeur lifts up the transcendence of suffering as essential to both Scripture and being human. "It is surely only through an act of reading, which is also an act of interpretation, that this reader passes from Psalm 22 to the Book of Job . . . In this way we are led at the end of a long periplus, to reread the Psalms of Lamentation in the light of the controversies of the Book of Job. The 'why' of Psalm 22 is then extracted, under the shock of this encounter, from the context of trust safeguarded by the "My God, My God" of invocation. In being so removed from its initial setting, the 'why' of Psalm 22 is lifted up as a question expecting another answer than the one imposed by the prophets, *a question that is left hanging.*" (emphasis mine)[8]

LaCocque quotes his conversation partner's previous insights about the complexity of scripture's textual struggle with suffering, evil and God's presence:

> "We cannot overemphasize therefore the unmediated juxtaposition, in the Hebrew Bible, of the liturgical and hymnic affirmation of the omnipotence of God and the confession of the persistence of evil, a confession that is itself raised to the lyrical plane of the lamentation. The relation of the full sovereignty of God to the end of time only underscores the dissonance between the proclamation of omnipotence and the confession of the 'terror of history.'"[9]

---

7. Ricoeur, "Lamentation as Prayer," 226.
8. Ricoeur, "Lamentation as Prayer," 227.
9. Ricoeur, "Fides Quaerens Intellectum: Antecedents bibliques?"; from LaCocque,

Furthering Interfaith Biblical Scholarship

Psalm 22 is unlike any other Lamentation text, because it is central to Christianity's origin story, the Passion. Jesus the Judean is the embodiment, the not-yet Incarnation of God's suffering presence of which both Ricoeur and LaCocque write.

We find a curious echo of Ricoeur and LaCocque in the work of the Jewish poet and early Zionist intellectual Haim Nahman Bialik: "So much for the language of words. But, in addition, "there are yet to the Lord" languages without words: songs, tears and laughter. *(I would include anger!)* And the speaking creature has been found worthy of them all. These languages being where words leave off, and their purpose is not to close but to open. They rise from the void. They *are* the rising up the void . . ."[10]

Bialik the Jewish poet who immortalized both the generation that perished in the biblical wilderness ("The Dead of the Wilderness") and those massacred in pogroms ("The City of Slaughter") adds an immediate impulse to Ricoeur's challenge of, ". . . a question left hanging . . ." This classic Song of Lamentation is not limited to the biblical voice and experience. Surely both LaCocque and Ricoeur were transformed by language rising up out of the void of the Shoah. LaCocque notes about his intellectual and spiritual conversation partner. ". . . 'saviors' rescuers of sanity and righteousness, did blunt the absoluteness of evil. They were among the 'lamed-waw,'" the thirty-six just who redeem the world in each generation, according to Jewish tradition. Paul Ricoeur was one of them, unknowingly to himself of course, but not to us, his witnesses. In the darkness of our terrible times, he was a beacon, and he remains so for generations to come."[11]

We offer this inadequate reflection on two men who refused to be silenced by all the empty languages that rose up out of the destructive voids of the twentieth century. André LaCocque and Paul Ricoeur engaged in the acts that are the most resilient ways to refute self-destructive lamentation; they taught how to read and re-read the sacred in response to any . . . *question that is left hanging.*

"My God, My God, Why Have You Forsaken Me?," 209.

10. Bialik, "Revealment and Concealment in Language," 27 (previously published by *Commentary*, 1927), 27.

11. LaCocque, "Reading Scripture with Paul Ricoeur: Homage," 18.

A RESPONSE WITH NEW QUESTIONS—JAMES MOORE

My colleague has ended his portion of our dialogue with the image of a question left hanging. In fact, our relationship began with a question—would you want to teach together, an invitation extended in a hallway at Valparaiso University where a young rabbi had decided to take on a teaching load in addition to serving his congregation. That question has led to more than forty years of collaboration, indeed, friendship that has produced both a lifelong dialogue and several joint publications, the first of which was an essay on team teaching a class on Jewish-Christian dialogue. After four decades of dialogue, we now come to the question left hanging with the clear intent to show both the dialogue between André LaCocque and Paul Ricoeur as well as a dialogue between this rabbi/professor Joseph Edelheit and a pastor/professor James Moore by reflecting on both an intriguing Psalm 22 and an equally intriguing conversation between André LaCocque and Paul Ricoeur.

That image of a question left hanging is quite vivid if it is applied not merely to Psalm 22 but also to the words from the gospels that place in the mouth of Jesus this very Psalm, this question left hanging. The implication becomes, then, profound for Christians and for Jewish-Christian dialogue. For Paul Ricoeur, the Psalm both in its context of worship and in Christian understanding of the "passion narrative" is revealed as a critical clash between two views (from the end or the beginning of the Psalm) that is resolved only by a rehabilitation of the meaning and value of the Psalm as a prayer of lament as my colleague has developed so fully. Ricoeur concludes his reflection on Psalm 22 with thoughts that reveal both the basic argument of the essay as well as his interaction with André LaCocque in this volume on *Thinking Biblically*. This also shows why for him, the question must be "left hanging." Ricoeur writes:

> Another conclusion for the rehabilitation of the prayer of lamentation would be that what we might call its agonistic character has to be preserved. Looked at from the point of view of its end, the movement from lamentation to praise seems to unfold within a single "being-with-God." Looked at from its beginning, the prayer is a movement that starts from the silence of God and never loses its aspect of being a struggle for renewed trust.[12]

---

12. Ricoeur, "Lamentation as Prayer," 231.

This brief summary of Ricoeur's analysis says much about Ricoeur's approach to the interpretation of the Psalm as well as his relation and interaction with André LaCocque. Before taking up this analysis, however, we can digress a bit since in this case we have more than the text. André consented to an interview at the meeting of The Society for Ricoeur Studies annual meeting just before his death. In that interview, he talked about the motivation for producing *Thinking Biblically*, which began simply as a set of conversations. He invited Paul to engage in these reflections during a low point in Ricoeur's life.[13] Considering the well-being of his friend, André invited Paul to engage in reflecting on texts as a kind of therapy. Knowing this, we can see more clearly that the reflections on Psalm 22 are consequential not only as an important component of the religious traditions but also as a personal statement that Ricoeur makes in the midst of his emotional struggles.

Given that insight, we can return to the analysis of Psalm 22 outlined so well in the above section of Ricoeur's essay. We ask first of all why would a text need rehabilitation? Of course, we also see that it is not just the text but also the worshippers who come to offer this prayer that needs rehabilitation. The notion of rehabilitation in fact alerts us to the interpretive approach that Ricoeur so often uses especially in the earlier years, a structural approach. In fact, Ricoeur chooses this approach as a literary critic but also because he does not see himself as a Biblical scholar. Thus, he gladly makes use of Biblical scholars and historical criticism to help provide basic information that can then inform his structural analysis.

This means, of course, that the relationship between Ándré and Paul was a natural fit for Ricoeur and André as scholars. Indeed, his entire essay on Psalm 22 (also for the entire book project) takes the lead from André. He consistently remarks on what André's analysis has revealed both to make use of the information and also to contrast the two approaches. André is led to see that there is a problem with the Psalm in that it seems to move too quickly from despair at the beginning to praise at the end. This creates a problem since both André and Paul see the Psalm as a prayer of lamentation, a prayer offered by worshippers in the midst of deep despair—"Why, O Lord, have you forsaken me?" Can such worshippers so easily hang on to their hope and trust in God? If Ricoeur has figuratively joined these worshippers, can he so easily accept that quick move to hope and trust?

---

13. André LaCocque interview with Joseph Edelheit, Society for Ricoeur Studies Annual Meeting, 2022.

The answer to that question is revealed for Ricoeur by asking about the structure of the lament. Thus, the nature of the prayer will shift depending on how one understands the structure—from the end or the beginning. Ricoeur implies that it is the latter that preserves the full meaning of the text in that the struggle and questioning with God that opens the Psalm must be preserved even as the hope expressed at the end is recovered as a "not yet." This discovery found by reflecting on Psalm 22 then becomes an insight into how all laments can be understood. Even a fulfillment of hope does not eliminate the despair and pain of the sense of abandonment. To add another dimension to this assertion (as the only way to rehabilitate the lament) I am reminded of the claim that Elie Wiesel made in the anguish in the years after his "liberation." He simply asked the question whether the hope for the messiah is vanquished by the horror of the present. He asks whether if the messiah is to come why was this not the appropriate time? Is it not too late now?[14]

Ricoeur's analysis, like that of LaCocque, leaves the Psalm to its original context for the most part. It is a lament voiced by a people in exile. However, for these two Christians the reflection cannot be left there as it is clear something must be said of the way the Psalm is inserted into the gospel text of both Mark and Matthew. We can follow André's analysis which again is the beginning point for Ricoeur. The words from the cross must be taken as part of a received tradition. That is, the words cannot be understood in the context of the crucifixion narrative unless they are understood as part of the entire Psalm (both despair and praise). Even more, it is best seen as a way to link Jesus and the moment with the entire history of the laments of the people. Jesus speaks in this way not merely for himself but for the whole people. But then we are led to ask what this means given Ricoeur's structural analysis.

If Ricoeur reads the Psalm correctly (the structure demands looking from the beginning), then the opening words demand that the struggle with God remains. The crucifixion is not, cannot be read as a victory but rests in the not yet while the struggle, the pain and despair remain. It is a "not yet moment." The supposed victory proclaimed in much of Christian theological tradition cannot remove the anguish. We dare not run too quickly to the moment of hope, but we leave this in a "not yet. "The dialogue presents us with a question for Christian theologians then to pursue.

---

14. Wiesel, *Messengers of God*.

What does this reading of the crucifixion mean for Christian teaching and for Jewish-Christian dialogue?

My colleague has concluded his reflection by drawing on Haim Nahman Bialik, for which I respond with a person whose life of faith was completely anchored in his unending dialogue for the sake of his Christianity, A. Roy Eckardt. Eckardt, at least in his initial theological response to the Shoah, concludes that Christians must now understand the crucifixion *as if* Jesus is still on the cross. He is "not yet" risen for that could not do justice to address the horror of the Shoah.[15] Much like Ricoeur's argument that only a reading from the beginning can rehabilitate the Psalm and the gospel, Echardt contends that only a Jesus *"not yet"* risen can rehabilitate Christian theology after the Shoah. It is not clear that Eckardt offers a fully developed view for Christian theology and for dialogue (he later changes this view) which perhaps is the only way that dialogue can proceed for our time when horror seems all too present for us.

Surely André LaCocque and Paul Ricoeur were compelled, as is my colleague and co-author in dialogue to remain present to each other especially when we studied, reflected, and accepted that surely this is "a question left hanging."

BIBLIOGRAPHY

Bialik, Haim Nahman. "Revealment and Concealment in Language." *Commentary* (1927) 27.

Eckardt, A Roy, and Alice Eckhardt. *Long Night's Journey into Day.* Detroit. Wayne State University Press, 1982.

LaCocque, André. "My God, My God, Why Have You Forsaken Me?" In André LaCocque and Paul Ricoeur, *Thinking Biblically: Exegetical and Hermeneutical Studies*, 187–209. Chicago: University of Chicago Press, 1998.

———. "Reading Scripture with Paul Ricoeur: Homage." In *Reading Scripture with Paul Ricoeur*, edited by Joseph Edelheit and James Moore, 15–20. Lanham, MD: Lexington, 2022.

LaCocque, André, and Paul Ricoeur. *Thinking Biblically: Exegetical and Hermeneutical Studies.* Chicago: University of Chicago Press, 1998.

Ricoeur, Paul, "Fides Quaerens Intellectum: Antecedents bibliques?" *Archivio di Filosofia* 68 (1990) 38.

Ricoeur, Paul, "Lamentation as Prayer." In André LaCocque and Paul Ricoeur, *Thinking Biblically: Exegetical and Hermeneutical Studies*, 211–32. Chicago: University of Chicago Press, 1998.

Wiesel, Elie. *Messengers of God.* New York: Summit, 1976.

---

15. Eckardt and Eckardt, *Long Night's Journey into Day*, 125ff.

5

Imagine I Am Sitting There
An Interreligious Perspective on Matthew 23

RACHEL S. MIKVA

Matthew 23 *Then Jesus said to the crowds and to his disciples,* [2] *"The scribes and the Pharisees sit on Moses's seat;* [3] *therefore, do whatever they teach you and follow it, but do not do as they do, for they do not practice what they teach.* [4] *They tie up heavy burdens, hard to bear, and lay them on the shoulders of others, but they themselves are unwilling to lift a finger to move them.* [5] *They do all their deeds to be seen by others, for they make their phylacteries broad and their fringes long.* [6] *They love to have the place of honor at banquets and the best seats in the synagogues* [7] *and to be greeted with respect in the marketplaces and to have people call them rabbi. . . .*
[13] *"But woe to you, scribes and Pharisees, hypocrites! For you lock people out of the kingdom of heaven. For you do not go in yourselves, and when others are going in you stop them.* [[14] *Woe to you, scribes and Pharisees, hypocrites! For you devour widows' houses and for the sake of appearance you make long prayers; therefore you will receive the greater condemnation.]* [15] *Woe to you, scribes and Pharisees, hypocrites! For you cross sea and land to make a single convert, and you make the new convert twice as much a child of hell as yourselves. . . .*
[23] *"Woe to you, scribes and Pharisees, hypocrites! For you tithe mint, dill, and cumin and have neglected the weightier matters of the*

> *law: justice and mercy and faith. It is these you ought to have practiced without neglecting the others.* ²⁴ *You blind guides! You strain out a gnat but swallow a camel!*
> ²⁵ *"Woe to you, scribes and Pharisees, hypocrites! For you clean the outside of the cup and of the plate, but inside they are full of greed and self-indulgence.* ²⁶ *You blind Pharisee! First clean the inside of the cup and of the plate, so that the outside also may become clean.* (NRSV)

I AM SITTING IN the church as the preacher begins a sermon on the lectionary reading from the Gospel according to Matthew, a portion of the "seven woes" of chapter 23.[1] She offers the necessary caveats: its scathing critique of scribes and Pharisees is not meant as objective description, but as polemic. It should not be used, as it too often was (is?), to vilify Jews or Judaism. Chastened by Rosemary Ruether's condemnation of the schism between judgment and promise, whereby Christian exegesis applied every positive description of the people Israel in Hebrew Bible to the Christian community and every chastisement to the Jews,[2] the preacher directs the New Testament's censure toward the community of present-day Christian listeners. How are *we* closing off others from the kin-dom of heaven? How often do we pay lip service to the values of our faith, and violate them in practice? Or pay attention to the technical requirements and miss the deeper significance? Are we Christian only on the outside, to make a show of piety—a practice of vanity rather than service?

But I am a Jew, a rabbi, a teacher of text—a spiritual, biological, and intellectual descendant of the scribes and Pharisees.[3] Each word cuts deeply. The congregation is looking in a mirror to examine how pride distorts faith, but I am reflected on the other side, a woman who joyfully bears the title "Rabbi." I am the one who fingers the *tzitzit* ("fringes") on my *tallit* when I pray, delighting in the mystical way the knots and wrappings signal my connection and commitments to God.

The preacher's insightful teasing out of hypocrisy cannot help but resurrect the archetype of "pharisaism" as portrayed in the text. When her parishioners ponder the outside versus the inside of their cups, I fear that it feeds the trope of "legalism" as an epithet. Can they appreciate how my

---

1. Passages from the chapter appear in each year of the cycle: https://lectionary.library.vanderbilt.edu//daily-citationindex.php

2. Ruether, *Faith and Fratricide*, 228–32.

3. To complexify this association, see Cohen, "The Significance of Yavneh"; and Reed, "When Did Rabbis Become Pharisees?" 888–91.

ritual observances—including my kosher dishes—enlarge my ethical and spiritual capacities rather than obscure them? Do they meet God in the details of how we eat, talk, make love, labor, rest, and do business—or do they believe that God has no business there? The Book of Matthew advocates both the letter of the law and its spirit,[4] but later Christian interpretation rendered observance of Torah obsolete.

Each critique, even while urging contemporary Christians toward self-critical faith, is constructed from the bones of my ancestors. The congregation can pretend to be the Pharisees in order to examine their souls, but not without implicating mine. What if the canon enshrined a text of contemporary racist "lazy and dishonest" stereotypes? Could it be used to prod the faithful regarding work ethics and truth-telling—or only held at arm's length, teaching over against the terrifying othering embedded within? Woe to us, peoples of the book, who sometimes hold our texts more dear than the radiant image of the Divine shining through our neighbor's face.

Listening to the sermon, I remind myself that the passage's self-righteous fury has sometimes provided a valuable tool for transformation. Luther justified his virulent critique of the Catholic Church by stating, "I have Christ's example."[5] Frederick Douglass found voice in the gospel to challenge slavery as an institution that set burdens on others—burdens that those in power were not themselves willing to bear. He defended his faith by condemning the profound hypocrisy of white, Christian Americans who practiced only outward forms of religion while ignoring its greater claims for justice and mercy.[6]

But, the history does not calm my spirit. I notice counter-judgment in my internal response: rabbinic Judaism historically affirmed that the righteous of all nations could gain entry to *olam haba* (lit: the next world).[7] It is Christian exclusivism that shut out the majority of human souls from heaven, dividing the world into the saved and the damned. Examples of contemporary Christian hypocrisy flood my imagination. I would not say such things aloud of course, so my ungracious reaction makes no waves. In the church, I am invisible. When that thought crosses my mind, I realize what seems to be missing from the preacher's faithful efforts to redeem the

---

4. See, for example, Matt 5:17–19, 23:3, 23.

5. Luther, "Letter to Pope Leo X," in *Reformation Writings of Martin Luther*, 1:337. He refers to Matt 23:33 among other verses.

6. Douglass, "Appendix," in *Life of an American Slave*.

7. See, for instance, t. Sanhedrin 13:2, Maimonides, *Mishnah Torah Hilchot Teshuva* 3:5.

text. No one sees my wounds because the cure for the text is to erase me. Immediately, I think of André.

RESISTING ERASURE

When I arrived at Chicago Theological Seminary (CTS) as the first occupant of the Rabbi Herman E. Schaalman Chair in Jewish Studies, I invited Dr. André LaCocque to lunch. After all, he had been the one to invite Rabbi Schaalman to begin teaching at CTS decades before, and their long friendship had been key to establishing the chair. I also knew that Dr. LaCocque had created the Center for Jewish, Christian, and Islamic Studies—a prescient interreligious academic project that had gone quiet after his retirement but left a lasting imprint on the seminary's interreligious commitments. As we were reviving it, his experience would be of great value.

At lunch I learned of his childhood during the Shoah, when his family harbored Jews in Belgium; Dr. LaCocque never forgot how easy it is to use religion as a tool for division and demonization. Decades later, he and his beloved wife Claire sent their own children to an orthodox Jewish day school so they would know what it was like to be "the other." His biography was inspiring.

Still, I was taken aback when he opined during that first encounter that the key reason Christian seminary students need to learn about Judaism is to understand their theological and historical roots. What about being interested in religious difference out of respect for the living tradition, for teachings and practices that are important to other people today? His conviction appeared to erase Jews and Judaism as subjects, turning them into objects of Christian study to advance formation.

In focusing on historical rather than contemporary Judaism, I also feared that it perpetuated the dangerous mythology of *Spätjudentum*—literally "late Judaism"—seeing Judaism in the time of Jesus as the end of its story or significance. "Judaism is long since a dead religion," Friedrich Schleiermacher announced in 1799. Like other Protestants of his era, he was aware that there continued to be people who identified as Jews. He declared that the beauty of this faith, however, was "completely buried, and the whole constitutes such a remarkable example of the corruption and total disappearance of religion from a great body in which it was formerly found."[8] Theological justification for this notion of Jews subsisting without

---

8. Schleiermacher, *On Religion*, 113–14.

a living faith had circulated since the time of Augustine: "The Jews had been cursed by God and condemned to a nomadic, perpetually oppressed lifestyle as punishment for their participation in the crucifixion and as a concrete demonstration of the consequences of unbelief."[9]

Dr. LaCocque did not believe such calumnies of course and, as our relationship developed, I realized how unfounded my fears were. André was instrumental in ensuring that CTS was among the first Christian theological schools to reemphasize Jesus as a Jew, and to highlight ways in which the New Testament reflects internal Jewish controversies. As a scholar of Hebrew Bible, his insights continually challenged what R. Kendall Soulen identified as "structural supersession" in how Christian commentators read the dual canon.[10] In place of the usual emphasis on creation and "the fall," which then bypassed entirely God's involvement with the people of Israel in order to focus on the salvific role of Jesus, André saw all of Hebrew Bible as significant for imagining God's redemptive plan. He was unhappy when we decided to change the title of the core courses he once taught from "People and Faith of Israel" to "Interpreting the Hebrew Bible" so ordination committees would recognize what our graduates had studied. Christian students must be reminded at every turn, he argued, that this text—which he generally called the Prime Testament—is not "background" for Christianity.

So what did André mean when he suggested that Christians need to learn about Judaism so they can understand their own roots? He agreed that there was great value in engaging Jews and studying Judaism, coming to understand people who orient around religion differently—in their own terms. At the same time, he believed that Christians need a deeper investment in this work and, to do that, they need to understand how their own faith and wellbeing are at stake. He invoked Paul's image of the graft from the olive tree: "Remember that you do not support the root, but the root supports you" (Rom 11:18). If Christians understand themselves as a living tether to Jews and Judaism, you have a bulwark against the tragic othering we have witnessed throughout history.

I was not fully persuaded, given the dangers of such proximity. As Jonathan Z. Smith argues, while difference or "otherness" may be perceived as being either like-us or not-like-us, it becomes most problematic when it is too-much-like-us or when it claims to be-us. It is here that the real

---

9. Newman, "Death of Judaism," 456.
10. Soulen, *The God of Israel and Christian Theology*, 28–33.

urgency of theories of the other emerges, called forth not so much by a requirement to place difference, but rather by an effort to situate ourselves.[11]

Nonetheless, I appreciated André's commitment to dismantle anti-Jewish teachings and to resist erasure of Christianity's Jewish roots. He would be squirming in the pew alongside me.

REVISIBILIZING JUDAISM

I determined to carry his counsel with me even if I did not always agree, paying attention to how Judaism illuminates early Christianity and continues to impact Christian formation. Reading Matthew 23 through this lens immediately surfaces the Jewish nature of the critique.[12]

The Hebrew prophets frequently called members of the community to task for hypocrisy, for example. Jeremiah is portrayed standing in the Temple courtyard, incredulous that some of the people steal, murder, and commit adultery—violating God's teachings in serious ways—and yet come to the sanctuary and imagine that it will somehow protect them. "Do you consider this House, which bears My name, to be a den of thieves?" (Jer 7:1–11). In the next chapter, he proclaims, "How can you say, 'We are wise, and we possess the Torah of YHWH?' Assuredly, for naught has the pen labored, for naught the scribes!... Priest and prophet alike, they all act falsely" (Jer 8:8, 10).

Several rabbinic texts specifically indict hypocrisy among the Pharisees. While the early rabbinic movement included individuals who identified as Pharisees, their claim of stringent observance invited special scrutiny. The earliest layer of this discourse is tannaitic (1st–2nd century CE), but the earliest text in which the categories are explained is the Palestinian Talmud, *Berakhot* 9:5:7 (4th century):

שִׁבְעָה פְרוּשִׁין הֵן פָּרוּשׁ שִׁכְמִי. וּפָרוּשׁ נִקְפִּי. וּפָרוּשׁ קִיזָאי פָּרוּשׁ מָה הַנְּבְיָיה. פָּרוּשׁ אֲדַע חוֹבָתִי וְאֶעֱשֶׂנָּה. פָּרוּשׁ יִרְאָה. פָּרוּשׁ אַהֲבָה. פָּרוּשׁ שִׁכְמִי. טָעִין מִצְווֹתָא עַל כֵּיתְפָא. פָּרוּשׁ נִקְפִּי. אֲקֵיף לִי וַאֲנָא עָבֵיד מִצְוָה. פָּרוּשׁ קִיזָאי. עֲבַד חָדָא חוֹבָה וְחָדָא מִצְוָה וּמְקַזֵּז חָדָא בְחָדָא. פָּרוּשׁ מָה הַנְּבְיָיה. מָאן דְּאִית לִי מֶהֱנָא מְנַכִּי עָבֵד מִצְוָה. פָּרוּשׁ אֲדַע חוֹבָתִי וְאֶעֱשֶׂנָּה. הֵי דָא חוֹבָתָה עֲבָדִית דְּאַעֲבִיד מִצְוָה כְּוָותָהּ. פָּרוּשׁ יִרְאָה כְּאִיּוֹב. פָּרוּשׁ אַהֲבָה כְּאַבְרָהָם. אֵין לָךְ חָבִיב מְכוּלָּם אֶלָּא פָּרוּשׁ אַהֲבָה כְּאַבְרָהָם.

---

11. Smith, *Relating Religion*, 245. See also Freyne, "Vilifying the Other and Defining the Self," 117–43.

12. See Weinfeld, "The Charge of Hypocrisy."

> There are seven kinds of *perushim* (Pharisees): shoulder Pharisee, credit Pharisee, balancing Pharisee, "what is the deduction" Pharisee, "I will do it when I realize my guilt" Pharisee, fear Pharisee, love Pharisee. A shoulder Pharisee wears his fulfillment of commandments on his shoulder. A credit Pharisee figures, "Give me credit and I will fulfill a commandment." A balancing Pharisee commits one transgression and then observes one commandment to balance one against the other. A "what is the deduction" Pharisee thinks, "I will deduct this fulfilling of a commandment from what I have" [a checklist?]. A "I will do it when I realize my guilt" Pharisee says, "I committed this sin so I will fulfill a commandment like it." A fear Pharisee is like Job. A love Pharisee is like Abraham. No one is as beloved as a love Pharisee [one who fulfills commandments out of love], like Abraham.[13]

These images are not all negative, but they clearly reject ostensibly religious deeds that are performed for public acclaim or reward, or with a similarly transactional approach.

Numerous additional details in Matthew 23 echo Hebrew Bible. In v. 12, the image of humbling the exalted and exalting the humble resonates with Hannah's prayer (1 Sam 2:8) and other passages that valorize humility (e.g., Num 12:3; Isa 40:4; Prov 15:33; 18:12). Decrying the persecution of prophets,[14] lamenting the fate of Jerusalem (its earlier destruction by the Babylonian Empire), recalling God's seemingly futile efforts to guide the people—all these are very "Jewish." The chapter ends with a quote from Ps 118:26, "Blessed is the one who comes in the name of the Lord," a song that likely served as part of Temple ritual.

The similarities, which revisibilize the Jewishness of the early community of Jesus followers, also illuminate differences. While Christians hear in the Psalms quotation a promise of Jesus' return, for example, Jews recite the song as the climax of *Hallel* (lit: Praise, comprising Ps 113–118) at festivals and other occasions—and lift up that particular verse at Jewish weddings to celebrate the sacred purpose for which people have gathered. The author of Matthew holds the current generation responsible for all the innocent

---

13. See also b. Sotah 22b, where some of the categories and their explanations are different. *Avot d'Rabbi Natan (A)* 37:4 presents eight categories.

14. Isaac Kalimi compares details in the Gospels with the account in 2 Chr 24:20–22, concluding that they recount the same event despite differing details. He also notes that mentioning the murders of Abel and Zechariah as "bookends" suggests that the passages in Matthew 23 and Luke 11 "confirm a rising tripartite Biblical canon," with Genesis at the beginning and Chronicles at the end ("Murder of the Prophet Zechariah," 260).

blood shed by their ancestors, but the prophet Ezekiel insisted that people would suffer only for their own sins (Ezek 18; see also Jer 31:29–30). Even then, the prophet emphasized, those who repent will be forgiven. Reconciling Ezekiel's pronouncement with Torah passages that suggest Divine punishment endures to the third generation, the tannaitic sages limited it to a case in which the descendants perpetuate the sins of their ancestors (*Mekhilta de-Rabbi Ishmael, Baḥodesh* 6; *Sifra Beḥukkotai* 2:7). Yet apparent contrasts often lead back to similarities. Later Christian writers made the same argument as the rabbinic sages, reasoning that God does not act unjustly. Both communities of interpreters continued to struggle with the enigma of Divine justice.[15]

POLEMIC

Reflections on polemic also reveal complex dynamics of similarity and difference. Hebrew Bible polemicizes against Canaanites and even justifies war against them as Divinely commanded once their iniquity has reached its full measure (see Gen 15:16; Deut 7). It does not include much name-calling like one sees in Matthew 23 and other New Testament texts, but the Canaanites are presented as a threat, always luring Israel toward idolatry. In both scriptures, the polemic is not really addressed to the target, but to the insiders and the persuadeables—to emphasize how they should be different. Even though Matthew 23 repeats the trope, "Woe to you, scribes and Pharisees," Jesus is portrayed speaking to the crowds and his disciples (Matt 23:1).

Both Hebrew Bible's polemic against Canaanites and Matthew's polemic against Jewish leadership suggest a greater distinction between the communities and their practices than likely existed. New Testament scholarship in recent decades has focused on reading Matthew as a product of Jewish sectarian argument, believing that the author was active in the Galilee and directly competing with other Jewish groups for followers in the wake of the Temple's destruction in the late first century.[16] Anthony Saldarini argues, "Matthew's rancor against the leadership indicates that they, not he, had been successful in attracting most of the people of the

---

15. See Weiss, "Sins of the Parents," 9–10. Rabbinic theology is multivocal and contextual, so there are also passages that seem to affirm intergenerational punishment.

16. See, for example, Kampen, *Matthew within Sectarian Judaism*. Some scholars suggest a mixed city outside the land of Israel, such as Antioch.

Jewish community." Thus, the portrayal of Jesus' triumphant entry into Jerusalem and rhetorical victories in chapters 21–22 support the thesis that the book reflects an ongoing contest with a "rival reform movement." The author is fighting to "legitimate himself and his group as the true leaders of Israel, accurate interpreters of the Bible, and the authentic messengers of God's will."[17]

He utilizes a compelling strategy for the underdog, turning each potential strength of the adversary into a weakness. The merits of the scribes and Pharisees are erased by their failings. He acknowledges that they occupy the seat of authority for interpreting the tradition, for example, but he accuses them of abusing their power. They are committed and successful in making converts, but subsequently lead them on a doomed path. They are scrupulous in their tithes but miss the big picture. And they honor the prophets by building and decorating their tombs, but are implicated in their persecution and execution as well.[18] The emerging Christian community, still struggling against Roman oppression, could not have known how devastating this rhetoric of othering would become after they gained the reins of imperial power.

A notable difference emerges when comparing Matthew's critique of the Pharisees with what is found in early rabbinic texts. While dismissive of certain approaches to religious practice, the rabbinic passage does not create the same dichotomization of us and them. It is not polemical (from Greek, *polemikos*—warlike). It suggests a different strategy, illustrative of what Shaye Cohen calls "the end of Jewish sectarianism" in the wake of the Temple's destruction.[19] As minority populations in the Sassanian and Roman empires, Jews struggled to resist the unceasing imperial and cultural pressures that caused communities to fracture. *Lo titgodedu*—do not form factions, they warned (b. Yevamot 13b). Theologically, they attributed exile in part to baseless hatred among the diverse Jewish groups of the late Second Temple period. While they still determined which opinion to endorse as normative practice, they presented divergent teachings as authentic embodiments of Torah. It is likely that the rabbis considered the valorization

---

17. Saldarini, "Delegitimation of Leaders in Matthew 23," 661, 664.

18. See Simmonds, "'Woe to You . . . Hypocrites!'" He notes that Quintillian mentioned the rhetorical strategy of censuring someone with pretend praise, and Aristotle identified it as a technique of aggressive prosecutors.

19. Cohen, "The Significance of Yavneh."

of multivocality as the best strategy for gathering followers and retaining community cohesion.

Yet there is overlap here as well. Elements of this strategy are evident in Paul's work to reconcile Jewish and Gentile segments of the Jesus movement: *There is no longer Jew or Greek* (Gal 3:28; Col 3:11). In Romans 14–15, he acknowledges distinct practice and doctrine within the community and encourages followers not to quarrel over disputed matters. As portrayed in 1 Cor 11:19, he is not happy about divisions among the followers but surmises that the differences might be necessary to discern the best path; the subsequent chapter discusses diverse ways in which each person receives the Holy Spirit, comprising interdependent parts of the body of Christ.

Religious communities naturally shift between focusing on what separates them from others and what binds them together. Texts have afterlives, however. The polemic against the Canaanites might seem harmless, since their tribal identities were absorbed into the empires of antiquity. Yet a neo-pagan student in my Hebrew Bible course felt the sting of condemnation, especially because contemporary theists often reject the spiritual validity of her path. We also know that polemics get repurposed, casting some new adversary in the role of the other, in order to stigmatize or dehumanize them.

Many Christians have absorbed aspects of the New Testament's polemic, even those who believe they harbor no negative feelings about Jews or Judaism. Matthias Henze writes,

> During my presentations on Jesus and the law in several churches, I was struck by two sentiments that I heard repeatedly from people in the audience. The first: At the time of Jesus, Jews had a rather narrow understanding of the law. Their religious lives were largely organized around the interpretation of, and strict obedience to, the law, which they took to an extreme. And the second sentiment: Jesus overcame this form of religion and freed his followers from the law. Jesus abolished the law and replaced it with love and common sense.[20]

Amy-Jill Levine similarly describes the common misconception that observance of Torah was considered burdensome and Jesus sought to lighten the load. In fact, Jesus is often portrayed making it more stringent: Torah forbids murder, and Jesus expands it to include anger and insult (Matt 5:21–22). Torah forbids adultery, and Jesus expands it to include lust (Matt 5:28).

---

20. Henze, *Mind the Gap*, 115.

She mentions other misrepresentations that continue to shape Christian attitudes toward Judaism. They assume God was distant until Jesus called out "Father," even though the relationship of God and Israel has always been described and experienced in intimate, familial forms. They frequently misunderstand "impurity" to convey some kind of moral judgment and marginalization, when it is simply one of several common, temporary human states. They portray Jesus as liberating women from Jewish patriarchy, ignoring the fact that Jewish women in antiquity owned their own homes, served as patrons, studied with sages, appeared in the Temple and in synagogues, controlled their property, and had freedom of travel. Nothing Jesus did was radical when it came to women. Nor was he ministering to "outcasts" in the way many Christians imagine. Sinners and tax collectors were not cast out; those with diseases considered contagious were physically separated but still tended by the priests who would monitor their healing. Gentiles participated in the life of the community.[21]

These mischaracterizations are all residues of the polemic embedded in New Testament and later Christian literature. It may not be possible to strip such texts of their power to harm. Even when the pastor turned the critique to examine her own community's behaviors, it still reinforced images of the Pharisees. Our plural world demands that we cannot read or speak about religious "others" without imagining that they are sitting there.

DIFFICULT TEXTS

Would I prefer that Matthew 23 be excised from the lectionary and never read? There are many ways in which humans try to circumscribe the text: Marcion lobbied to jettison the entire Hebrew Bible from Christian scripture. Jefferson eliminated most of the supernatural elements in his edited version of New Testament, literally cutting and pasting passages to evoke his ethical deism. Elizabeth Cady Stanton gathered a committee to create *The Women's Bible*, selecting and commenting on specific passages to highlight women's existential equality and the patriarchal distortion of God's will. Selective memory is one of the best tools to excise difficulties, and lectionary frameworks sometimes make it official.

The lectionary cycle in Judaism, however, reads the Torah straight through, including first family dysfunction and instructions for genocide. Although it is more selective with prophetic and other texts, the readings

---

21. Levine, "Bearing False Witness."

do not shy away from problematic passages—kings misbehaving, people ignoring Divine instruction. We grapple with horrific images of Israel as a battered wife and retributive theology. The searing doubt of Ecclesiastes is read during Sukkot, the festival of our joy.

Scripture is not a Boy Scout manual, my teacher Rabbi Arnold Jacob Wolf used to bellow. It does not lay out in easy steps God's path of goodness. It is not to be read as a guidebook with all the answers. It has the *questions*. It is a syllabus for a life-long course in advanced ethics. Contradictions within the text, a multiplicity of interpretations, the clash with contemporary values—all these irritations are designed to create dialectical tension. We read closely, consider carefully, consult history, rub the sore spots—and we produce from the irritating grains of sand precious pearls of Scriptural instruction. We cannot simply spiritualize or ignore all the tough parts, because that is where the ethical work really happens: texts as tools of moral development.[22]

BIBLIOGRAPHY

Cohen, Shaye J. D. "The Significance of Yavneh: Pharisees, Rabbis, and the End of Jewish Sectarianism." *Hebrew Union College Annual* 55 (1984) 27–53.

Douglass, Frederick. *Narrative of the Life of an American Slave*. 1845. Reprint, New York: Viking Penguin, 1982.

Henze, Matthias. *Mind the Gap: How the Jewish Writings Between the Old and New Testament Help Us Understand Jesus*. Minneapolis: Fortress, 2017.

Kalimi, Isaac. "The Story About the Murder of Zechariah the Prophet in the Gospels and Its Relation to Chronicles." *Revue Biblique* 116 (2009) 246–61.

Kampen, John. *Matthew within Sectarian Judaism: An Examination*. New Haven: Yale University Press, 2019.

Levine, Amy-Jill. "Bearing False Witness: Common Errors Made About Early Judaism." In *The Jewish Annotated New Testament*, edited by Amy-Jill Levine and Marc Brettler, 501–4. Oxford: Oxford University Press, 2011.

Luther, Martin. "Letter to Pope Leo X." In *Reformation Writings of Martin Luther*. Translated by Bertram Lee Wolff. Cambridge: Lutterworth, 1952.

Mikva, Rachel S. "What Progressive Protestants Can Learn from Jewish Engagement with Scripture." *Theological Education* 50.1 (2015) 95–106.

Newman, Amy. "The Death of Judaism in German Protestant Thought from Luther to Hegel." *Journal of the American Academy of Religion* 61 (1993) 455–84.

Neusner, Jacob and Ernest S. Frerichs, eds. *"To See Ourselves as Others See Us": Christians, Jews, "Others" in Late Antiquity*. Scholars Press Studies in the Humanities Series. Chico, CA: Scholars, 1985.

---

22. See Mikva, "What Progressive Protestants Can Learn," 100.

Reed, Annette Yoshiko. "When Did Rabbis Become Pharisees? Reflections on Christian Evidence for Post-70 Judaism." In *Envisioning Judaism: Studies in Honor of Peter Schäfer on the Occasion of His Seventieth Birthday*, edited by Ra'anan S. Boustan et al., 860–95. Tübingen: Mohr Siebeck, 2013.

Rollens, Sarah, Eric Vanden Eykel, and Meredith J C Warren. "Confronting Judeophobia in the Classroom." *Journal for Interdisciplinary Biblical Studies* 2.1 (2020) 81–106.

Ruether, Rosemary. *Faith and Fratricide: The Theological Roots of Anti-Semitism*. 1974. Reprint, Eugene, OR: Wipf & Stock, 1997.

Runesson, Anders. *Matthew within Judaism: Israel and the Nations in the First Gospel*. Early Christianity and Its Literature 27. Atlanta: SBL Press, 2020.

Saldarini, Anthony J. "Delegitimation of Leaders in Matthew 23." *Catholic Bible Quarterly* 54 (1992) 659–80.

Schleiermacher, Friedrich. *On Religion: Speeches to Its Cultured Despisers*. Translated and edited by Richard Crouter. Cambridge Texts in the History of Philosophy. 1996. Reprint. Cambridge: Cambridge University Press, 2010.

Simmonds, Andrew R. "'Woe to You . . . Hypocrites!' Re-reading Matthew 23:13–36." *Bibliotheca Sacra* 166 (2009) 336–49.

Smith, Jonathan Z. *Relating Religion: Essays in the Study of Religion*. Chicago: University of Chicago Press, 2004.

Soulen, R. Kendall. *The God of Israel and Christian Theology*. Minneapolis: Fortress, 1996.

Weinfeld, Moshe. "The Charge of Hypocrisy in Matthew 23 and in Rabbinic Sources." *Immanuel* 24/25 (1990) 52–58.

Weiss, Dov. "Sins of the Parents in Rabbinic and Early Christian Literature." *Journal of Religion* 97 (2017) 1–25.

6

Isaiah 52:13—53:12
The Suffering Servant in Judaism, Christianity, and Modern Thought

BRIAN BRITT

INTRODUCTION

BIBLICAL SCHOLAR BREVARD CHILDS describes Isa 52:13—53:12 as "probably the most contested chapter in the Old Testament," a view echoed by Mordechai Schreiber, who adds that polemics in the past often led to violence and the killing of Jews.[1] While Immanuel Kant excluded the notion of substitute suffering from his moral philosophy, Friedrich Nietzsche exalted it in *Thus Spoke Zarathustra*, and Max Weber framed it in aesthetic terms. Other thinkers who engage the text's moral and religious meaning include Hermann Cohen and Jacob Taubes. Modern biblical scholars such as John J. Collins and Israel Knohl, meanwhile, seem to carry on the

---

1. Childs, *Isaiah*, 410. What Childs and Schreiber share is a sense that this passage of the Bible generates fierce disagreement. More openly than Childs, Schreiber explains the problem directly in terms of Jewish-Christian polemics (Schreiber 34). But it is Childs who wonders whether and how such external considerations belong in biblical scholarship: "To what extent does a proper exegesis derive from bringing a historical or literary perspective from outside the context of the book itself?" (410).

Christian–Jewish polemics that have surrounded this text since the time of the New Testament. This essay written in honor of André LaCocque surveys the reception of this "suffering servant" text in modern Christian and Jewish biblical scholarship and thought. I argue that, in contemporary engagements with Isaiah 53, literary features highlighted by philosophers provide important resources for challenging traditional Jewish–Christian polemics.

Biblical scholarship on Isa 52:13—53:12 centers on questions of history and language. But without conclusive evidence, disagreements over these questions can echo longstanding conflicts of interpretation. In the Hebrew Bible and most pre-Christian sources, the idea of vicarious suffering is very rare outside the context of priestly sacrifice.[2] Later Christian readings of the text tying it to the suffering and crucifixion of Jesus as the messiah differed from Jewish interpretations, often in polemical ways (see Origen, *Contra Celsum*, cited below). In fact, disagreements between biblical scholars frequently fall along the same polemical lines as traditional interpretations of the text, with Christian readers supporting messianic and Christological readings and Jewish readers associating the servant with a particular prophet (like Jeremiah) or the people of Israel in general.[3] A separate set of modern discussions on the text, with Immanuel Kant as a source, considers the moral meaning of the idea of substitute suffering.

The present essay addresses modern interpretations of the text with emphasis on two features of the text: the mechanism of substitute suffering associated with the "servant" and the servant's ugly appearance (Isa 53:2, 4–6). I argue that traditional sectarian differences on the meaning of Isa 52:13—53:12 (hereafter abbreviated as Isa 53) survive in modern scholarship and that Kant's engagement with the text, along with later thinkers Max Weber, Hermann Cohen, and Jacob Taubes, expands the text's modern reception and opens up ways to think beyond sectarian differences.

Kant's challenge to the idea of vicarious suffering in *Religion within the Boundaries of Mere Reason* (1793) adds something new to the long history of Jewish-Christian disputes over this text. Whereas Jewish-Christian debates center on the identity and theology of the servant, Kant raises the deeper question as to whether vicarious suffering can be morally justified. In the hands of Cohen, Weber, and Taubes, Kant's position leads to discussions about the history and suffering of the Jewish people. Through their

---

2. Hengel, "The Effective History of Isaiah 53," 93.
3. Moyaert, "Who Is the Suffering Servant?" 220–21.

engagement with Kant's position on vicarious suffering, these thinkers complicate standard Jewish-Christian divisions over the text, particularly through consideration of the text's aesthetic description of the suffering servant as ugly.

THE SERVANT OF ISAIAH 53 IN BIBLICAL RECEPTION AND BIBLICAL STUDIES

The idea of vicarious suffering may have roots in ancient Mesopotamian substitute king rituals.[4] The purpose of these rituals was to direct harm and evil omens away from the real king onto an alternate of lower status who sits temporarily on the throne before being sacrificed.[5] If there is even partial influence from this tradition on Isa 53, it leaves the uniqueness of the text, central to Jewish and Christians alike, in doubt.

In the context of the book of Isaiah, the fourth servant song in Isa 53 belongs to what most biblical scholars describe as Deutero-Isaiah, a text dating after the Babylonian exile, about a century and a half later than the setting of the first part of the book. The long internal history of Isaiah exhibits a larger pattern in the prophetic canon of maintaining a textual tradition after a catastrophic historical displacement. And like the book of Jeremiah, which depicts its central figure also as a righteous figure who suffers what James Sanders calls "prophetic agony," the text uses an emerging sense of written tradition to address historical crises of theodicy.[6]

The passage features striking contrasts, between the servant's exaltation and his damaged appearance (52:13–14) and between the majesty of the divine arm and the despised and unsightly appearance of the servant (53:1–3). The description of vicarious suffering vividly combines language of infirmity, sacrifice of livestock, and social status (52:4–9), placing special emphasis on the transgressions for which the servant suffers (פשע in 5a, 8b, 12a, 12b). In addition to its theological innovation, such striking imagery may contribute to its influence. One clue on how readers approached the text comes from the New Testament book of Acts, which describes an Ethiopian eunuch reading Isa 53:7–8 with help from the apostle Philip: "The eunuch asked Philip, 'About whom, may I ask you, does the prophet say this, about himself or about someone else?' Then Philip began to speak,

---

4. Walton, "The Imagery of the Substitute King Ritual," 734.
5. Walton, "The Imagery of the Substitute King Ritual," 736–38.
6. Sanders, *Torah and Canon*, 67–69.

and starting with this scripture, he proclaimed to him the good news about Jesus" (Acts 8:34–35). For followers of Jesus, the ambiguous identity and meaning of the servant are resolved.

An example of early rabbinic reception is the Targum to Isaiah 53, which characterizes the servant as messiah in ways that are analogous to but different from Christian readings of the text.[7] This polemic was fully underway early in the third century, when Origen wrote in his *Contra Celsum*: "At this the Jew said that these prophecies referred to the whole people as though of a single individual, since they were scattered in the dispersion and smitten, that as a result of the scattering of the Jews among the other nations many might become proselytes. In this way he explained the text: 'Thy form shall be inglorious among men' (Isa. 52:14); and 'those to whom he was not proclaimed shall see him' (52:15); and 'being a man in calamity' (53:3)."[8] The Jewish tradition of understanding the servant in a "collective" sense continues in the polemical tradition, for instance in a sixteenth-century Jewish exegesis from Lithuania.[9]

Jewish–Christian polemics continue among some biblical scholars. These polemics, notes Schreiber, center on the question of who the Servant is, a question he frames by saying: "Both sides cannot be right. Clearly, Isaiah had someone in mind," and that person, for Schreiber, is Jeremiah.[10] In the 2010 edition of *The Scepter and the Star*, a study of messianic themes in the Dead Sea Scrolls, John J. Collins acknowledges the proliferation of messianic reflection in the Hasmonean and Roman periods, but he forcefully argues that in pre-Christian literature "[t]here is still no evidence for a Jewish interpretation of Isaiah 53 in terms of a suffering messiah."[11] Collins describes this issue as a "Jewish-Christian debate" and skeptically analyzes scholarly claims to the contrary in the case of 4Q541, the Teacher Hymns, and the so-called "Self-Exaltation Hymn" (4Q491c), including a lengthy

---

7. Adna, "The Servant of Isaiah 53 as Triumphant and Interceding Messiah," 222–224. Adna presents a thorough reading of the Targum that includes discussion of whether its reading is polemical (Adna, 190–92).

8. Origen, *Contra Celsum*, 1.55, cited in Markschies, "Jesus Christ as a Man before God: Two Interpretive Models for Isaiah 53 in the Patristic Literature and Their Development," in *Suffering Servant*, 285.

9. Schreiner, "Isaiah 53 in the *Sefer Hizzuk Emunah* ('Faith Strengthened') of Rabbi Isaac ben Abraham of Troki," 418–61. Schreiner shows how this collective interpretation also appears in Rashi, ibn Ezra, and David Kimchi.

10. Schreiber, "The Real Suffering Servant," 35.

11. Collins, *The Scepter and the Star*, 144.

refutation of Israel Knohl's reading of the latter text as evidence for a Jewish messiah before Jesus modeled on the suffering servant.[12]

Knohl's reading of texts found at Qumran leads him to argue that a Jewish messiah identified with Isa 53 preceded Jesus. Collins observes that Knohl takes speculation on the "Self-Glorification Hymn" farther than anyone else, even dramatizing the life of the so-called "messiah before Jesus."[13] Like the scholars who fix the identity of the "servant" of Isaiah 53, typically in terms of Jesus, Knohl fixes the identity of the speaker of these Qumran texts. Knohl thus uses the same interpretive approach as the Christian reading of Isaiah 53 he seeks to overturn.

In his analysis, Collins applies two standards of precision that may be unwarranted by the evidence: the distinction between Judaism and Christianity, and a concept of messiah *exclusive of* references to the suffering servant. In the first case, there is the historical analysis of the gradual emergence of Christianity as a tradition and identity distinct from Judaism, along with cultural studies of the continued blurring of this boundary.[14] In the second case, Collins depends on a taxonomy of models of messiah, as king, priest, prophet, and heavenly messiah that permit little overlap or ambiguity. Yet as Collins and other scholars admit, ideas of a Jewish messiah take many forms in many texts that abound in allusion and ambiguity, making their meaning and reference difficult to specify.[15]

Against this view stands not only Israel Knohl but also Michael Wise, Jon Levenson, and Martin Hengel, who concludes that some Jewish texts before Jesus interpret Isa 53 messianically in terms of vicarious suffering: these include some Greek and Hebrew (Q) versions of the text, and "perhaps Dan 11–12, the *Aramaic Apocryphon of Levi* 4Q540–541, and the *Testament of Benjamin* 3:8."[16] Levenson situates the "suffering servant" in the larger context of Christian identifications of Jesus with several texts in the Hebrew Bible, particularly the binding of Isaac in Gen 22. Ascribing a "potent midrashic logic" to the text, Levenson strikingly argues that Paul's use of this typology leads to exclusivist models of Christianity, in contrast to the relatively inclusive Jewish worldview of the period.[17]

---

12. Collins, *The Scepter and the Star*, 164–70.
13. Knohl, *The Messiah before Jesus*, 5–15.
14. See, for example, Boyarin, *Judaism*, 106–11.
15. Collins, *The Scepter and the Star*, 18.
16. Hengel, "The Effective History of Isaiah 53," 75–76.
17. Levenson, *The Death and Resurrection of the Beloved Son*, 201, 215–18.

One way out of this polemic is to affirm the text's inherent ambiguity as part of a literary design. Hans-Jürgen Hermisson, for instance, argues that "The special feature of these texts—their floating metaphorical, tradition-bound expressions—allows no biographical interpretation in detail."[18] Benjamin Sommer argues that the suffering servant is a detailed intertextual allusion to Jeremiah as well as earlier passages from Isaiah (e.g., ch. 6). Sommer shares Hermisson's recognition of the text's ambiguity, attributing debates on the text's meaning to the "allusive artistry with which it was composed."[19] Sommer's approach challenges the scholarly tendency to splice texts out of literary and canonical context like laboratory specimens. Inherently ambiguous and embedded in literary tradition, the servant of Isa 52–53 calls primarily for hermeneutical and aesthetic analysis rather than simple historical and theological glosses. A further resource for analyzing these sectarian conflicts of interpretation is the question raised by Kant on the moral justification for vicarious suffering.

KANT'S CHALLENGE TO VICARIOUS SUFFERING AND COHEN'S RESPONSE

Immanuel Kant's *Religion Within the Boundaries of Mere Reason* (1793) challenges the rationale of vicarious suffering: "[T]his original debt... cannot be erased by somebody else. For it is not a *transmissible* liability which can be made over to somebody else, in the manner of a financial debt... but the most *personal* of all liabilities, namely a debt of sins which only the culprit, not the innocent, can bear."[20] Later in the book, Kant relegates vicarious suffering to the domain of mystery: "Inasmuch as reason can see, therefore, no one can stand in for another by virtue of the superabundance of his own good conduct and his merit; and if we must *assume* any such thing, this can be only for moral purposes, since for ratiocination it is an unfathomable mystery."[21]

By assigning the vicarious suffering of Isa 53 and its Christian application to the domain of mystery, Kant challenged any attempt to understand atonement theology as rational and begged the larger question of how to distinguish rational from non-rational accounts of such moral ideas. As

---

18. Hermisson, "The Fourth Servant Song in the Context of Second Isaiah," 46.
19. Sommer, *A Prophet Reads Scripture*, 96.
20. Kant, *Religion within the Boundaries of Mere Reason*, 89.
21. Kant, *Religion within the Boundaries of Mere Reason*, 144.

Daniel Bailey shows, German biblical scholars frequently cite Kant's claim as they combine historical questions of biblical texts with theological ones.[22] One Christian option is to associate the Christian doctrine of incarnation with the domain of mystery, but to do so poses a dilemma for the biblical scholar, since such a non-rational claim is available to theologians but not to historical biblical scholars.[23] For anyone invested in the ethical reasoning of Kant, this judgment against vicarious suffering poses a significant challenge, particularly for biblical scholars.[24]

Over a century later, the Jewish neo-Kantian Hermann Cohen responded to the challenge of reconciling the "vicarious sufferer" with Kant's notion of ethical autonomy by making a distinction between guilt and suffering: "Consequently the man, the Messiah, is conceivable as representative not of the guilt of men and peoples but of the suffering, which otherwise would have to be their punishment. Only through the Messiah's taking the earthly suffering of man upon his shoulders does he become the ideal image of the man of the future, the image of mankind, as the unity of all peoples. He becomes through this not a Tantalus or Sisyphus but Atlas who supports the moral world of the future."[25] Here Cohen reads Isaiah 53 through the lens of Kant: "Not only does the sufferer suffer innocently, but he suffers *for* the guilty one."[26]

---

22. See Bailey, "Concepts of *Stellvertretung* in the Interpretation of Isaiah 53," esp. 239–40.

23. One scholar reviewed by Bailey, Otfried Hofius, shares Kant's appraisal of vicarious suffering and argues that only the Christian incarnation and not Isa 53, can overcome Kant's concern (Bailey, "Concepts of *Stellvertretung*," 239–41).

24. Bailey shows how biblical scholars respond to Kant's criticism of *Stellvertretung* not just with history and text but also with theology: "Christian scholars would not now be debating the issue of Jesus and the Servant, either in agreement with or in reaction against nineteenth-century criticism that Christianity would be irrational if it laid a passage like Isaiah 53 at its heart. It was philosophical and doctrinal criticism that in part gave rise to historical criticism" (Bailey, "Concepts of *Stellvertretung*," 232).

25. Cohen, *Religion of Reason*, 264; the German reads: "Erst durch diese Unterscheidung wird die Identität verständlich, die zwischen Gerechtigkeit und Liebe bei Gott bestehen kann. Die Leiden werden die „Züchtigungen der Liebe". Und so wird nun auch der Mensch, der Messias, denkbar als Stellvertreter; nicht etwa der Schuld der Menschen und der Völker, aber des Leidens, das sonst ihre Strafe sein müßte. Der Messias wird da- durch erst das Idealbild des Menschen der Zukunft, der Menschheit, als der Einheit der Völker: daß er das Erdenleid des Menschen auf seine Schultern nimmt" (Cohen, *Die Religion der Vernunft*, 310).

26. Cohen, *Religion of Reason*, 283.

In taking on this suffering, the servant/messiah shifts punishment and retribution from the realm of divine justice to become "a goal for moral culture and control."[27] At the same time, Cohen accepts the Kantian appraisal of vicarious suffering as opaque to human understanding. After all, his book, *The Religion of Reason out of the Sources of Judaism*, closely echoes Kant's *Religion within the Boundaries of Mere Reason*. But in addition to distinguishing guilt from the servant's suffering, Cohen also projects the servant onto Jewish people and history, which embodies "the world-historical idea of messianic mankind." Paraphrasing Isaiah 53:3–5, Cohen continues, "These servants of the Lord have always been despised and pierced through, cut off from the land of life . . . The messianic people suffer vicariously for mankind. This opinion about the mission [*Mission*] of Israel cannot be an exaggeration, if the messianic realization of monotheism is the historical task [*Aufgabe*] of the religion of Judaism."[28] Cohen applies the text's theodicy to the people of Israel in general:

> The problem of *evil* which traverses the whole of biblical literature, is here transferred from the individual to the historical image of the peoples. . . Only Israel suffers from the persecutions of the idol worshipers, and Israel has the calling not only to maintain the true worship of God but also to spread it among the peoples. . . This historical suffering of Israel gives it its historical dignity, its tragic mission [*Mission*], which represents its share in the divine education of mankind . . . to suffer for the dissemination of monotheism, as the Jews do, is not a sorrowful fate; the suffering is, rather, its tragic calling [*Beruf*], for it proves the heartfelt desire for the conversion of the other peoples, which the faithful people feels.[29]

The people of Israel represent, then, an exception and a model of Kantian ethics: "There is no other means but suffering to bring about this dignity in its purity. This tragic suffering has the final good as its end, and therefore despises all transitory, eudaemonistic prosperity."[30]

The servant/messiah has shifted punishment and retribution to "a goal for moral culture and control"[31] but, while Cohen's messiah is a person

---

27. Cohen, *Religion of Reason*, 314.
28. Cohen, *Religion of Reason*, 267. German: *Die Religion der Venunft*, 315.
29. Cohen, *Religion of Reason*, 283–4. German: 333.
30. Cohen, *Religion of Reason*, 284.
31. Cohen, *Religion of Reason*, 314.

who assumes the suffering of others, his idea of Jewish history embodies "the world-historical idea of messianic mankind."[32]

THE UGLY SERVANT IN MODERN THOUGHT

In the expression that the servant "had no form or comeliness that we should look at him, and no beauty that we should desire him," Isa 53:2 draws attention to the appearance of the servant before elaborating on the servant's vicarious suffering. Modern thinkers Max Weber and Jacob Taubes include this detail in their discussion of the text, thereby adding an aesthetic dimension to a moral and theological one. This aesthetic dimension of the problem, like the literary ambiguity invoked by Hermisson and others, is central to the biblical text but overlooked among biblical scholars and religious thinkers alike.

Neither Kant nor Cohen addresses the ugliness of the servant, but in declaring vicarious suffering a mystery, Kant takes one step in that direction, away from reason and toward the domain of faith, which elsewhere he associates with the aesthetic category of the sublime.[33] And by extending the servant's suffering to the Jewish people as a tragic quality, Cohen invokes a literary and therefore aesthetic category. But Weber introduces a different aesthetic analysis, the idea of the ugly servant as crucial to the meaning of Isaiah 53.

For Max Weber, the servant's ugliness is crucial to understanding the meaning of his suffering and relates, as for Cohen, to the Jewish people in general. In his 1917 address, "Science (*Wissenschaft*) as Vocation," Weber cites Isa 53 with Ps 22 to illustrate the association of ugliness with the sacred:

> If we know anything today, it is that something can be sacred not merely *despite* not being beautiful, but *because* and *insofar as* it is not beautiful. We used to know this—there are proofs in Isaiah 53, in Psalm 21 [sic: 22]. We know too that something can be beautiful not merely *despite* its not being good, but *because* it is not good—certainly since Nietzsche, and before him the same idea could be found among the "Flowers of Evil," as Baudelaire called his book of

---

32. Cohen, *Religion of Reason*, 267. German: 315.

33. "The majesty of the law (like the law on Sinai) instills awe…[and] rouses a *feeling of the sublimity* of our own vocation that enraptures us more than any beauty," (Kant, *Religion Within the Boundaries of Mere Reason*, 48, n.).

poems. And everyone knows that something can be true despite, and by virtue of, not being beautiful or sacred or good.[34]

Weber's broad interests reflect his education in the sources of nineteenth century Idealism and his use of this model of education (*Bildung*) to inform modern thought.[35] His lecture on science reflects his attempt to draw from traditional sources to inform contemporary challenges in scholarship.

Weber elaborates on the ugliness of the servant in *Ancient Judaism*: "Many are horrified by the Servant of YHWH because he is uglier than others."[36] Weber finds the idea of the servant pleading for sinners typical of the Bible and also some precedent (in Exod 32:32) for the idea of dying for others' sins, though he finds the case of the Servant of Isa 53 distinctive. For Weber, the Servant is alternatively identified with a prophet and the people of Israel, whom he identifies as a "pariah people":

> Thereby the Servant of God and the people whose archetype he is, become the deliverers of the world. Thus, should the Servant of God even have been conceived as a personal savior, then he qualified only by voluntarily taking upon himself the pariah situation of the Exile people and by suffering without resistance and complaint misery, ugliness, and martyrdom . . .The situation of the pariah people and its patient endurance were thus elevated to the highest station of religious worth and honor before God, by receiving the meaning of a world historical mission [*Mission*].[37]

Associating Isa 53 with Ps 22, Weber elaborates further on the ugliness motif: "The mood of Deutero-Isaiah, the work feeling (41:14) and the positive evaluation of self-abasement and ugliness, has had broad ramifications in Jewry as well as in Christendom up to Pietism."[38] For Weber, the elevation

---

34. Weber, "The Scholar's Work," 30. Two other relevant biblical references in the lecture are the mention of Abraham's death after a long life in Gen 25:8 and a paraphrase of Isa 55:8— "his ways were not our ways, his thoughts not our thoughts" (Weber, "The Scholar's Work," 19, 22).

35. Ringer, *Max Weber: An Intellectual Biography*, 16.

36. Weber, *Ancient Judaism*, 373.

37. Weber, *Ancient Judaism*, 375–376. German: *Das Antike Judentum*, 392.It is noteworthy that Weber, writing two years after Cohen, uses the term "Mission" to describe a similar idea of the historical purpose of the Jewish people.

38. Weber, *Ancient Judaism*, 376. LaCocque and Paul Ricoeur both link Isa 53 to Ps 22 in their collaborative essays on Psalm 22: LaCocque, "My God, My God, Why Have You Forsaken Me?" and Ricoeur, "Lamentation as Prayer"; in *Thinking Biblically: Exegetical and Hermeneutical Studies*, 207, 225.

of the ugly suffering servant in Isa 53 informs Christian soteriology as well as the idea of the Jews as a pariah people. Like Cohen's idea of the "tragic calling" of the Jewish people, Weber's idea of the Jews as a pariah people was not original to him, and as Arnoldo Momigliano shows, it had roots in nineteenth-century ideas about the Jewish people.[39] Writing at the end of World War I and before the Holocaust, Cohen and Weber both reflected contemporary understandings of the history and life of the Jewish diaspora as precarious but sustainable.

In a remarkable essay on the justification of ugliness in Christianity, Jacob Taubes traces the influence of Isa 53 on such early Christian sources as the Acts of Peter, the Sybilline Oracles, and Clement of Alexandria.[40] Starting with Nietzsche's account of Paul's theology as a "transvaluation of the religious, ethical, and aesthetic values of antiquity," Taubes traces the theme of humiliation in the crucifixion in 1 Corinthians through a number of early Christian sources. Like Weber, Taubes is interested in the exaltation of the humble, in this case the Corinthian congregation of early Christians: "the social standing of the congregation—its pariah-existence—is for Paul a consequence and expression of the same divine weakness and folly whose sign is the cross."[41] But while the ugliness of Christ reflected the humiliation of Isa 53 and the crucifixion, its articulation was inconsistent. Clement of Alexandria at once explains Jesus's ugliness as a way to focus on his teachings and elsewhere praises his beauty, while Origen argues that Jesus's beauty or ugliness is effectively in the eye of the beholder, with believers seeing his beauty. And it was not until centuries later that images of the torture and crucifixion of Jesus would become widespread in Christian art.[42]

Taubes goes on to note that "it is precisely the heresiologists Irenaeus and Tertullian in their struggle against Gnosticism who propagated the tradition of the ugly Christ."[43] For Taubes, Tertullian's full-throated description of Jesus as ugly served to challenge Gnostic views of Jesus's perfection;

---

39. Momigliano, "A Note on Max Weber's Definition of Judaism as a Pariah-Religion," 313–15. Weber's knowledge of religious texts and thought was not unusual for his time. Though his social, economic, and historical research was not explicitly theological, he was closely involved with religious institutions like the Evangelical-Social Congress (Ward, "Max Weber and the Lutherans," 208–210).

40. Taubes, "The Justification of Ugliness in Early Christian Tradition," 91.

41. Taubes, "The Justification of Ugliness," 83.

42. Taubes, "The Justification of Ugliness," 91–92, 94–96.

43. Taubes, "The Justification of Ugliness," 92.

the gospel accounts of Jesus's life, culminating in the Passion and death, are only possible, argues Tertullian, for a human whose body is neither heavenly nor even beautiful.[44]

Unlike Weber and Cohen, Taubes does not articulate a notion of Jews as a tragic or pariah people. Nor does he endorse the harmony between Judaism and Christianity. In "The Issue Between Judaism and Christianity," Taubes includes the suffering servant in a thorough rejection of the compatibility of Judaism and Christianity. In an extended discussion of Gershom Scholem's study of Sabbatianism, Taubes recognizes similarities between this seventeenth-century messianic movement and the suffering servant, but he denies that this Jewish movement descended from Christianity. Rather, both cases reflect a conflict between belief in a messiah and belief in the central place of *halakhah* in Jewish life.[45] Taubes critically decries the decline of *halakhah* as leading to "all the disguised anti-halachic (antinomian) and Christian assumptions current in modern secularized Christian society."[46] The Jewish preference for the "romance of a mythologized East European Jewry" in place of Torah and *halakhah* as a defining feature of the tradition leaves it powerless to resist "the Pauline rejection of the law" and Christianity in general: "For what greater 'romance' can there be than the incarnation of God in flesh?"[47]

Separated in time by the Holocaust, Taubes and Cohen both linked the suffering servant to the place of Judaism in majority Christian history and culture. But it is nearly impossible to imagine Taubes or any other post-Holocaust thinker writing the following words by Cohen about Jewish suffering in the tradition of the suffering servant: "The election to the teaching of the unique God is at the same time the election to vicarious suffering for the idolatrous peoples, as for all peoples who have not yet matured to the knowledge of the unique God . . . Israel's greatest happiness . . . is now balanced by vicarious suffering."[48] For Cohen and Taubes, the reception history of Isa 53 relates directly to the history of Jewish-Christian relations. A third option, introduced by Immanuel Lévinas, is to relate the servant more generally to the encounter with the other: "[S]ubstitution entails bringing

---

44. Taubes, "The Justification of Ugliness," 93.

45. Taubes, "The Issue between Judaism and Christianity: Facing Up to the Unresolvable Difference," 55–56.

46. Taubes, "The Issue between Judaism and Christianity," 56.

47. Taubes, "The Issue Between Judaism and Christianity," 58.

48. Cohen, *The Religion of Reason*, 433–34.

comfort by associating ourselves with the essential weakness and finitude of the other; it is to bear his weight while sacrificing one's interestedness and complacency-in-being, which then turn into responsibility for the other."[49] Lévinas, who lived through the Holocaust, related this ethical construal of substitution to the biblical categories of sacrifice and holiness.[50] Cohen, Taubes, and Lévinas thus represent three distinct ways of understanding the servant in dialogue with Kant's challenge to vicarious punishment as well as the history of Jewish-Christian relations. Their three accounts of the servant respond to Kant's challenge of irrationality by reserving a space beyond reason for the historical and moral act of substitute suffering.

BIBLICAL STUDIES, SECTARIANISM, AND THE AESTHETIC

The biblical scholars whose readings of Isa 53 align with Jewish or Christian theology belong to a long tradition of Jewish-Christian polemic. And the concern that biblical scholarship mixes all too easily with sectarian positions is nothing new. Partly in response to the work of David Friedrich Strauss, Nietzsche's *The Antichrist* asks: "What do I care for the contradictions of 'tradition'? How can legends of saints be called 'tradition' at all! The stories of saints are the most ambiguous literature in existence: to apply to them scientific procedures *when no other records are extant* seems to me wrong in principle—mere learned idling."[51] This concern to subject biblical ambiguity to scientific analysis continues to bear on biblical scholarship about the servant in Isa 53. As the author of *Thus Spoke Zarathustra* understood very well, prophetic discourse is inherently ambiguous, and so while we may be able to discern something about the *sense* or meaning of the term "servant" in our text, it seems contrary to the spirit of prophetic texts to determine with any certainty the *reference* of this term.

---

49. Lévinas, "Responsibility and Substitution," 228.

50. Lévinas, "Responsibility and Substitution," 229. Paul Ricoeur cites Lévinas's idea of substitution in his essay on Psalm 22, "Lamentation as Prayer," 226.

51. Nietzsche, *The Anti-Christ*, 152. See also *Thus Spoke Zarathustra*, whose biblical allusions include Isa 52–53, as when the Jester says to Zarathustra: "You are hated by the good and the just, and they call you their enemy and despiser"; and later when Zarathustra says, "The work of a suffering and tortured god, the world then seemed to me . . . [but] this god whom I created was man-made and madness, like all gods," *Thus Spoke Zarathustra*, 21, 30–31.

But despite Nietzsche's provocations to biblical scholars, it may be Kant's assignment of vicarious suffering to the domain of religious mystery that best uncovers their theological interests. Kant's distinction between reason and mystery also contributes to modern expressions that distinguish the religious from the secular in Judaism and Christianity. Since Kant, modern interpreters of Isa 53 must reckon not only with the ancient text but also with a landscape organized by two divisions: Christian and Jewish; rational and extra-rational. With Kant and Nietzsche, one can understand Isa 53 as beyond the domain of reason and scholarly efforts to apply rational means to assign it rational meaning misguided. And scholars who exceed the boundaries of their own rationalistic methods are more likely to reinscribe deeply ingrained Jewish-Christian polemics.

It may be that Kant's religious and ethical philosophy illustrates what Nietzsche meant when he wrote, "All great things bring about their own destruction through an act of self-overcoming... thus Christianity *as a dogma* was destroyed by its own morality; in the same way Christianity *as morality* must now perish, too."[52] The traces of Christian thought in Kant's ethics, for example in the categorical imperative and the idea of human dignity, complicate any pre-Kantian distinction between Judaism and Christianity. After Kant, one can depict Kant on the one hand as the self-overcoming of Christianity and on the other as a way of splitting Christianity (and Judaism) into rational and extra-rational parts. For a text like Isa 53, Kant's designation of vicarious suffering as non-rational means that the category of messiah itself, central to Jewish and Christian theodicies and even to "secular" political thought, defies the rule of reason. Kant's complex legacy shears any theological and sectarian away from biblical scholarship, but it leaves the text, with all its literary and aesthetic ambiguity, untouched.

CONCLUSION

The Kantian objection to the servant's vicarious suffering comes from a modern, rational conception of morality and guilt tied to the autonomous self.[53] Cohen acknowledges the problem and articulates a messianic and Jewish response: the servant represents the tragic history of the Jewish people, a view comparable to Weber's notion of the Jews as a pariah people.

---

52. Nietzsche, *The Genealogy of Morals*, 161.

53. Janowski, "He Bore Our Sins: Isaiah 53 and the Drama of Taking Another's Place," 450–52, 71.

Lévinas and Taubes avoid casting Jewish people as perennial victims; Lévinas places sacrifice and suffering at the heart of ethical encounters with the other, while Taubes finds the ugly servant of Isa 53 flourishing more in Christian theology than in a Judaism defined by *halakhah*. Lévinas and Taubes represent two distinct models of moving beyond Jewish-Christian polemics over Isa 53 without denying history or resorting to a tendentious notion of Judeo-Christianity.[54]

Overlooking the aesthetics of Isa 53, particularly the ugly servant, many biblical scholars reiterate the Jewish-Christian polemics that characterize its history of interpretation. Weber's and Taubes's attention to the servant's ugliness suggests a new way of seeing the text beyond the Jewish-Christian divide, since the text's surprising ennoblement of ugliness finds distinct lines of interpretation among pre-modern and modern Jewish and Christian, exegetes. Two moderns who pluralize the servant, Cohen and Weber, read the servant as the people of Israel whose history of suffering illustrates the redemptive dynamics of Isa 53. Taubes identifies the ugly servant more with early Christians and reminds his readers that Judaism places more emphasis on *halakhah* than on messianism.

While some biblical scholars engaged in sectarian polemics over Isa 53, the philosophers found complexity in the text. Kant's claim about vicarious suffering shines a light on what made Isa 53 so original, and the ambiguity on which Nietzsche insisted made the question of labelling the servant seem ludicrous. Weber and Taubes show how the servant's ugliness raises broader questions of value, how the aesthetic relates to the moral and theological. Other biblical scholars, like Hermisson and Sommer, share the philosophers' regard for the text's ambiguous richness. For them, the startling images of the ugly, humiliated servant whose suffering "makes many righteous" belong to a biblical tradition concerned less with sectarianism than making meaning out of disaster.

BIBLIOGRAPHY

Adna, Jostein. "The Servant of Isaiah 53 as Triumphant and Interceding Messiah: The Reception of Isaiah 52:13–53:12 in the Targum of Isaiah with Special Attention to the Concept of the Messiah." In *The Suffering Servant: Isaiah 53 in Jewish and*

---

54. See, e.g., the survey of Talmudic accusations against Christians and Jesus, from disgraceful birth and sexual promiscuity to eternal punishment with Titus and Balaam, where Jesus' punishment is immersion in boiling excrement in Schäfer, *Jesus in the Talmud*.

Christian Sources, edited by Bernd Janowski and Peter Stuhlmacher, 189–224. Grand Rapids: Eerdmans, 2004.

Bailey, Daniel P. "Concepts of *Stellvertretung* in the Interpretation of Isaiah 53." In *Jesus and the Suffering Servant*, 223–50. Harrisburg PA: Trinity, 1998.

Boyarin, Daniel. *Judaism: The Genealogy of a Modern Nation*. New Brunswick, NJ: Rutgers University Press, 2019.

Cohen, Hermann. *Die Religion der Vernunft*. Leipzig: Fock, 1919.

———. *Religion of Reason Out of the Sources of Judaism*. Translated by Simon Kaplan. New York: Ungar, 1972.

Childs, Brevard S. *Isaiah*. Old Testament Library. Louisville: Westminster John Knox, 2001.

Collins, John J. *The Scepter and the Star: Messianism in Light of the Dead Sea Scrolls*. 2nd ed. Grand Rapids: Eerdmans, 1995.

Hengel, Martin, with Daniel P. Bailey. "The Effective History of Isaiah 53 in the Pre-Christian Period." In *The Suffering Servant: Isaiah 53 in Jewish and Christian Sources*, edited by Bernd Janowski and Peter Stuhlmacher, 75–146. Translated by Daniel P. Bailey. Grand Rapids: Eerdmans, 2004.

Hermisson, Hans-Jürgen. "The Fourth Servant Song in the Context of Second Isaiah," in, *The Suffering Servant: Isaiah 53 in Jewish and Christian Sources*, edited by Bernd Janowski and Peter Stuhlmacher, 16–47. Translated by Daniel P. Bailey. Grand Rapids: Eerdmans, 2004.

Janowski, Berndt. "He Bore Our Sins: Isaiah 53 and the Drama of Taking Another's Place." In *The Suffering Servant: Isaiah 53 in Jewish and Christian Sources*, edited by Bernd Janowski and Peter Stuhlmacher, 48–74. Translated by Daniel P. Bailey. Grand Rapids: Eerdmans, 2004.

Kant, Immanuel. *Religion within the Boundaries of Mere Reason and Other Writings*. Edited and translated by Richard Crouter. Cambridge Texts in the History of Philosophy. Cambridge: Cambridge University Press, 1998.

Knohl, Israel. *The Messiah before Jesus: The Suffering Servant of the Dead Sea Scrolls*. Translated by David Maisel. Berkeley: University of California Press, 2000.

LaCocque, André. "My God, My God, Why Have you Forsaken Me?" In André LaCocque and Paul Ricoeur, *Thinking Biblically: Exegetical and Hermeneutical Studies*, 187–209. Translated by David Pellauer. Chicago: University of Chicago Press, 2003.

Levenson, Jon. *The Death and Resurrection of the Beloved Son: The Transformation of Child Sacrifice in Judaism and Christianity*. New Haven: Yale University Press, 1993.

Lévinas, Emmanuel. "Responsibility and Substitution." In *Is It Righteous to Be? Interviews with Emmanuel Lévinas*, edited by Jill Robbins, 228–33. Translated by Maureen Gedney. Stanford: Stanford University Press, 2001.

Markschies, Christoph. "Jesus Christ as a Man before God: Two Interpretive Models for Isaiah 53 in the Patristic Literature and Their Development." In *The Suffering Servant: Isaiah 53 in Jewish and Christian Sources*, edited by Bernd Janowski and Peter Stuhlmacher, 225–323. Translated by Daniel P. Bailey. Grand Rapids: Eerdmans, 2004.

Momigliano, Arnoldo. "A Note on Max Weber's Definition of Judaism as a Pariah-Religion." *History and Theory* 19 (1980) 313–18.

Moyaert, Marianne. "Who Is the Suffering Servant? A Comparative Theological Reading of Isaiah 53 after the Shoah." In *Comparing Faithfully: Insights for Systematic Theological Reflection*, edited by Michelle Voss Roberts, 216–37. New York: Fordham University Press, 2016.

Nietzsche, Friedrich. *The Anti-Christ*. In *Twilight of the Idols and The Anti-Christ*. Translated by R. J. Hollingdale. London: Penguin, 1990.

———. *The Genealogy of Morals*. Translated by Walter Kaufmann and R. J. Hollingdale. New York: Vintage, 1967.

———. *Thus Spoke Zarathustra*. Translated by Walter Kaufmann. London: Penguin, 1978.

Ricoeur, Paul. "Lamentation as Prayer." In André LaCocque and Paul Ricoeur, *Thinking Biblically: Exegetical and Hermeneutical Studies*, 211–32. Translated by David Pellauer. Chicago: University of Chicago Press, 2003.

Ringer, Fritz. *Max Weber: An Intellectual Biography*. Chicago: University of Chicago Press, 2004.

Sanders, James A. *Torah and Canon*. Philadelphia: Fortress, 1972.

Schäfer, Peter. *Jesus in the Talmud*. Princeton: Princeton University Press, 2007.

Schreiber, Mordechai. "The Real 'Suffering Servant': Decoding a Controversial Passage in the Bible." *Jewish Bible Quarterly* 37 (2009) 35–44.

Schreiner, Stefan. "Isaiah 53 in the *Sefer Hizzuk Emunah* ('Faith Strengthened') of Rabbi Isaac ben Abraham of Troki." In *The Suffering Servant: Isaiah 53 in Jewish and Christian Sources*, edited by Bernd Janowski and Peter Stuhlmacher, 418–61. Translated by Daniel P. Bailey. Grand Rapids: Eerdmans, 2004.

Sommer, Benjamin. *A Prophet Reads Scripture: Allusion in Isaiah 40–66*. Stanford: Stanford University Press, 1998.

Taubes, Jacob. "The Issue between Judaism and Christianity: Facing up to the Unresolvable Difference." In *From Cult to Culture: Fragments toward a Critique of Historical Reason*, edited by Charlotte Elisheva Fonrobert and Amir Engel, 45–58. Stanford: Stanford University Press, 2010.

Taubes, Jacob. "The Justification of Ugliness in Early Christian Tradition." In *From Cult to Culture: Fragments Toward a Critique of Historical Reason*, 76–97.

Walton, John H. "The Imagery of the Substitute King Ritual in Isaiah's Fourth Servant Song." *Journal of Biblical Literature* 122 (2003) 734–43.

Ward, W. R. "Max Weber and the Lutherans." In *Max Weber and His Contemporaries*, edited by Wolfgang J. Mommsen and Jürgen Osterhammel, 203–14. London: Allen & Unwin, 1987.

Weber, Max. *Ancient Judaism*. Translated and edited by Hans H. Gerth and Don Martindale. Glencoe, IL: Free Press, 1952. German: *Das Antike Judentum*. Tübingen: Mohr, 1921.

Weber, Max. "The Scholar's Work." In *Charisma and Disenchantment: The Vocation Lectures*. Edited by Paul Reitter and Chad Mellmon. Translated by Damion Searls. New York: New York Review of Books, 2020.

7

Gender, Animality, and Ecology in Genesis 2–3
Reflections on the Hermeneutics of Subversion

KEN STONE

WHEN I FIRST VISITED Chicago Theological Seminary in 1996, prior to beginning to teach there myself, I had the opportunity to sit in on one of André LaCocque's classes on women in the Hebrew Bible—or, as he often referred to it, the Prime Testament. Although it was an elective course, the classroom was quite full. As another faculty member noted at the time, students were aware that a beloved professor would soon retire officially, and they were eager to have a chance to study with him on a topic with which he had become associated. One of the texts for the course, in addition to the Bible itself, was LaCocque's own book *The Feminine Unconventional: Four Subversive Figures in Israel's Tradition*; and students were engaging it on the day of my visit.[1] In the years since then, some of his former students have told me that *The Feminine Unconventional* remains one of their resources for ministry, especially when preaching on the book of Ruth. His students need not have worried that his contributions were coming to an end, however. Far from actually "retiring," André LaCocque went on

---

1. LaCocque, *The Feminine Unconventional*.

to publish many more books after he moved to Emeritus status, including several focused on what he called "subversive" women in the Bible.[2]

There can be little doubt that LaCocque was led to pursue his research and teaching interests in women and the Bible in part by his responsiveness—his felt "response-ability"—to the contemporary concerns of his students and the ethos of the school where he taught, an ethos he also helped to shape. Many of those students were women from diverse backgrounds who were responding to a call to ministry, often in the face of sex discrimination; and his seminary colleagues included the feminist theologian Susan Brooks Thistlethwaite, who was also writing on women and biblical interpretation.[3] That attention to gender in biblical interpretation continues at Chicago Theological Seminary today, often in forms shaped by still newer approaches to biblical scholarship, from Stephanie Crowder's womanist hermeneutics to my own queer readings.[4]

A significant characteristic of LaCocque's writings on women and the Bible is his attention to the multiplicity or heterogeneity of biblical literature. In this respect his work stands in the tradition of biblical scholars who emphasize the theological and hermeneutical significance of "the diversity of scripture."[5] But such diversity should not be mistaken for a happy pluralism. As James Barr once noted, the Bible seems at times to be less like a polite dialogue and more "like a battlefield, in which different traditions strive against one another."[6] Although Barr's military language may be discomfiting, it does encourage us to rethink the hermeneutical strategies we bring to conflicts involving the Bible, including conflicts around gender. Rather than falling into the trap of assuming that the Bible holds a single, clear perspective on such conflicts, or attempting to harmonize two or three diverse perspectives found in it, we might see the existence of conflicting perspectives inside the Bible as an opportunity to take up tactical positions within the context of specific struggles that shape either the ancient writing of the Bible or its contemporary interpretation—or, as in the case of gender, both.

This seems to me to be one way of understanding LaCocque's approach to arguments about women and the Bible. His interpretation of Ruth, for

---

2. For example LaCocque, *Romance, She Wrote*; LaCocque, *Ruth*; LaCocque, *Esther Regina*.

3. Thistlethwaite, "Every Two Minutes."

4. See for example Crowder, *When Momma Speaks*; Stone, *Practicing Safer Texts*.

5. Hanson, *The Diversity of Scripture*.

6. Barr, "The Bible as a Document of Believing Communities," 28.

example, understands it as, in part, a kind of postexilic counterargument to certain views represented by the books of Ezra and Nehemiah, which in contrast to Ruth would prohibit intermarriage between a Judahite man and a Moabite woman.[7] Note that this proposal goes beyond suggesting that diverse views on intermarriage can be found in the Bible. LaCocque is making the more radical suggestion that we can plausibly understand the book of Ruth as a counter-offensive against beliefs promoted by other biblical texts. To be sure, this counter-offensive is contained within a beautiful novella with literary characteristics that lead some scholars to doubt that "this gentle and humane story" could have served as a polemic.[8] But LaCocque's hermeneutical orientation recognizes that the aesthetic qualities of a book like Ruth do not rule out its embeddedness in social conflict. Rather, a close reading of it indicates that its literary features are precisely why it is more persuasive than a rant. Even if one does not go as far as LaCocque does in attributing polemical motives to the writer of Ruth, one has to acknowledge that the book stakes out a different position on intermarriage between Judahites and Moabites than Ezra and Nehemiah, or even Deuteronomy 23:3 (Heb. 23:4). In that respect, the book is "subversive" within the Bible as a whole.

Similarly, LaCocque argues that the writer of Song of Songs, who in his view is likely to have been a woman, can be understood as actively contesting views about women and women's sexuality that are found in such prophetic books as Hosea. The potential harm caused by this prophetic rhetoric is made clear by feminist and womanist studies of it which are cited by LaCocque, such as that of Renita Weems.[9] But a critique of Hosea's approach to women is already carried out, in LaCocque's view, by the Song's "intertextual" use of language and imagery that are also found in Hosea. By recontextualizing this language and imagery, the writer of Song of Songs creates "not just a secular love song but . . . a defiant, irreverent, subversive discourse, which at times constitutes a satirical pastiche of prophetic metaphors and similes."[10] Note the recurrence of the term "subversive," which we saw already in *The Feminine Unconventional*. LaCocque defends this view of the Song through characteristically close readings of it that are influenced by both the modern literary-theoretical notion of "intertextuality"

---

7. LaCocque, *The Feminine Unconventional*; LaCocque, *Ruth*.
8. Collins, *Introduction to the Hebrew Bible*, 565.
9. Weems, *Battered Love*.
10. LaCocque, *Romance, She Wrote*, 12.

and the use of this notion to study Jewish Midrash.[11] But in the present context, the details of his argument about Song of Songs are less important than a recognition of LaCocque's hermeneutics of gender and subversion. Skillfully deploying literary analysis, a dialogue with Jewish sources, an emphasis on the heterogeneity of scripture, and both historical critical and interdisciplinary tools, LaCocque re-reads the Song of Songs in a way that demonstrates its differences from Hosea and other prophetic books with respect to women's sexual agency, as well as its relevance for both ancient conflicts and contemporary ones.

It is crucial to note, however, that the creativity which LaCocque brought to the hermeneutics of gender did not lead him to deny the patriarchal nature of biblical literature. One might even say that a frank acknowledgment of the Bible's patriarchal assumptions led him to articulate the interpretations that he did. If the Song of Songs, for example, can be characterized as "subversive discourse," it is precisely because the discourse of biblical books such as Hosea is indisputably patriarchal in its representations of women's sexuality and, so, in need of the subversion that LaCocque not only finds in the Song, but also enacts himself, through his own subversive interpretation of the Song and its relationship with Hosea. Recognition of the Bible's patriarchy does not lead to the conclusion that the Bible should be dismissed as some archaic artifact from a barbaric past. Rather, it summons one to respond with interpretation. It is not accidental that LaCocque, a friend of and sometimes collaborator with the great French hermeneutic philosopher Paul Ricoeur,[12] subtitles his book on Song of Songs "a hermeneutical essay." For it is only through hermeneutics—the practices of interpretation—that the Bible comes alive for us as a resource and dialogue partner in contemporary conflicts such as those involving gender and sexuality.

In the remainder of this chapter, I consider another text that caught LaCocque's hermeneutical attention, a text in which, as he explicitly acknowledges, one also finds a "patriarchal framework."[13] In his book on the Yahwist's creation myth in Genesis 2–3, LaCocque observes that "patriarchalism" is "pervasive" in the story. Moreover, the perspective on sexuality that shapes the story privileges heterosexuality, while "celibacy and homosexuality are totally outside the text's purview," a fact that makes the text

---

11. For example, Boyarin, *Intertextuality and the Reading of Midrash*.
12. See for example LaCocque and Ricoeur, *Thinking Biblically*.
13. LaCocque, *Trial of Innocence*, 9.

"incomplete."[14] LaCocque cautions against overstating these characteristics of the narrative, however. As one would expect, his treatment of it encourages us to read and interpret it further.

I will therefore take up LaCocque's hermeneutical challenge by reconsidering certain elements of the Yahwist's story that do involve gender. More specifically, I am interested here in how the story's views on gender are inextricably intertwined with its views on another issue that has received increasing scholarly attention in recent years, the matter of animality. My observations are shaped by my interdisciplinary engagement with contemporary animal and ecological studies, as well as queer studies and its rethinking of gender.[15] Thus I take a somewhat different approach to Genesis 2–3 than LaCocque does.

But it is important to note that LaCocque also considers the text's perspective on animality. While the relationship between animality and gender is not a primary focus for him, his discussion hints that the issues are not entirely separate, either. After all, the creation of two humans out of one in Gen 2:21–23, and with it the creation of human sexual difference, follows from God's recognition in 2:18 that the first human should not be alone and needs appropriate companionship. Immediately after this recognition, God creates "every living thing of the field and every bird of the sky" out of the same earth or soil, the *adamah* (2:18), from which the first human, the *adam*, has already been created (2:7). This sequence implies that God's creation of the animals is a kind of first attempt to provide for the human suitable companions. LaCocque cautions against finding in these animals a "false start," since the text does go on to assert that the human will need a closer partner than the other earth creatures. Thus God acts again, taking a part of the human and creating out of it a woman, and hence human sexual difference. But as LaCocque notes, there already "exists between humanity and animality a potential kinship or communion," one that he finds compatible not only with their shared substance (the earth or soil) but also with the vision of human and animal *shalom* in certain prophetic texts (he cites for example Isa 11:6–9 and 65:25, and Hos 2:20). This "communion" may take the shape of cross-species communication: "There was originally no hindrance, it seems, to the human finding some animal to converse with; proof of it is the dialogue between Eve and the

---

14. LaCocque, *Trial of Innocence*, 10.

15. Stone, *Reading the Hebrew Bible with Animal Studies*; Stone, "The Garden of Eden and the Heterosexual Contract."

serpent in Genesis 3."[16] LaCocque is right to recognize the importance of cross-species communication, which is a fascinating topic in its own right, quite apart from its presence in biblical myth.[17] And there are other points of connection between humans and animals as well. The statement of 2:7 that God animates the first human being by "breathing into its nostrils the breath of life" (2:7) calls to mind such texts as Psalm 104, which asserts (with different vocabulary) that "all" creatures, human and animal, depend upon the "breath" or "spirit" of God for life (Ps 104:29–30).[18]

LaCocque's identification of "a potential kinship or communion" in Genesis 2 "between humanity and animality" may also have some significance for ecological hermeneutics. For while the book of Genesis has long played a role in attempts by its readers to articulate views on gender and sexuality, it has also become a focal point for contemporary discussions of the ecological implications of the Bible. Historians point out that certain interpretations of Genesis have been used to justify the exploitation of the earth and its creatures, understood as resources for humans.[19] Such interpretations seize upon the opening chapter of Genesis, usually referred to by scholars as the Priestly creation account, which refers to humans being made in "the image of God" and charges them with multiplying and filling the earth, and having "dominion over the fish of the sea and over the birds of the air and over every living thing that moves upon the earth" (1:26–27), living things who later come to "fear" the humans who eventually eat them (9:1–7). These elements of Priestly discourse have been, and sometimes still are, used to justify human domination of the earth and its nonhuman creatures. As Theodore Hiebert notes, the reference to the "dominion" or "rule" of humans, who are said to be created in "the image of God," has "dominated conversations about the Bible and ecology" and created "much consternation" among ecologists. It assigns a "special role" to humans, which is "to rule . . . take charge of, or be responsible for other life. There is no way to diminish the hierarchical reality and power" of this Priestly language.[20] Armed with such an understanding of Genesis 1, readers of the

---

16. LaCocque, *Trial of Innocence*, 105.

17. See further Stone, "Wittgenstein's Lion and Balaam's Ass."

18. See further Stone, "All These Creatures Look to You"; Hiebert, "Air, the First Sacred Thing."

19. See Thomas, *Man and the Natural World*.

20. Hiebert, "Genesis," 85.

Bible, especially in the modern West, have declared themselves justified in exploiting the earth's resources for human use and profit.

Now this interpretation of Genesis 1 is not the only way in which its ecological implications can be understood. After all, the chapter does not *simply* exalt human beings. It also describes God's methodical creation of a beautiful cosmos out of the primordial forces of chaos. It represents God as pronouncing all of the created elements, including the animals, to be "good" (Gen 1:4, 10, 12, 18, 21, 25, 31). And it urges other-than-human living beings such as, explicitly, birds and sea creatures, to be fruitful and multiply, filling the seas and the skies (Gen 1:20–22), activities which are contrary to the extinction of animal life that is currently taking place across the earth due to human activities.[21] Thus Genesis 1 might have been taken by readers as an affirmation of God's desire for the flourishing of animal and plant life throughout God's creation, an affirmation that is taken even further by such texts as Psalm 104.[22] Hiebert notes that even with the story's troubling emphasis on human hierarchy and rule or dominion, "the priestly writer places the world at the center of his theology . . . The primary vocation God gives humans is earth-oriented, to take charge of all living things. God makes the archetypal human responsible for the earth and its life, albeit from a dominant position."[23] Hiebert recognizes here a point with which LaCocque would have agreed: that even texts which have been interpreted in damaging ways, such as, in this case, the Priestly creation story with its emphasis on human rule, can sometimes be re-read to highlight textual elements that subvert dominant understandings.

Still, Hiebert believes there are other texts in Genesis that draw a more ecologically promising picture than the Priestly account in chapter 1. More specifically, he argues across multiple publications that the Yahwist account in Genesis 2–3—the same text that captures LaCocque's attention in *The Trial of Innocence*—is the product of a subsistence agricultural society and reflects the agrarian orientation of its writer. That writer, attuned to elements of the natural world with which farmers in ancient Israel had to engage, "views humans not as separated from nature but as oriented to the world and closely integrated with it." The humans are created from fertile soil, the *adamah* (as already noted), and are closely related to both the earth

---

21. See Kolbert, *The Sixth Extinction*.

22. See further Stone, *Reading the Hebrew Bible with Animal Studies*, 164–81; Stone, "All These Look to You"; Stone, "Reading Elisha's She-Bears."

23. Hiebert, "Genesis," 85.

and its other-than-human creatures, who are, like the humans, referred to as "living beings." (2:7, 19). Indeed, "the human is created to serve the earth" from which it was taken (2:15) and is "positioned as the earth's servant, rather than its ruler, as in Gen 1:26."[24] Note that Hiebert is intentionally contrasting the view of humans and the earth found in Genesis 2–3 with that found in Genesis 1. He goes on to suggest, moreover, that "Just as the Yahwist attributes to the first archetypal human his own agrarian identity, so he represents God with this agrarian character as well. The Yahwist's creator is a divine farmer, planting the garden in fertile soil (2:8–9), walking through the garden to inspect it (3:8), and watering it with rainfall (2:5)."[25]

Hiebert's interpretation of the Yahwist therefore provides us with an account of this text that usefully connects its ancient context of origin with our contemporary context of reception. At a time when people of faith are wrestling with both ecological problems and a legacy of using biblical rhetoric to justify the human activities that have made these problems more severe, Hiebert gives greater attention to the Yahwist creation story in order to suggest that some parts of the Hebrew Bible are more helpful than others in offering resources for readers who are rethinking our relations to the earth and its creatures. And his argument has influenced other scholars such as Timothy Beal, who, searching for religious resources with which to face today's ecological crises, finds in Genesis 2–3 a positive "sense of earth-creaturely interdependence," indeed, a "dirty spirituality" which understands humanity, *adam* from the *adamah*, as "God-breathed earth, animated by a force of life shared with all other earth creatures."[26] The hermeneutic that leads to such interpretations, like LaCocque's hermeneutics of gender, plays upon the heterogeneity of biblical traditions, highlighting differences among them (such as differences between the Priestly and Yahwist creation accounts) in order to lift up portions of biblical literature that may provide resources for modern readers wrestling with environmental devastation. It also aligns the interpretation of Genesis 2–3 with a wider effort on the part of biblical scholars to take seriously the agricultural context of ancient Israel, and the influence of that context on biblical thought and imagery.[27]

---

24. Hiebert, "Genesis," 83; see also Hiebert, *The Yahwist's Landscape*; Hiebert, "The Human Vocation."

25. Hiebert, "Genesis," 84.

26. Beal, *When Time Is Short*, 91.

27. For example, Davis, *Scripture, Culture, and Agriculture*.

But here we should note a cautionary point. An agricultural reading of Genesis 2–3 is certainly more ecologically resonant than a traditional reading of Genesis 1, with its references to the "dominion" or "rule" of humans created in "the image of God." Nevertheless, an emphasis on agriculture carries some potentially negative ecological connotations of its own. Agriculture today, which is often practiced on an industrial scale, is widely recognized as one of the most significant sources of environmental damage thanks to such matters as deforestation, pesticides, methane and other emissions, and the pollution, diversion, and overuse of water. Such contemporary problems would seem to have little to do with the interpretation of ancient biblical texts, which were written long before the rise of industrial agriculture. But some observers doubt that ancient agriculture and modern problems can be separated completely from one another. The ecological theorist Timothy Morton, for example, calls attention to Genesis 2–3, with its association between agriculture and God's curse on the ground (3:17–19), in the course of arguing that our current ecological crises are grounded in an "agrilogistics" that is continuous with the emergence of ancient Mesopotamian agriculture.[28] For Morton, the agricultural legacy of the ancient world that gave us the Bible has contributed to our environmental problems. Some archaeologists also suggest that human impacts on the environment which are associated with the contemporary term "Anthropocene," signaling the fact that we are now living in an era when human modification of the earth is extensive enough to justify the designation of a new geological epoch, can actually be traced to the ancient emergence of intensive agriculture rather than, as is more often the case, to the industrial revolution or capitalism.[29]

Modern industrial agriculture also has devastating consequences for the lives of animals. Indeed, concern about the treatment of domesticated animals has been a major impetus for the rise of animal studies, and concerns about animal welfare and animal rights, in the humanities and social sciences. To be sure, the literary setting for the story in Genesis 2–3 is a mythical world in which humans are not yet eating animals. At first glance, then, animal agriculture might seem irrelevant to it. But the story of Cain and Abel that follows in Genesis 4, also associated with the Yahwist, is premised on the existence of "flocks" of domesticated animals (4:2–5; the term

---

28. Morton, *Dark Ecology*, 38–40.
29. Smith and Zeder, "The Onset of the Anthropocene."

may include both sheep and goats) whose sacrifice is not only permitted but represented as more acceptable to God than offerings of produce.

The thoroughgoing significance of the domestication of animals for our understanding of biblical literature and the world that produced it has been underscored most recently by David Carr.[30] But what does this have to do with gender and Genesis 2–3? In an earlier article on "competing construals of human relations with 'animal' others in the "Primeval History" (Genesis 1–11), Carr argues that the Yahwist account, which he refers to as "non-P primeval history," is characterized by "what might be termed 'differentiation by triangulation,' where the relation of the first (implicitly) male subject is simultaneously defined vis-à-vis both women *and* animals." Carr, like Hiebert and Beal, points out that the story in Genesis 2–3 opens with an "account of the creation of the (hu)man out of the earth as an animal-like creature, a נפש חיה ("living being" [2:7]), who is progressively differentiated from animals and then women."[31] Here we have a close but complex relationship between human-animal difference and human sexual difference. The differentiation of human and animal is not accomplished all at once but involves "a longer process of distinguishing humans from animals," a process, moreover, that is not strictly linear. After the creation of the first human, the animals are "fashioned" from the same *adamah*; but then the woman is created "from a part of the human," which seems to distinguish her from the animals.[32] The unique closeness of her relationship to the man, in contrast to the relation between humans and animals, is emphasized by the text, as LaCocque also notes. At a later point, the differentiation of the human pair from non-human animals is emphasized by, among other things, the animal-skin tunics that God gives them to wear (3:21). Yet when the woman is punished, "she, along with the animals, is now defined as both different and under the man" and is named by him (3:20) in a manner that uses "the same naming formula (. . . 'call a name to/for') that the human used earlier in naming animals (2:20)."[33] At times the woman is clearly distinguished from animals, and at other times she is more closely associated with them than the man is, and subordinated to the man as they are. "Differentiation by triangulation" seems not to be a

---

30. Carr, "The Bible and the Domestication of the World."
31. Carr, "Competing Construals of Human Relations with 'Animal' Others," 256.
32. Carr, "Competing Construals of Human Relations with 'Animal' Others," 256–57.
33. Carr, "Competing Construals of Human Relations with 'Animal' Others," 258.

smooth process moving towards its tidy conclusion but rather a complicated, and sometimes contradictory, ordeal.

Carr goes on to observe that "the Eden narrative . . . reflects the contradictions implicit in the distinctions it draws, in part by way of the snake character who initiates the plot in Gen 3." The snake moves across boundaries that we normally use to distinguish humans from animals. It is, in the words of Amy Kalmanofsky, "a hybrid figure. Although an animal, it embodies qualities such as walking, talking, and cunning that typically are associated with humans."[34] It knows more than the humans about the trees in the garden and God's motivation in forbidding the humans from eating of the tree of knowledge of good and evil. It is able to speak with the humans, not because God has opened its mouth (as happens, for example, with the she-donkey who converses with Balaam in Num 22:28) but rather because, as LaCocque disarmingly puts it, "communication between humans and animals used to be no problem."[35] And its punishment by God in 3:14–15, which includes a specification that the snake will henceforth move on its belly, indicates that at one time it walked upon legs, like many other animals including humans.

Carr, however, calls attention not only to the punishment of the snake, but to the larger series of punishments that appear in Gen 3:14–19. All three characters—the man, the woman, and the snake—are punished; and they are punished in ways that reflect the world in which the writer lived. The punishments recognize that life in ancient Israel could be hard for all of them. As Carr notes, however, the punishment of the woman explicitly includes subordination to the man: "the woman is bound into a role of reproductive toil—multiplied conceptions, desire for her husband, and his ruling over her (3:16)."[36] Carr, then, like LaCocque, is very clear about the fact that Genesis 2–3 is shaped by a patriarchal perspective.

Now many discussions of Gen 3:16 pay insufficient attention to the fact that both sexual reproduction and heterosexual desire are represented in 3:16 as punishments for women rather than ideals for human existence. Readers of the Bible are perhaps a bit nervous about the implication that having children, and desiring men, are understood as negative features of life for women. Yet in the ancient world, such a conclusion makes sense. Childbirth, explicitly acknowledged as a painful hardship in the text, would

---

34. Kalmanofsky, *Gender-Play in the Hebrew Bible*, 31.
35. LaCocque, *Trial of Innocence*, 155.
36. Carr, "Competing Construals of Human Relations with 'Animal' Others," 258.

have been dangerous for most women, who risked dying in childbirth at a higher rate than many women in modern industrial societies.[37] A woman's sexual desire for men, on the other hand, makes both pregnancy and the risk of dying in painful childbirth more likely. It is therefore understandable that childbirth and heterosexual desire might have been viewed with some suspicion, as phenomena that women would have been better off without. As Rebecca Alpert puts it in her discussion of Jewish lesbian approaches to Torah, the text acknowledges as a "descriptive" matter that "childbirth is both painful and dangerous, yet women it endure it anyway."[38] Recognition of these negative consequences of both heterosexual desire and sexual reproduction, for women, alongside the subordination of women to men, may be especially significant within the framework of LGBT or queer readings.[39]

In any case, as Carr notes about the punishments meted out on the woman, "she, along with the animals, is now defined as both different and under the man." The "final certification" of this differentiation and subordination comes in 3:20 where, as noted above, the woman is named by the man using the same language that was applied earlier to the naming of the animals by the first human (2:19–20).[40] Carr points out that the differentiation and subordination of both women and animals is followed in the Yahwist's narrative by the stories of Cain and Abel, and of Noah and his sons, which further differentiate Israelite men from such groups as Kenites, Canaanites, and others through tales of symbolic ancestors. The text is not interested in these groups of people as such, but rather "features these characters as diverse 'others' vis-à-vis its construction of the Hebrew male subject."[41] We might conclude from Carr's analysis that women, animals, and men who represent other ethnic groups in the Yahwistic narrative function primarily to highlight the emergence of Carr's "Hebrew male subject," a patriarchal subject, with whom the assumed male Israelite audience can identify.

This is a grimmer assessment of the Yahwist than one finds in, for example, Hiebert's ecological reading. In comparison with Hiebert, Carr characterizes the Yahwist's narrative in a more negative light even than the Priestly narrative in Genesis 1, which, while emphasizing the hierarchy

37. See Meyers, *Rediscovering Eve*.
38. Alpert, *Like Bread on the Seder Plate*, 25.
39. Stone, "The Garden of Eden and the Heterosexual Contract," 55–56.
40. Carr, "Competing Construals of Human Relations with 'Animal' Others," 258.
41. Carr, "Competing Construals of Human Relations with 'Animal' Others," 259.

between humans and animals, makes no reference to the subordination of women to men (though other priestly texts do support such subordination). In Carr's words, "where the non-P [i.e., Yahwist] primeval history constructs an implicitly Hebrew male self over against multiple binaries of animal, female, and various ethnic others, P develops just one of these binaries—that of godlike humans versus the nonhuman creatures they rule."[42] The Priestly story has had a more damaging legacy for our treatment of animals and the environment, and yet it arguably leaves room for a more egalitarian relationship between women and men. We do not have to do here with good and bad texts, but rather with two different stories that lend themselves to both positive and negative consequences, depending upon the issues highlighted in their interpretation.

Carr briefly connects the dynamics of gender, species, and ethnicity found in the Yahwist story to a discussion of such dynamics that the French philosopher Jacques Derrida organized around the neologism "carnophallogocentrism." Space and focus do not permit a full explication of this term here.[43] Derrida, however, uses it to discuss the relationship between, on the one hand, constructions of the dominant, Western, male subject and, on the other hand, women, animals, and men who, for various reasons including race, ethnicity, nation, and homosexuality, are also excluded from the construction of an idealized notion of "Man."[44] Although Derrida is primarily focused on the construction of the dominant subject in modernity, his discussions of animality elsewhere note that the roots of our contradictory notions about animals can be traced back to the ancient world, a point he makes by engaging not only Greek myths but also, significantly, the Yahwist's stories about Adam and Eve in Genesis 2–3 and Cain and Abel in Genesis 4.[45]

Like LaCocque, then, Carr recognizes the patriarchal nature of Genesis 2–3. But how thoroughly patriarchal must we understand it to be? Are there ways to read the story that are, to return to LaCocque's term more "subversive"? It is tempting to answer this question simply by appealing to the Priestly narrative in chapter 1, where no hierarchy is identified between the male and female, who are both created in the image of God. Such a tactic would ground a subversive hermeneutics in a recognition of the

---

42. Carr, "Competing Construals of Human Relations with 'Animal' Others," 262.
43. But see Stone, "Judges 3 and the Queer Hermeneutics of Carnophallogocentrism."
44. See Derrida, "Eating Well."
45. See Derrida, *The Animal That Therefore I Am*.

diversity of scripture comparable to that found in some of LaCocque's other writings on women and the Bible. But there is a potential cost to deploying such a hermeneutical strategy in this case. By grounding gender equality in the particular understanding of the image of God found in Gen 1:26–28, one risks reinforcing the rule over, and domination of, the earth and its creatures that are also referred to in the chapter and that has contributed to our current ecological crises, as Hiebert reminds us.

Here it is useful to note instead a distinction between the respective interpretations of the Yahwist's tale by Carr and LaCocque. As both scholars observe, the history of interpretation of this story contains at least two different understandings of the gendered nature of the first human created in 2:7. In one stream of interpretation, the first human, the *adam* created from the *adamah*, is already implicitly male.[46] In a second stream of interpretation, however, the *adam* is not created as male, but rather as an androgynous earth creature who is only subsequently divided into man and woman.[47] While Carr agrees with the first interpretation, LaCocque aligns himself with the second one, noting that an understanding of the first human as an "androgyne" is also supported by "Rashi and most of the Jewish tradition."[48]

I have suggested elsewhere, in a queer reading of the Genesis creation accounts, that there is no definitive way to resolve this difference in interpretations on the basis of the text alone.[49] The story is simply too full of tensions and contradictions, which result in part from its difficult project of trying to imagine a moment of creation that does not yet entail a binary logic of gender and sexuality, even though such logic overdetermines the world of the text's author as well as that of most readers. Nevertheless, the tension in this text between the reality of life now, and a different form of life that one can imagine in the distant past, may offer opportunities to apply a subversive hermeneutic to Genesis 2–3. For one need not subscribe to Christian notions of "the Fall" in order to see that Genesis 2–3 is shaped by a conviction that human life would ideally take a different shape than the shape it currently has. In that respect the story contains a critique of the world that the Yahwist knew. But this characteristic of the story also allows readers to interpret it in ways that contribute to a critique of the world of

---

46. See for example Chapman, "The Breath of Life."
47. So, famously, Trible, *God and the Rhetoric of Sexuality*.
48. LaCocque, *Trial of Innocence*, 120.
49. Stone, "The Garden of Eden and the Heterosexual Contract."

the reader. One can read the series of punishments in 3:14-18 backward, as it were, recognizing in these verses a description of circumstances of life that are *other* than ideal. These circumstances can then be contrasted with earlier stages of the narrative in order to see that the storytellers could imagine a better way of life—and so too, perhaps, can the story's readers.

This way of reading the text is most often deployed as a critique of the subordination of women to men. For if we see in the text that the man's "rule" over the woman (3:16), while no doubt reflecting the patriarchal world of ancient Israel, did not exist from the beginning of the story or from the moment of the creation of sexual difference (where the two humans are represented as corresponding partners for one another, "bone of my bones and flesh of my flesh" [2:23]), we may emphasize this earlier, foundational moment in the narrative, prior to male domination, as a textual rallying point in support of sexual equality. But variations on this hermeneutical move are also possible. Starting from the recognition in 3:17-19 that agricultural life as it actually existed at the time of the Yahwist was difficult, and that plants for food could only be grown with much sweat and toil, we may emphasize an earlier moment in the story when agriculture looked more like care for a garden planted by God. This contrast can then serve as one basis for a critique of agricultural systems that actually exist, which fall short of the original ideal and have such devastating consequences for human agricultural workers, for animals, and for the environment. And even a queer reading of the story might emphasize the contrast between the troubling representation of sexuality and gender in the punishments in 3:16, or the bodily shame implied by 3:7-10, and the more innocent relationship between the humans that initially exists in 2:21-25 or, for that matter, the existence of a transgender human (LaCocque's "androgyne") who is originally created from the earth in 2:7.[50]

So also I want to suggest, by way of conclusion, that this type of subversive hermeneutical move may be applied to the status of animals in the Yahwist text, and specifically to their relations with humans. It is clear that 3:14-15 results in negative consequences for the snake, who, like the woman and the man, stands in for some larger group of living beings in the world of the author. It is possible to read the punishment of this snake as a symbolic understanding of snakes alone, distinguishing them from other animals because snakes crawl on the ground.[51] But the "enmity" which now

50. Stone, "The Garden of Eden and the Heterosexual Contract."
51. Kalmonofsky, *Gender-Play in the Hebrew Bible*, 31.

emerges between the offspring of the snake and the offspring of the woman may also have at least some connection to a new tension in this text between humans and animals as a group, comparable to the tension that also emerges in the Priestly tradition when humans are given permission to eat animals and animals come to fear humans (Gen 9:1–5). As Carr observes, "animals are treated as ever more ancillary objects" by the Yahwist following the announcement of the snake's punishment in 3:14–15.

Yet this more negative representation of the relationship between animals and humans can also be contrasted with earlier moments in the Yahwist's narrative. It contrasts with the fact that the animals and the first human are all created out of the same soil. It contrasts with the fact that the animals are brought to the humans before the creation of a second human when God determines that the first human needs companionship. And it contrasts with the fact that, as LaCocque noted, animals and humans are initially represented as communicating with one another. None of these features of the story will turn Genesis 2–3 into a manifesto for animal rights. But by recognizing with André LaCocque that the Yahwist imagined an earlier time when sexual hierarchy did not yet exist and humans and animals lived and communicated with one another in "a potential kinship or communion," we may be inspired to live together once again in "kinship or communion" across both sexual difference and species difference.

BIBLIOGRAPHY

Alpert, Rebecca. *Like Bread on the Seder Plate: Jewish Lesbians and the Transformation of Tradition*. New York: Columbia University Press, 1997.

Barr, James. "The Bible as a Document of Believing Communities." In *The Bible as a Document of the University*, edited by Hans Dieter Betz. Polebridge Books 3. Chico, CA: Scholars, 1981.

Beal, Timothy. *When Time Is Short: Finding Our Way in the Anthropocene*. Boston: Beacon, 2022.

Boyarin, Daniel. *Intertextuality and the Reading of Midrash*. 2nd ed. Indianapolis: Indiana University Press, 1994.

Carr, David M. "The Bible and the Domestication of the World." *Biblical Interpretation* 31 (2023) 579–601.

———. "Competing Construals of Human Relations with 'Animal' Others in the Primeval History (Genesis 1–11)." *JBL* 140 (2021) 251–69.

Chapman, Cynthia. "The Breath of Life: Speech, Gender, and Authority in the Garden of Eden." *JBL* 138 (2019) 241–62.

Collins, John J. *An Introduction to the Hebrew Bible*. 3rd ed. Minneapolis: Fortress, 2018.

Crowder, Stephanie Buckhanon. *When Momma Speaks: The Bible and Motherhood from a Womanist Perspective*. Louisville: Westminster John Knox, 2016.

Davis, Ellen. *Scripture, Culture, and Agriculture: An Agrarian Reading of the Bible.* New York: Cambridge University Press, 2009.
Derrida, Jacques. *The Animal That Therefore I Am.* Edited by Marie-Louise Mallet. Translated by David Wills. New York: Fordham University Press, 2008.
———. "'Eating Well,' or the Calculation of the Subject." In *Points . . . : Interviews, 1974–94,* edited by Elizabeth Weber, 255–87. Translated by Peggy Kamuf. Stanford: Stanford University Press, 1995.
Hanson, Paul D. *The Diversity of Scripture: A Theological Interpretation.* Overtures to Biblical Theology. Philadelphia: Fortress, 1982.
Hiebert, Theodore. "Genesis." In *The Oxford Handbook of the Bible and Ecology,* edited by Hilary Marlow and Mark Harris, 81–94. Oxford Handbooks. New York: Oxford University Press, 2022.
———. "Air, the First Sacred Thing: The Conception of *Ruach* in the Hebrew Scriptures." In *Exploring Ecological Hermeneutics,* edited by Norman Habel and Peter Trudinger, 9–19. Atlanta: SBL, 2008.
———. "The Human Vocation: Origins and Transformations in Christian Traditions." In *Christianity and Ecology: Seeking the Well-Being of Earth and Humans,* edited by Dieter T. Hessel and Rosemary Radford Ruether, 135–51. Religions of the World and Ecology. Cambridge: Harvard University Press, 2000.
———. *The Yahwist's Landscape: Nature and Religion in Early Israel.* New York: Oxford University Press, 1996.
Kalmanofsky, Amy. *Gender-Play in the Hebrew Bible: The Ways the Bible Challenges Its Gender Norms.* New York: Routledge, 2017.
Kolbert, Elizabeth. *The Sixth Extinction: An Unnatural History.* New York: Holt, 2014.
LaCocque, André. *Esther Regina: A Bakhtinian Reading.* Rethinking Theory. Evanston, IL: Northwestern University Press, 2007.
———. *The Trial of Innocence: Adam, Eve, and the Yahwist.* Eugene, OR: Cascade Books, 2006.
———. *Ruth: A Continental Commentary.* Translated by K. C. Hanson. Continental Commentaries. Minneapolis: Fortress, 2004.
———. *Romance, She Wrote: A Hermeneutical Essay on Song of Songs.* Harrisburg, PA: Trinity, 1998.
———. *The Feminine Unconventional: Four Subversive Figures in Israel's Tradition.* Overtures to Biblical Theology. 1990. Reprint, Eugene, OR: Wipf & Stock, 2005.
LaCocque, André, and Paul Ricoeur. *Thinking Biblically: Exegetical and Hermeneutical Studies.* Trans. David Pellauer. Chicago: University of Chicago Press, 2003.
Meyers, Carol. *Rediscovering Eve: Ancient Israelite Women in Context.* New York: Oxford University Press, 2012.
Morton, Timothy. *Dark Ecology: For a Logic of Future Coexistence.* New York: Columbia University Press, 2016.
Smith, Bruce, and Melinda A. Zeder. "The Onset of the Anthropocene." *Anthropocene* 4 (2013) 8–13.
Stone, Ken. "'All These Look to You': Reading Psalm 104 with Animals in the Anthropocene Epoch." *Interpretation* 73 (2019) 236–47.
———. "The Garden of Eden and the Heterosexual Contract." In *Bodily Citations: Religion and Judith Butler,* edited by Ellen Armour and Susan M. St. Ville, 48–70. Gender, Theory, and Religion. New York: Columbia University Press, 2006.

———. "Judges 3 and the Queer Hermeneutics of Carnophallogocentrism." In *The Bible and Feminism: Remapping the Field*, edited by Yvonne Sherwood, 261–76. New York: Oxford University Press, 2017.

———. *Practicing Safer Texts: Food, Sex and Bible in Queer Perspective*. Queering Theology Series. London: T. & T. Clark, 2005.

———. "Reading Elisha's She-Bears: Biblical Interpretation, Extinction Studies, and the Wildness of God." *Biblical Interpretation* 31 (2023) 602–22.

———. *Reading the Hebrew Bible with Animal Studies*. Stanford: Stanford University Press, 2018.

———. "Wittgenstein's Lion and Balaam's Ass: Talking with Others in Numbers 22–25." In *The Bible and Posthumanism*, edited by Jennifer Koosed, 75–103. Semeia Studies 74. Atlanta: SBL, 2014.

Thistlethwaite, Susan Brooks. "Every Two Minutes: Battered Women and Feminist Interpretation." In *Feminist Interpretation of the Bible*, edited by Letty M. Russell, 96–109. Philadelphia: Westminster, 1985.

Thomas, Keith. *Man and the Natural World: Changing Attitudes in England 1500–1800*. New York: Oxford University Press, 1983.

Trible, Phyllis. *God and the Rhetoric of Sexuality*. Overtures to Biblical Theology. Philadelphia: Fortress Press, 1978.

Weems, Renita. *Battered Love: Marriage, Sex, and Violence in the Hebrew Prophets*. Overtures to Biblical Theology. Philadelphia: Fortress, 1995.

8

The Dialectic of Praxis and the Theology of Work

BO-MYUNG SEO

ANDRÉ LACOCQUE'S *WORK AND Creativity* was the last book published during his long and fruitful scholarly life. The book reveals his erudition and wide-ranging intellectual interests, well-known to his former students and the readers of his books alike. How this book may differ from many of his earlier works is not his passion for interpretation and wish to bring in multiple disciplinary voices to bear upon the reading of scriptures but the extent of their presence. Partly function of the theme of the book, work, and its method, the dialectic, we see him invoking and discussing political philosophers and psychoanalytic thinkers, touching upon both the material and anthropological dimensions of work. I take LaCocque's insights in the book to be an important contribution to the theology of work, one that begins with the welcoming of the dialectical understanding of work contained in the Bible and its presence in human experience. LaCocque's engagement with the philosophers in the book is reminiscent of his collaboration with Paul Ricoeur, in whose memory the book is dedicated. My intention in this essay is as follows: 1) to discuss the problem of work in capitalism utilizing the dialectical insights found in his book; 2) to point out some possible ways of relating LaCocque and Ricoeur's thoughts on work; 3) focusing on the idea of work as a praxis, I formulate some suggestions for a contemporary theology of work.

CONTEXTS

The context for LaCocque's book is the same one that inspired so many, since Marx, to offer their analyses and critiques. This, of course, is capitalism and its negative impact on the dominant human experience of work. The realization that work, under capitalism, became a problem—previously unknown in history—is common to much of modern discourses on work. There is no modern discourse on work, whether it is philosophical, theological, or sociological, without this realization. LaCocque's is no exception. That the human experience of the condition of work has not changed much since the 19th century speaks to the failure, or the success, of capitalism. People may differ on the nature of the problem, but the reported human experience of that problem tends to be remarkably similar. Take, for example, the experience of alienation, which was so brilliantly analyzed in the 1840s by Marx, and how the workers in the digital economy of the 21st century speak of the same but more intensified experience of alienation. Given how even the work of low-wage workers today is performed around symbolic numbers and data, it is difficult to identify the nature and cause of the alienation. Moreover, the blurring boundary between the human and non-human in the post-human future means that more is at the stake than just human social relations. The feeling of alienation is just one example, since such experiences as unfreedom, degradation, exploitation—historically associated with industrial capitalism—are still part of the working class experience of work.[1] The freedom from the burden of work that was to come with deployment of more machines, as predicted by Herbert Marcuse, may have alleviated the intensity of physical exertion from work but added to the psychological and even ontological sense of alienation.

The long history of criticism of work in capitalism is countered by the more dominant discourse on work in the modern West that has extolled and glorified the virtues of work—as what gives meaning to being human,

---

1. My sources for thinking about the contemporary work class experience of work included popular books such as *On the Clock: What Low-Wage Work Did to Me and How It Drives America Insane*, written by Emily Guendelsberger. In particular, I found her discussion of "cyborg work" incisive in naming what work for many Americans was becoming today.

as what mobilizes the nation, and as being a divine gift to human beings. Nietzsche's case against modern, industrial, work as a manifestation of nihilism of his era is countered by Ernst Jünger and Martin Heidegger, for whom the idea of the human as a worker was both a destiny and a new principle for their vision of the world.[2] And Marx's critique against work was famously countered by Weber's thesis on the Protestant work ethic.

Christian theology has done much to elevate the value of work in the modern West, giving it a religious aura as a calling and vocation. While it was not possible for any theologian to ignore the problem with work in the nineteenth century, the Marxist call for revolutionary changes was not an option for many theologians. Weber's re-discovery of Luther's notion of vocation and the Puritan work ethic was a boon for theologians who were interested in a different understanding of work. But Weber's justifiably important thesis was produced in order to counter the dialectical, secular understanding of history, and its popularity in the United States was not unrelated to the context of the Cold War. Out of his interpretation of Luther and Calvin, the ideas of vocation and 'calling' were advanced as what motivated the work ethic of the Calvinists and puritans that paved the way for the emergence of capitalism. Against the Marxist critique of work, Weber presented the Lutheran idea of workers being called by God to be working at their current place of work. While it is easy to dismiss his ideas as inadequate or even wrong, as they can potentially perpetuate the situations of exploitation and alienation and provide justifications for why we have to endure bad work, Weber's theory had impact that went far beyond the field of theology. It was part of my upbringing in Korea, for example, to believe what characterized the American ethos was its work ethic: honest, diligent, and vocational. No doubt I came to believe it because it was taught to me as such, with a corollary suggestion that what's ailing the non-Western world is precisely the lack of such characteristics. If this was part of a colonial propaganda, nothing for me made it more effective than the ideas of the puritan work ethic and the calling advanced by Max Weber. More recent

---

2. Nietzsche on multiple occasions expressed his disgust for what became of work in the modern period. He would ask, for example: "And has anyone noticed that, consequently, it is the modern, noisy, time-consuming, self-satisfied, stupidly proud industriousness which, more than anything else, gives people an education and preparation in "un-belief"? (Nietzsche, *Beyond Good and Evil*, 51). Jünger's influential book written in 1932, *The Worker: Dominion and Form*, was an inspiration for Heidegger. I am also familiar with this totalitarian vision of the world as found in North Korea and South Korea after the Korean War.

reflections on work, however, tend to begin with the understanding that the vocational perspective on work is inadequate not just to account for the problem of work in the post-industrial world but to meet the complex understanding of work to be found in the Bible. In the end, this theory—to be equally attributed to Luther's originality and Weber's interpretive power, in my estimation—is problematic because it does not address the issue from the workers' perspective and turns it into a matter of doctrine.

THE DIALECTIC OF WORK

My understanding of the term "work" and its use in this essay is built around a sensibility toward what people who bear the burden of work in our society do to earn their living. Today they are referred as low-wage workers or the "bottom-half." To be sure, work has wider meanings and implications, as it is now used in reference to virtually all human activities. This is a sign that work has become a defining, totally consuming human activity, which in turn requires a dialectical understanding.

I can offer two possible reasons as to why LaCocque was interested in interpreting work dialectically. First, it's because human work explains and embodies what dialectic is. Work, for instance, makes dialectics concrete as it provides real life experiences from human existence. A second and related reason is because recent theological reflections on work have not been dialectical or not dialectical enough. Needless to say, both assume that he was concerned about the state of human work in capitalism and the possibility of redeeming it toward greater justice of God. The idea of work as a dialectical theme is well-grounded in LaCocque's book, because work was central to the two thinkers most responsible for keeping the spirit of dialectic alive in modern thought: Hegel and Marx. For Hegel, it is the spirit that moves the dialectic, while for Marx it is the emancipatory human action or praxis.

My own view on the importance of a dialectical understanding of work can be briefly stated as follows. The dialectic of work resists the regimes of total work, while anticipating a wholistic, emancipatory understanding of work. It is based on a prior dialectical understanding of what it is to be human, which assumes the human ability to say 'no' to refuse and negate the conditions of domination. It assumes contradiction to be inherent in all social relations. But it also assumes the presence of others who share the emancipatory goal of social relations. Ultimately, dialectic is built upon a hope for the transformation of the world. Praxis is the practice of dialectic that assumes the achievement of a better world is an object of human work performed in solidarity. In the twentieth century such an understanding of dialectic and praxis came into theological consciousness through Latin American liberation theology.

What seems central to the dialectical conception of work is the acceptance of the negative moment in the unfolding process of work, without moving on too quickly toward a positive resolution. Assuming that dialectic is a movement through the productive opposition or contradiction, there's a tendency to underestimate the reality of contradiction and its burden in order to claim its productive function. I understand one meaning of Adorno's negative dialectic to be that of asking us to take "negation" in dialectic more seriously. In terms of the history of work in capitalism, this means to take the idea of non-work seriously as a possibility, not as a blasphemy, or at least to take the critiques of work seriously, not just as a prelude to a positive theology of work. Here I recall the words of Henri Lefebvre: "Workers, let us remember, have as their historical mission the negation of work."[3] Perhaps sensing the non-dialectical nature of the Lutheran theology of vocation, Bonhoeffer gave a dialectical twist in claiming that a call to work in the world is at the same time a call to responsibility for the world, and to say at times 'no' to the world.[4]

It is from Hegel that we learn about how the dialectic presupposes not a relative opposition but absolute opposition. This helps it from degenerating into a dualism and to achieve a *coincidentia oppositorum* rather than a synergistic unity. The dialectical thinking in Christian theology since Hegel is nowhere more passionately articulated and argued for than in the work of Thomas Altizer. The dialectical theology there would begin with the idea that God became human in self-negation, so that humanity may become like God, and is extended to the end of dialectical negation on the cross. That the Spirit,[5] history, or even human beings come to their

---

3. Lefebvre, *Critique of Everyday Life*, vol. 3, 167. As a warning against the propensity to think of Marx's ideas on work only as positive and productive, Lefebvre says on the same page that Marx was "the thinker of the negative."

4. Bonhoeffer, *Ethics*, 251.

5. I don't feel the need to explain what this term means, but it is central to Hegel's thought and to understanding modern German philosophy. The foreignness of this term to the non-European mind was reiterated for me by Adorno's passing remark in *Critical Models* that the "absolute importance of spirit" he learned in Europe was not "absolutely valid in America" (239).

self-consciousness through negation is basic to his thought. Such a dialectical thinking also makes sense of the problem of the modern West which, for someone like Altizer, was the result of the triumph of the liberal, colonial, thinking in the West. Altizer understood Herbert Marcuse to have provided a 'dialectical assault' on the logic of capitalist domination, and it was Marcuse's work that LaCocque quotes on a number of occasions to make sense of the problem of work in capitalism.

LACOCQUE'S DIALECTICAL-BIBLICAL THEOLOGY OF WORK

LaCocque pursues a study of work as a way to illustrate how dialectical criticism works in hermeneutics, but what comes out clearly in the book is his interest in the state of work in capitalism and its implications for human life in general. He understands work to be at the center of dialectical tension in human life and an important part of the biblical conception of humanity. The theme of dialectic is also to be found in his method of bringing philosophy and the biblical tradition to speak to each other, at times in affirmation and other times in tension. But it is in human work that we have a real-life instantiation of dialectic, which for LaCocque is already witnessed in the Bible. This begins with the idea of God as a dialectical being, who found self-negation to be necessary for the realization of the divine self-consciousness. God's act of creation is already a dialectical work, as it is bound to encounter resistance from the created order, "be it cosmic monsters or human beings." LaCocque says God is "a field of opposites—an urgent invitation to a dialectical interpretation."[6] God's divine, dialectical nature is realized through God's own work. Not just dialectical, work has an ontological dimension that applies to both God and humanity. LaCocque pushes this idea further: "Nothing can be more averse to disincarnation than work. Work is incarnation par excellence."[7] That is, the dialectical in the idea of divine becoming human is to be witnessed in the idea of God's work as God's self-revelation. If that is the ideal of human work, i.e., work as humanity's self-realization, we can find an analogue in Marx's insistence that human beings create themselves through labor. Pushing this

---

6. LaCocque, *Work and Creativity*, 39.
7. LaCocque, *Work and Creativity*, 77.

idea further, we can say that God undergoes self-development, even self-creation, through the dialectical work of divine creation.

Through a meticulous analysis of the book of Genesis, LaCocque narrates the biblical account of work from its Edenic condition to its state after the Fall. In this account, work before the Fall was a divine gift, a way for humanity to participate in the continuing work of creation and become co-creators with God, and as such it belonged to the very essence of being human. But this offer was negated through the Fall, causing human work to become toil and drudgery, destructive and negative. So, the contradiction is built into the nature of work we inherited, both as a gift to cherish and a curse to bear, a symbol of glory and a sign of rebellion. In the modern world, this dialectical analysis of work continued in the Marxist tradition, particularly as to how work became a symbol of alienation, domination, and exploitation in capitalism, and how "instead of self-realization, work [became] self-negation" and the workers "homeless."[8] If Marxism envisions an ideal, classless society, where human work will be self-realizing and self-fulfilling, the Biblical vision of work and the task for the theological reflection on work for LaCocque is the recovery of work as a redemptive and creative act, even a form of worship.

For LaCocque, God's creative work then serves as a model for human work. Human creativity in turn comes to its finest expression in art, which is "the apex of humanity's work." Although it is not developed further by LaCocque, I can continue this thought by saying that it is through art that human beings create themselves in imitation of God. Artistic activity, to the extent that it is work, rescues human activity from the reaches of 'total work' and becomes a dialectical act of freedom. LaCocque would share the sentiment contained in the following words of Ted Cohen: "Art is that human activity . . . that we do just because we do not have to. It is, therefore, the activity in which we show ourselves to be free, human beings."[9]

PAUL RICOEUR ON DIALECTIC AND WORK

The way LaCocque carries on a dialectical discussion of work in dialogue with philosophical authors and provided biblical responses to their criticisms is reminiscent of his collaboration with Paul Ricoeur in *Thinking Biblically: Exegetical and Hermeneutical Studies*. Thinking about how Ricoeur

8. LaCocque, *Work and Creativity*, 40.
9. Cohen, *Serious Larks*, 87.

might have joined LaCocque's discussions leads me to two of Ricoeur's writings: "Word and Work" (1955) and "What is Dialectical?" (1974).[10] I will limit myself below to simply suggest some points of convergence in their thoughts.

In 1955, Ricoeur joined the discussion over the nature of work that many of his peers in France and indeed in Europe were already engaged in. The issue of work—whether expressed as the problem of "total work," glorification of work, work society, or civilization of work—was generating anxiety and distress among the intellectuals both in and outside the Marxist tradition. Ricoeur's way of getting into the discussion was a dialectical one, juxtaposing words or speech to the dominant ethos of work. Rather than seeking a revolutionary overcoming of the condition of work, he wanted to temper the discourse on work that equated being human with being a worker, by suggesting that there is something just as important and yet irreducible to work: the word. He wanted to preserve this irreducibility of the word in dialectical tension with work, but it was the word, particularly in its artistic representations, that spoke more to human creativity. While both are needed, it is the word that is "at the roots of a project of a civilization, even the project of a civilization of work."[11] The recognition of the creativity and the power of the word, however, cannot be complete without the words of the scripture and their theological possibility. Ricoeur was led to ask: "Is it possible that a theology of the word coincides in the end with a theology of work? Perhaps." I can then think of LaCocque's book on work as a rejoinder to Ricoeur's question. LaCocque would say that, prior to the need for work to be dialectically juxtaposed by the word, the sacred word itself is dialectically formulated, as the speech that forms the word negates the plentitude of the divine being that does not require anything from the outside for its perfection. Further, LaCocque would say that in order for work to be what it can become—without the distortion and exploitation of its modern, capitalist manifestations but full of creative and redemptive possibilities—it has to be dialectically connected to the word.

I believe it is out of a similar intuition that Lévinas said: "Language . . . is a first action over and above labor, an action without action, even though speech involves the effort of labor, even though, as incarnate thought, it

---

10. "Word and Work" was published in 1955 as a chapter in *History and Truth*, which was three years before the publication of Hannah Arendt's *The Human Condition*. "What is Dialectical?" was a lecture given by Ricoeur in 1974 at the University of Kansas, later collected in *Freedom & Morality*.

11. Ricoeur, *History and Truth*, 218.

inserts us into the world, with the risks and hazards of all action. At each instant it exceeds this labor by the generosity of the offer it forthwith makes of this very labor."[12] LaCocque would add to Lévinas' last sentence in saying that is why labor needs to be an offering to the word, the first and divine word. But the world of work, the world of 'risks and hazards,' comes to us in the face of the Other for Lévinas. It comes to us precisely as the word that speaks of the world—the world of work, with its 'risks and hazards,' distortion, and exploitation. If the word offers the world to us, LaCocque would say in agreement with Lévinas that our work should be an offering to the face of the Other, in humility and solidarity. The connection between the word, this time not as spoken but written, and work can also be found in Thoreau, who famously declared in *Walden* that people "labor under a mistake."[13] If so, then people work not out of a sense of calling or as a result of fate or sin but out of ignorance and a commitment to wrong things. Thoreau was not just advocating the virtue of being self-sufficient through the work done with hands or how that is liberating and self-fulfilling, but also writing as a labor done with hands, thereby positing a dialectic of the written word and work. This particular dialectic for LaCocque is to be resolved through interpretation and not primarily through human activity. The resolution of a dialectic can never only be textual, but dialectic interpretation of a text can lead to motivations or impetus for human action, a praxis. The movement of Ricoeur's thought from that of interpretation theories to theories of action is not entirely unrelated to the problematic presented by the totalization of work. It was, I think, an attempt to find human activity that is irreducible to work that led thinkers like Ricoeur and Arendt and others even unconsciously to explore the nature of human action.[14] By the same token, the entire industry of discourse on human action in the middle of the 20th century was an attempt, in so many disciplines, to carve out a space for human action that is not reducible to work. One way in which Ricoeur's texts can expand the dialogue with LaCocque concerns the role of human action as a praxis to bring about a resolution to the dialectic of work.

12. Lévinas, *Totality and Infinity*, 174.

13. Thoreau, *Walden*, 5.

14. Richard Bernstein delineated the history and philosophy of how a movement from hermeneutics and praxis emerged in his books, *Praxis and Human Action* and later in *Beyond Objectivism*. He wrote: "In exploring the fusion of hermeneutics and *praxis*, I intend to show how the implicit *telos* within philosophic hermeneutics requires us to move beyond hermeneutics itself" (*Beyond Objectivism*, 114).

In the text of his 1974 lecture, Ricoeur refers to praxis as being central to dialectic, saying "praxis is dialectic at work."[15] He finds Marxism to be limited in its reduction of praxis to class struggle, which in turn is understood to be the paradigmatic example of the dialectic.[16] This means historical materialism that theorizes the dialectical also limits the scope of dialectical thought. The problem with this reduction is that it forgets the "dialectical features of human experience." If praxis is human action understood dialectically, it should also account for and be accountable to the dialectical character of human experience. For Ricoeur, it was not Marx but Hegel who paid attention to the dialectical character of human experience, hence it is in Hegel that "the notion of work received a more complete interpretation."[17] But it is also the case that Marx's analysis of work in capitalism, especially around alienation, as I noted earlier, continues to be accountable to the human experience of work as unfulfilling, alienating, and exploitative. The dialectical in human experience for Ricoeur is formed not so much out of the economic and political experience of negation but more out of social relations that require negation in responses and answers to others, and even to nature. This for Ricoeur is dialectical human experience that is closer to the historical essence of humanity. In this quick reading, it seems Ricoeur would want to engage LaCocque around the notion of praxis and experience.

LaCocque's use of praxis is decidedly theological. Praxis is not human action, as is the case in Marxism, performed to bring about revolutionary transformation of society and an end to capitalism along with its distortions and alienations. Such a transformation should be envisioned as a consequence rather than the goal of human activity in the world. The goal of human activity is to cooperate with God's standing invitation for human beings to become co-creators with God. He says, "the universe is incomplete and on the relative side rather than the absolute as long as human work is distorted and factually crippled. Here lies the significance of human praxis."[18] That is, he affirms the ability of human beings to regain, through praxis, the "nobility and glory of work," so that it can achieve the status of

---

15. Ricoeur, "What Is Dialectical?," in *Freedom & Morality*, 183.

16. Ricoeur was surely not alone in his criticism of praxis as advanced in Marxism. For example, Gadamer also lamented how we have forgotten what praxis is under the distortion of Marxism.

17. Ricoeur, "What Is Dialectical?," in *Freedom & Morality*, 185.

18. LaCocque, *Work and Creativity*, 71.

"living sacrifice" and "spiritual worship." But LaCocque does not say how human work can be free from distortion, perhaps being content to let it be inferred from the dialectical critics of the Frankfurt School, who called for "a different praxis."[19] Inferring the different praxes proposed by figures like Marcuse and Adorno is not an easy task, because they famously argued in the 1960s over the very nature of praxis, each claiming to be faithful to Marx. I would think Adorno's view of praxis that cautioned against praxis turning into a force of domination and stressed the non-identity of theory and praxis better serves LaCocque's theological purpose, which is to retain the primacy of the word, theory, of the Bible. Though he doesn't dwell upon it, LaCocque says in plain but prescient words how the force of praxis needs to be tempered: "Paradoxically as it may seem to some, exegesis and philosophy have led us to a decisive option for a praxis marked by humaneness and compassion. The crucial biblical notion of love is not a far-fetched abstraction."[20]

DIALECTIC AS A PRAXIS

Using the ideas presented above, I will in this part of the essay develop some suggestions for a theology of work, particularly along the line of the notion of praxis. I would like them to be relevant to the contemporary condition of work, but it should be noted again that, despite all the changes in the governing faces of capitalism in the West, there has been a remarkable consistency since the days of industrial capitalism on how the low-wage workers or workers on the margins of society experience their daily work. It is not a fate or necessity that comes with being low-wage workers in an affluent society, but a part of how capitalism works as a system. So, until a systematic change is possible, thinking about redemptive, creative work can only be a hopeful and even a utopian exercise. But it is the standpoint of hope and redemption that gives legitimacy to theology's claim to speak of God and for God.

To offer some further reflections on dialectic and praxis, I assume that dialectic not only assumes the priority of praxis but is meaningful only to the extent it is praxis. Praxis is human activity that is consciously performed with emancipatory and transformative goals in mind. The dialectic imagines such goals in praxis, and this imagination is possible through the

---

19. LaCocque, *Work and Creativity*, 71.
20. LaCocque, *Work and Creativity*, 71

recognition of the moments of resistance and negation as being integral to the movement. The priority of praxis does not reduce theory to being a propaganda-wing of praxis. The dialectic assumes the non-identity and the tension between the two. Theologically, it was the liberation theology of Latin America that reformulated the idea of praxis as a central notion with which to call for fundamental changes in society and to present a challenge to the dominant Western theology. And it is the inspiration from this development of praxis that I will draw from in talking about work as a praxis and the possibility of a theology of work.

Liberation Theology's primary contribution to Christian theology had to do with its conception of theology as a second act which gives primacy to praxis, thereby making theology a matter of reflection on Christian praxis. As in Marx, praxis for liberation theology was a social practice done for the sake of transformation of the world. Mere reflection upon the world or even construction of doctrines is no longer the goal of theology, which is now famously defined as "a critical reflection on Christian praxis in the light of word."[21] The elevation of orthopraxis as the norm for theology, in addition to the idea of doing theology from the underside of history, still holds power and promise as a source for theological reflection. The dialectical relation between praxis and orthopraxis removes the relation of theory and praxis from the center of discussion for liberation theology, as it affirms the primacy of doing over mere believing.

The idea of praxis in Liberation Theology is untenable without a dialectical understanding of history and the Christian life. The central dialectic has to do with the interaction between faith and action or theory and practice. The experience of the poor in the world, for example, demands a reflection on faith through the lens of that experience. The commitment toward the transformation of the world comes out of this new dialectical reflection. It is praxis in human activity that reflects this commitment.

Despite the different contexts, I believe the insights of liberation theology can be transposed into being a resource for a contemporary theology of work. As I already alluded to it earlier, this theology can begin with the idea of work as a praxis. I think of it also as a way to broaden LaCocque's reflections on work and to continue the theologically motivated dialectical thinking on work. I will offer the following as a way to flesh out the idea: Understanding work dialectically in this account means that the human experience of work that forms the basis of praxis is to be preserved. It is

---

21. Gutierrez, *A Theology of Liberation*, 15.

not just to be overcome in a quick resolution of the dialectic; preserving or tarrying with that negative moment (perhaps as a "dangerous memory"). Part of human reality experienced by most people in the world is the recognition that praxis is formed out of a historical consciousness (For example, praxis for Gutierrez is always a historical praxis). Any resolution of this dialectic needs to be measured by the reality and memory of this experience. The same measure applies to any attempt to recover the redemptive dimension of work as God intended.

To understand human work as a form of praxis means that we are not called to work, because we are called into being—to be and to act—prior to our work. To have a coherent sense of what work is about, we need a prior sense of what it means to be human. I believe this is in agreement with LaCocque's position to say that human beings are at their best when they are able to exercise autonomy, freedom, and engage in creative work and that this idea is a part of the biblical tradition. This is what Liberation Theology offers by insisting on the liberative dimension of human existence—that human beings do and should seek liberation from oppression—as being normative, and this anthropology is posited as the measure with which human praxis is to be judged. The idea of orthopraxis rescues praxis from being juxtaposed only against theory. It resists the imposition of theory on work, which can turn work into an abstract, fate-laden endeavor. To go back to the discussions in the 1960s around Adorno's allegedly shifting views on praxis, the idea of orthopraxis helps us to resist the temptation of the pseudo-praxis of unreflective, immediate action.

When work is a praxis, the worker retains the option to resist and negate the system and the work imposed through it. It is not part of a worker's right but a demand of a liberative faith. It is this option to negate work that propels the dialectic of work. Negation here means to both resist the stigma that comes with non-work and to embrace the critique of the state of work in capitalism. To be called a praxis, work should aspire to being the kind of human activity, borne out of a liberative understanding of God, the Bible, and faith. This places limits around what work is or is to be about, but it does not turn work into an ideology or oppressive praxis or a form of actionism. The reality, however, is that work done by low-wage workers is already ideological and oppressive, often to the point of being demeaning to our sense of what it means to be human. If anything, the praxis-oriented work would seek to liberate work toward more humane, non-alienating, and non-exploitative conditions.

A quick detour might be helpful in lessening the potential incredulity with regard to seeing work as a praxis. Alisdair McIntyre offers a philosophical vision for work that can serve as analogue. Despite all his criticisms of modernity, he is not under the illusion that capitalism will or has to go away before the possibility of fulfilling human work can be realized. His vision for work is related to the notion of practice, which he famously defined as "any coherent form of socially established cooperative activity through which goods internal to that form of activity are realized in the course of trying to achieve those standards of excellence which are appropriate to, and partially definitive of, that form of activity."[22] This vision, which is further elaborated on with actual corporate examples from around the world in *Ethics in the Conflicts of Modernity*, assumes the possibility that workers can be treated not just as a means to the ends around profit established by the company but as agents who can, in their work, pursue the common good central to the community in which they live.[23] The ideal of work as a practice, in which the worker works on becoming an ethical, creative, and free human being, depends on the availability of such workplaces. This vision, however, is not a dialectical vision of work and does not incorporate the contradictions built into work under capitalism or the changing social conditions of work. This is a vision rarely realized in the workplace of low-wage workers, but it can be posited as an ideal situation or a normative condition for free and creative work. The fact that people are not able to perform their work as a practice is not just due to the nature of their work, particularly for low-wage workers, but also because of the difficulty in ascertaining what the achievement of excellence internal to the ends of today's work can be. It is because the ends and the goods internal to work are either hard to recognize or nameable only in terms of external, material productivity. The recognition of this difficulty from the perspective of ideological distortion is what a theological conception of work as a praxis should aim toward.

This brief reference to McIntyre's Aristotelian vision of work as a practice is meant to help us better imagine praxis as a norm for the dialectical theology of work. This act of imagination is barely off the ground in this essay. But I think it is what LaCocque's book encourages for the future.

---

22. McIntyre, *After Virtue*, 187

23. In relationship to a fishing community in Denmark, McIntyre talks about the possibility that "work is not a means to an external end but is constitutive of a way of life, the sustaining of which is itself an end" (*Ethics in the Conflicts of Modernity*, 179).

BIBLIOGRAPHY

Adorno, Theodore. *Critical Models: Interventions and Catchwords*. New York: Columbia University Press, 2005.
Bernstein, Richard. *Beyond Objectivism: Science, Hermeneutics, and Praxis*. Philadelphia: University of Pennsylvania Press, 1983.
———. *Praxis and Action, Contemporary Philosophies of Human Activity*. Philadelphia: University of Pennsylvania Press, 1971.
Bonhoeffer, Dietrich. *Ethics*. New York: Simon & Schuster, 1995.
Guendelsberger, Emily. *On the Clock: What Low-Wage Work Did to Me and How It Drives America Insane*. New York: Hachette Book Group, 2019.
Gutierrez, Gustavo. *A Theology of Liberation: History, Politics, and Salvation*. Translated and edited by Sister Caridad Inda and John Eagleson. Maryknoll, NY: Orbis, 1973.
Jünger, Ernst. *The Worker: Dominion and Form*. Evanston: Northwestern University Press, 2017.
LaCocque, André. *Work and Creativity: A Philosophical Study from Creation to Postmodernity*. New York: Lexington, 2020.
Lefebvre, Henri. *Critique of Everyday Life*, vol. 3: *From Modernity to Modernism*. Translated by John Moore. London: Verso, 2008.
Lévinas, Emmanuel. *Totality and Infinity: An Essay on Exteriority*. Translated by Alphonso Lingis. Duquesne studies: Philosophical Series 24. Pittsburgh: Duquesne University Press, 1969.
McIntyre, Alisdair. *After Virtue: A Study in Moral Theory*. Notre Dame: University of Notre Dame Press, 1981.
———. *Ethics in the Conflicts of Modernity: An Essay on Desire, Practical Reasoning, and Narrative*. Cambridge: Cambridge University Press, 2016.
Nietzsche, Friedrich. *Beyond Good and Evil: Prelude to a Philosophy of the Future*. Edited by Rolf-Peter Horstmann and Judith Norman. Translated by Judith Norman. Cambridge Texts in the History of Philosophy. Cambridge: Cambridge University Press, 2002.
Ricoeur, Paul. *History and Truth*. Evanston, IL: Northwestern University Press, 1965.
———. "What Is Dialectical?" In *Freedom & Morality*, edited by John Bricke, 173–89. Humanistic Studies 46. Lawrence: University of Kansas Press, 1976.
Thoreau, Henry David. *Walden*. Princeton: Princeton University Press, 2004.
Weber, Max. *The Protestant Ethic and the Spirit of Capitalism: And Other Writings*. Edited, translated and with an introduction by Peter Baehr and Gordon C. Wells. New York: Penguin, 2002.

9

Creative and Destructive Work
Greek and Slavic Distributaries of Hebrew Biblical Lifeblood

ISAIAH (YESHAYAHU) GRUBER

Judge: Answer! Why didn't you work?

Defendant: I did work. I wrote poems...

Judge: And who recognized that you are a poet? Who reckoned you among the poets?

Defendant: No one. And who reckoned me among the human race?

Judge: And did you study this?...

Defendant: I didn't think that this came from education.

Judge: From what, then?

Defendant: I think it is...from God...

—Excerpt from the first trial of Joseph Brodsky, 18 Feb. 1964[1]

---

1. As transcribed by Frida Vigdorova; my translation (I.G.).

ON A PERSONAL NOTE...

IN NOVEMBER 2017 I traveled from Israel to Chicago for the annual convention of the Association for Slavic, East European, and Eurasian Studies. As I was staying with my Aunt Judy, a longtime friend of the LaCocque family, she took an interest in my paper on concepts of work in monastic traditions and passed it along to André. At that time Prof. LaCocque was nearing the completion of his study on biblical and philosophical notions of work and creativity. Thus began our personal and professional connection. He cited my unpublished paper in his book,[2] and eventually we began to correspond as well.

In 2020–2021 I was privileged to interview André LaCocque twice. These conversations, which sadly proved to be among the very last of his public appearances, are available from the Israel Bible Center under the titles "Biblical Work and the Jewish Jesus" and "Creative Life and Crushing Toil." Sharing from his mind and soul, André expressed his fundamental conviction in this way: "The Torah is a call to fulfill things with love, with compassion, with creativity, with happiness . . . The Torah is allowing the human being to vibrate with the will of God, with the intention—the deep, ultimate intention of the Creator. And this is, I think, *true* happiness—not the distorted one, not the fantasy, but the reality."[3]

Throughout his career, Prof. LaCocque enjoyed the friendship and collaboration of outstanding luminaries of French and Jewish thought, including Martin Buber, Emmanuel Lévinas, Paul Ricoeur, and Zwi Werblowsky, to name but a few. One of these connections is of special interest to me personally. During 1962–1963, André was invited to participate in a weekly study group at the Jerusalem home of André Chouraqui, a remarkable scholar whose unique "Judeo-French" version of *La Bible* has exerted a significant influence on my own thinking about biblical concepts and translation practices. Taken as a whole, Prof. LaCocque's own life and work bear witness to a deep yearning for Truth to break through the stale and harmful molds that so often entrap those who, we are told, bear the stamp of a divine Creator—not least in the historically traumatic realm of Jewish-Christian relations.

2. LaCocque, *Work and Creativity*, 13 n. 37. The present chapter is largely based on my earlier manuscript (Gruber, "Conventions and Transgressions"). It seems most fitting finally to publish that research here, in the present collection devoted to the memory of Prof. LaCocque.

3. LaCocque, "Creative Life."

"TO REJOICE IN HIS TOIL . . ."[4]

What *is* work? Professors sitting in their studies "work"; child laborers sent down into constricting, dangerous mineshafts "work"; musicians and garbage collectors and healthcare workers and weapons manufacturers all "work." Politicians and CEOs work, but often in very different ways from those they govern. Work, then, is not one thing; it is millions or billions of different livelihoods and lifetimes—the organic, vital thorax of human existence that clearly unites and yet, at the same time, oh-so-patently divides us all.

In the interpretation of André LaCocque, "Work is both private and universal; it is both properly mine and also the fruit of encountering the other."[5] Nor is this by any means the only paradox inherent in this most inescapable of daily realities. To reflect on human work(s) means to consider "its Janus-like nature of creativeness and destructiveness; its meaningfulness and absurdity; its distortions and glory."[6] Indeed, how ever can one "rejoice in one's toil," which the ancient Hebrew philosopher Qohelet makes out to be the best of lots in life?

Work, then, is both blessing and curse; it is drudgery and eureka and meaning and despair and banality and robustness and savage necessity all wrapped up together. It is self-expression and self-sacrifice; it is glory and honor and the theft of glory and honor. It elevates one person while debasing another. It kills; it gives life . . . Every day we see work that evidently emanates from Hell, enflamed with malice and oppression, or (more often) from that Kafkaesque nightmare of an infinite loop of endlessly bland and pointless tasks that serve no edifying purpose. And yet, when imbued with truth and meaning and willing sacrifice, genuine human work is—as Joseph Brodsky so bravely asserted when dragged before the Soviet court—a gift of the very Creator, a divine expression of love for humanity.

Perhaps we should attempt not to square this circle, but rather to understand it a little better. A great deal of conventional if unspoken assumptions—indeed, of lifestyles and beliefs and transgressions—rest on adaptations, borrowings, interpretations of Scripture. Certainly this has been true from antiquity until today in both Jewish and Christian contexts, and with regard to labor no less than other matters. It is therefore

---

4. Eccl 5:19 (cf. 3:22).
5. LaCocque, *Work and Creativity*, 82.
6. LaCocque, *Work and Creativity*, 82.

worthwhile to look back from time to time at the historical, linguistic, and cultural underpinnings of our sociological realities. This essay will address one subset of that giant task by investigating a selection of conceptions of work as they developed within the Greek and Slavic realms, with a particular focus on certain Christian monastic traditions.

The notion of creative, serving, and worshipful work functions in the Hebrew Bible as a key "lifeblood" flowing throughout its manifold stories, laws, and prayers. Yet in practice—in history and in religions—this uplifting notion of work has all too easily succumbed to a very different idea and reality: drudgery, toil, onerous labor. How and why did that conceptual shift occur? Is the problem merely down to the undeniably flawed nature of human life? Or does translation, as usual, lie at the core of this dilemma?

FROM THE HEBREW BIBLE TO MUSCOVITE MONASTERIES

The question of the nature of monastic work can be approached in multiple ways. One approach is to read prescriptive texts (community rules, epistles, and the like) to acquire an image of a given monk's or monastery's ideal lifestyle. Thus, for instance, numerous scholars have analyzed the writings of the fifteenth-century Muscovite monastic leaders Nil Sorsky and Iosif Volotsky, often opposing their views of the ideal community and, more recently, discovering significant commonalities between them.[7] A second approach is to look empirically at whatever evidence remains of monasterial activity in practice. In the Muscovite period, monks and nuns were explorers, traders, landowners, bankers, farmers, salt miners, musicians, scribes, recluses, and more—not to mention religious and political functionaries. A number of studies on prominent Muscovite monasteries such as Solovki, Iosifo-Volokolamsk, and Kirillo-Belozersk have provided considerable detail on these activities.[8]

Yet there is also a third approach: examining the underlying concepts that delineated the very possibilities for thinking, speaking, writing, and

---

7. See, e.g., Goldfrank, *Monastic Rule*; Pliguzov, *Polemika v russkoi tserkvi*; Sinitsyna, "Tipy monastyrei"; Goldfrank, *Nil Sorsky*; and the literature they cite.

8. See, e.g., Spock, "Solovki Monastery"; Semiachko, *Knizhnye tsentry*; Naidenova, "Vnutrenniaia zhizn' monastyria"; Dmitrieva, *Bytnye i opisnye knigi*; Dykstra, *Russian Monastic Culture*; Gruber, *Orthodox Russia in Crisis*; Brodskii, *Solovki*; and a wealth of other studies.

acting on the topic of *work* or *labor*. Though perhaps a bit nebulous sounding at first blush, this way of getting at the problem should logically precede, complement, and aid in consideration of the questions raised by the other approaches. Put crudely, how could an Orthodox Christian conception of monastic work integrate both the labor of Simeon Stylites, which reportedly consisted of bowing up and down for literally an entire generation while standing on an elevated platform in an attempt to avoid people, and that of the Solovki elders, who traveled on grand tours of the land as they conducted massive salt-trading and banking businesses? Why did such disparate enterprises seem equally legitimate as forms of the special higher calling of monkish work?

As generally understood, the monastic venture depended for its *raison d'être* on a presumed dichotomy between "the world" and the community of God and, concomitantly, between work directed toward profane purposes and holy service to the Lord. By retreating to or establishing a different sphere of activity, monks and nuns sought to create space for a lifestyle and form of labor they regarded as superior, more wholesome, and more godly. Their ideas stemmed in large part from readings of biblical texts,[9] which named God himself as the first worker (at the beginning of Genesis), spoke of "service" or "work" for God, and provided prototypes of ascetic living (such as John the Baptist). Yet the biblical concepts also underwent significant mutations as they passed from Hebrew into Greek and then Slavic before undergirding the worldview of Muscovite monks and nuns.

Here we will undertake a brief overview of such transformations in the monastic discourse of work.[10] Though one of the most universal of human ideas, the concept of *work* can be conceived in a surprising number of different ways; for instance: as any action; as activity directed toward accomplishing some practical task; or as activity directed toward some broader purpose (to cherry-pick from three of the 47 definitions and sub-definitions of the English word in the *OED*, aside from additional meanings within phrases).[11] Since every language and culture develops unique conceptualizations, trans-linguistic phenomena such as religion automatically spawn multiple variations of themselves as they spread. This occurs even

---

9. See, e.g., Weckman, "Bible Interpretation."

10. A thorough survey of all such linguistic transformations and the relevant monastic literature could easily occupy an entire volume or even series of volumes; here I will attempt only to trace a few of the most salient moments, with a consideration of likely influences on the Muscovite context and realia.

11. *OED*, s.v. "work."

without any conscious human effort, simply by virtue of the fundamental nature of human language. The point could be pressed even further: Ludwig Wittgenstein famously argued that every single language participant has a different impression of each word or concept.[12]

To keep this investigation within some necessary bounds, I will take as my starting point just the two most common Biblical Hebrew (BH) nouns often translated as "work."[13] The first of these is מלאכה (mel'akhah), introduced in Gen 2:2:

> And on the seventh day God ended his *mel'akhah* which he had done; and he rested on the seventh day from all his *mel'akhah* which he had done.

In the rest of the Pentateuch *mel'akhah* appears frequently as the name for the activity similarly forbidden to the "sons of Israel" and all others "within their gates" on the Sabbath and sacred holidays. As a result, the meaning of the word sparked extensive discussion in the Jewish tradition. The rabbis have traditionally regarded it as denoting forms of "creative activity"; i.e., imitation of divine Creation. Other interpretations are also possible, including mystical ones: intriguingly, *mel'akhah* apparently shares a root with מלאך (*mal'akh*), customarily translated as "angel" (or more literally, "messenger").[14] In any case, the Hebrew word seems to have expressed a notion similar to "craftsmanship,"[15] and resting from one's *mel'akhah* on

---

12. Wittgenstein, *Philosophical Investigations*.

13. In a further study it could be helpful to expand the analysis by adding the next most common nouns, e.g.: עמל, פעל-פעלה. Note also that here I consider related verbal forms only in specific cases that help to advance the discussion; their full inclusion would add hundreds more instances while still giving a very similar picture.

14. Perhaps because the *mal'akh* is an agent sent to carry out divine *mel'akhah*?

15. See esp. Exod 31:3, 5; 35:24, 31, 33, 35; 36:1–8, etc. (N.B.: Here and below biblical references are given according to traditional English numeration.) Note that the Jewish Greek Septuaginta (LXX) translations, discussed below, did not always try to have correspondence on the level of words/concepts, but instead sometimes to translate the broader sense (which is also the usual modern translation preference). Evidently they also relied to some extent on different textual traditions than have been preserved in Hebrew to this day (see Tov, *Textual Criticism*). For LXX's limited use of τέχνη and related τεχνίτης, usually for very specialized crafts and not as a general equivalent for מלאכה, see Exod 28:11; 30:25; Deut 27:15; 1 Kgs 7:2; 1 Chr 22:15, 28:21, 29:5; Song 7:2; Jer 24:1; 36:2. Compare the similarly limited and specialized usage in NT at Acts 17:29; 18:3; 19:24, 38; Heb 11:10; Rev 18:22.

the Sabbath explicitly represented an imitation of God's pausing of his own skillful work of Creation.[16]

GREEK VARIATIONS ON A HEBREW THEME

For our purposes, the most important question is how this Hebrew concept transferred into Greek. In approximately the third century BCE the Jewish translators of the Septuagint (LXX) rendered *mel'akhah* as ἔργον (*ergon*) in 133 of the 167 places that this word appeared in what we know as the Hebrew Bible. If one adds closely related words like ἐργασία (*ergasia*), that number rises to 156 out of 167, or 93.4%.[17] The significance of this dominant translation choice lies in the fact that the given Greek concept lacked the complex nuance of the Hebrew and naturally had its own different connotations as well. *Ergon* could be defined generally as "work" in the sense of "anything that is done"; *ergasia*, as "doing something," with usages usually tending toward "business, trade."[18] The translated meaning thus shifted to human "activity" *per se*, especially commerce, instead of "craftsmanship" and "creativity."

The second Hebrew word, עבדה (*'avodah*), appears 145 times in the biblical corpus. Its root meaning is connected to "servitude," in senses including working as a forced laborer for Egyptian pharaohs and serving a particular god or gods by means of one's lifestyle and offerings. The LXX translators utilized more than thirty different Greek equivalents for this single Hebrew word, thereby destroying any possibility of recognizing a

---

16. E.g., Exod 20:10–11. Note, however, that biblical *mel'akhah* cannot be equated with actual "creating," which is a different Hebrew concept (ברא) often said to refer exclusively to God's ability (though that traditional dictum does not seem to be entirely borne out by the evidence).

17. In MT and LXX: Gen 2:2, 3; 33:14; 39:11; Exod 12:16; 20:9, 10; 22:8, 11; 31:3, 5, 14, 15; 35:2, 21, 24, 29, 31, 33, 35; 36:1, 2, 3, 4, 5, 6, 7, 8; 38:24; 39:43; 40:33; Lev 7:24; 11:32; 13:48, 51; 16:29; 23:3, 7, 8, 21, 25, 28, 30, 31, 35, 36; Num 4:3; 28:18, 25, 26; 29:1, 7, 12, 35; Deut 5:13, 14; 16:8; Judg 16:11; 1 Sam 8:16; 15:9; 1 Kgs 5:16; 7:14, 22, 40, 51; 9:23; 11:28; 2 Kgs 12:11, 14, 15; 22:5, 9; 1 Chr 4:23; 6:49; 9:13, 19, 33; 22:15; 23:4, 24; 25:1; 26:29, 30; 27:26; 28:13, 19, 20, 21; 29:1, 5, 6; 2 Chr 4:11; 5:1; 8:9, 16; 13:10; 16:5; 17:13; 24:12, 13; 29:34; 34:10, 12, 13, 17; Ezra 2:69; 3:8, 9; 6:22; 10:13; Neh 2:16; 4:11, 15, 16, 17, 19, 21, 22; 5:16; 6:3, 9, 16; 7:70, 71; 10:33; 11:12, 16, 22; 13:10, 30; Esth 3:9; 9:3; Pss 73:28; 107:23; Prov 18:9; 22:29; 24:27; Jer 17:22, 24; 18:3; 48:10; 50:25; Ezek 15:3, 4, 5; 28:13; Dan 8:27; Jonah 1:8; Hag 1:14. Cf. Hatch and Redpath, *Concordance to the Septuagint*, s.v. ἔργον, ἐργασία, ἐργάσιμος, λειτουργία, etc.; Muraoka, *Hebrew/Aramaic Index*, s.v. מלאכה.

18. See LSJ, s.v. ἔργον.

unitary conception across multiple passages when reading the text in Greek or any future derivative translation (such as Slavic). However, some of these renderings do fall into groups of closely related translations: e.g., words belonging to the *ergon* family, or to the λειτουργία (*leitourgia*) family. The latter group translated a plurality of the occurrences of *'avodah*—about 43%.[19] Aside from the fact that most passages received a significantly different translation, this frequent *leitourgia* equivalence posed problems in and of itself. In the Hellenistic world the term signified "public service," especially pagan rituals paid for by private citizens out of their own pockets.[20] That meaning overlapped only to a small extent with the semantic range of Hebrew *'avodah*, thus stripping the latter of most of its substance.

The second most frequent LXX translation for *'avodah* was none other than the *ergon* family mentioned above, which accounted for about 35% of the total occurrences.[21] In fact, in the LXX corpus the single word *ergon*, with the general meaning of "something done," amalgamated at least 27 distinct Biblical Hebrew concepts, thus effectively effacing the differences among them.[22] In addition, even the most common translation preferences could easily be reversed: e.g., the LXX for 1 Chronicles 26:30 renders *mel'akhah* as *leitourgia* and *'avodah* as *ergasia* (the opposite of the usual pattern). It goes almost without saying, then, that the same Hebrew word could receive multiple Greek translations even within a single short passage, and that one or another of the Hebrew words might go untranslated in cases when they appeared together.[23]

---

19. In MT and LXX: Gen 29:27; 30:26; Exod 1:14; 2:23; 5:9, 11; 6:6, 9; 12:25, 26; 13:5; 27:19; 30:16; 35:21, 24; 36:1, 3, 5; 38:21; 39:32, 40, 42; Lev 23:7, 8, 21, 25, 35, 36; 25:39; Num 3:7, 8, 26, 31, 36; 4:4, 19, 23, 24, 26, 27, 28, 30, 31, 32, 33, 35, 39, 43, 47, 49; 7:5, 7, 8, 9; 8:11, 19, 22, 24, 25, 26; 16:9; 18:4, 6, 7, 21, 23, 31; 28:18, 25, 26; 29:1, 12, 35; Deut 26:6; Josh 22:27; 1 Kgs 12:4; 1 Chr 4:21; 6:32, 48; 9:13, 19, 28; 23:24, 26, 28, 32; 24:3, 19; 25:1, 6; 26:8, 30; 27:26; 28:13, 14, 15, 20, 21; 29:7; 2 Chr 8:14; 10:4; 12:8; 24:12; 29:35; 31:2, 16, 21; 34:13; 35:2, 10, 15, 16; Ezra 8:20; Neh 3:5; 5:18; 10:32, 37; Ps 104:14, 23; Isa 14:3; 28:21; 32:17; Lam 1:3; Ezek 29:18; 44:14. Cf. Hatch and Redpath, *Concordance to the Septuagint*, s.v. δουλεία, ἐργαλεῖον, ἔργον, ἐργασία, κάτεργον, λατρεία, λατρευτός, λειτουργία, λειτουργικός, etc.; Muraoka, *Hebrew/Aramaic Index*, s.v. עבודה.

20. See LSJ, s.v. λειτουργία.

21. See the same verses as in n. 19 above.

22. Hatch and Redpath, *Concordance to the Septuagint*, s.v. ἔργον; Muraoka, *Hebrew/Aramaic Index*, s.v. מלאכה, עבודה, etc.

23. Twenty-eight verses contain both words: Exod 35:21, 24; 36:1, 3, 5; Lev 23:7, 8, 21, 25, 35, 36; Num 28:18, 25, 26; 29:1, 12, 35; 1 Chr 9:13, 19; 23:24; 25:1; 26:30; 27:26; 28:13, 20, 21; 2 Chr 24:12; 34:13.

Even this brief examination of the two main Biblical Hebrew words expressing conceptions of "work" should suffice to demonstrate that the LXX translation shuffled and rearranged the concepts of the original—probably for reasons of "fluidity" and overall sense in the target language—to such an extent that the latter could not be reconstructed. The Greek reader would receive at best a homogenized and distorted impression of the sense of the original concepts. It must be said, of course, that problems of this nature (*inter alia*) beset any translation. However, not every translation comes to form the basis for precise linguistic formulae asserted as divine truth within some religious or political system, as would be the case with the LXX! With this in mind, it becomes evident that any theological conclusions about the biblical depiction of *work*, if based either directly or indirectly on the LXX, would simply have no chance of expressing the original textual intentions and would instead formulate some different meaning.[24]

Ancient Jewish-Greek sources that depended on the LXX often manifested some awareness of this problem. In the first century CE, for example, both Philo of Alexandria and Jacob of Jerusalem (rechristened "James" in English) attempted to explain the Hebraic notion of אמונה (*'emunah*) to an audience handicapped by its LXX-based usage of πίστις (*pistis*), a pair of words customarily but selectively translated into English as "faith."[25] The Hebrew concept implied stability and endurance, whereas the Greek "equivalent" referred primarily to a mental conviction or the cause thereof.[26] Virtually all similar Hebrew-Greek word pairs suffered from similar disjunctions and incongruities. For his part, Philo—though seemingly wise to the gulf between the languages[27]—explained away the differences with an

---

24. This is the case even if one is willing to presume perfectly skilled and intellectually honest interpreters.

25. See Philo, *Quod Omnis Probus Liber Sit*, 7.45, *De plantatione*, 17.70, *De Confusione Linguarum*, 31-32, *Quis rerum divinarum haeres sit*, 21.100-102, 22.108-111, *De profugis*, 27.152, *De mutatione nominum*, 39.220-221, *De Josepho*, 43.258, *Quaestiones et solutiones*, 2.13, 3.58; Jas 1-2.

26. See LSJ, s.v. πίστις.

27. As indeed others before him; compare the well-known prologue to the book of Ben Sirach, apparently written by the author's grandson and translator in the second century BCE: "Wherefore let me intreat you to read it with favour and attention, and to pardon us, wherein we may seem to come short of some words, which we have laboured to interpret; for the same things uttered in Hebrew, and translated into another tongue, have not the same force in them. And not only these things, but the law itself, and the prophets, and the rest of the books, have no small difference, when they are spoken in their own language" (Brenton, *Septuagint Version*, Sir *prol*. [15-26]).

argument that would come to be repeated and elaborated within Christianity for centuries. Philo claimed that the LXX translators had been miraculously directed by "the purest of spirits" to "prophetically" select absolutely perfect equivalents in the target language in every case.[28]

Philo's own works, however, belied any theory of exact conceptual correspondence between the Hebrew original and the Greek translation. Constrained by the Greek vocabulary, in one essay he described *ergon*—"work" in the sense of "doing something"—as forbidden on the Sabbath. Yet recognizing the problematic nature of such a claim vis-à-vis the biblical text, he hastened to qualify this LXX translation by specifying certain specific types of forbidden activity.[29] The collection that would later be called the New Testament (NT) originally emanated from the same first-century Jewish-Greek cultural environment. Its vocabulary also reveals the stark changes in fundamental concepts that resulted from a shift to Greek via the LXX. The NT employs the word *ergon* 176 times, but usually in the plural (*erga*)—a pattern already evident sometimes in LXX. Such usage gave this term the primary meaning of particular *deeds*, often described as good or evil. That narrow prosaic meaning is distant from the Hebrew notion of *mel'akhah* as practicing a creative craft (or something along those lines).

As for *leitourgia*—the LXX's favorite translation of Hebrew *'avodah*—it appears only six times in the whole NT corpus (and related forms are similarly infrequent). Such limited usage probably reflected a recognition of the proper Greek meaning of the word: the few NT occurrences have an almost technical connotation, relating specifically to forms of temple service or other public functions.[30] Evidently this word had been judged incapable of denoting the broader meanings of "service-work" to be rendered to God or to people. The resulting void was filled largely by relying on a concept that had been rare in LXX, and *never* used there for either *mel'akhah* or *'avodah*: Greek κόπος (*kopos*), signifying "striking" or "beating," and by extension "toil, trouble, suffering, fatigue, weariness, hard work."[31] In the language of

---

28. Philo, *De vita Mois.*, 37–40; cf. Ruzer, "Hebrew Bible or Septuagint," 2. Philo's works came to be incorporated into the Christian tradition, on which see (e.g.) Runia, *Philo in Early Christian Literature*; Runia, "Philo of Alexandria."

29. Philo, *De vita Mois.* 2.211, 220; *Special Laws* 2.59, 64, 66; cf. Jassen, *Scripture and Law*, 151.

30. Luke 1:23; 2 Cor 9:12; Phil 2:17, 30; Heb 8:6; 9:21.

31. The related verbal form κοπιάω is similarly common in NT, but also never used in LXX for any forms related to Hebrew *mel'akhah* or *'avodah*. See Hatch and Redpath, *Concordance to the Septuagint*, s.v. κοπιᾶν, κόπος; Muraoka, *Hebrew/Aramaic Index*, s.v.

the NT this concept now became the common term for "labor," including ordinary "work" in agriculture or any other field. For instance, in 1 Cor 3:8:

> Now the planter and the waterer are united; and each one shall receive his own reward according to his own *kopos*.[32]

Such linguistic shifts—no doubt influenced by contemporary realities in the Roman world—naturally filtered and recast the very possibilities of discourse that could pass through to the subsequent Eastern Orthodox Christian tradition. In place of the multiplicity of distinct Biblical Hebrew concepts, the Greek-speaking Christian world inherited the following basic notions of *work*: a) a generic word for "doing something" that made no distinction among different kinds of activity (*ergon*); b) the same word in plural, used for specific good or bad deeds (*erga*); c) a word for public ritual service and no other kind of work (*leitourgia*); and d) a word for "toil" (*kopos*) whose meaning did not properly correspond to any of the main words for *work* in Biblical Hebrew, but was actually closer to other BH concepts.[33]

Some effects may be seen already in the Rule of Pachomius, who is generally credited with establishing Christian communal monasticism in the first half of the fourth century. The Greek version of his foundational monastic document refers several times to the work or labor of monks by means of the *ergasia* family of words. Thus, for instance:

> Now while working (*ergazomenōn*), they shall not speak through the matter, but rather meditate or keep quiet.[34]

Why, in the Pachomian conception, was it better and holier not to talk while working? Influenced by Jerome's Latin version, William Graham translates the precept as follows:

> At work, they shall talk of no worldly matter, but either recite holy things or else keep silent.[35]

עבודה, מלאכה; LSJ, s.v. κοπιάω, κόπος.

32. Cf, e.g., Eph 4:28 (κοπιάτω).

33. Generally speaking, these Greek concepts correspond better to (e.g.) Hebrew מעשה, פעל-פעלה, עמל.

34. "Ἐργαζομένων δέ, μηδεὶς λαλήσῃ διὰ τῆς ὕλης, ἀλλὰ μελετήσωσιν ἢ ἡσυχάσωσιν." Boon, *Pachomiana Latina*, 177.

35. Graham, *Islamic and Comparative Religious Studies*, 278. The Latin version reads: "Operantes nihil loquentur saeculare, sed aut meditabuntur ea quae sancta sunt, aut certe silebunt." Boon, *Pachomiana Latina*, 32.

The intention thus seems to have been to eliminate any "profane" actions and thereby sanctify the monks' work. In Hebrew this idea would have been hard to express: the quintessential act of weekday *mel'akhah* was the divine Creation, with speech as its very core ("And God said: Let there be light"; Gen 1:3). Pachomius, or whoever created the Greek version of the Rule ascribed to him, of course knew that God had spoken his creative works or deeds (*erga* in the LXX of Genesis 2). However, here, as in so many other cases, the Hellenistic linguistic and cultural concepts overrode the original biblical intentionality, which could no longer be discerned or even reconstructed. Speech did not form an essential component of *ergon* or *ergasia*; nor was it in any way evident in Greek that Creation had represented a particular *kind* of work, rather than just "something done" (which latter would have been portrayed by a different concept in BH).

DISSIPATION OF THE ORIGINAL

The Pachomian model eventually came to dominate in medieval Christian monasticism; but it merged to a certain extent with a contrasting approach that had sought to escape normal earthly labor and toil altogether. Ancient Manichean monks, in the words of Peter Brown, "considered that they were fully entitled to the [financial] support of the faithful because, being freed from the shame of physical labor, they were engaged in the 'weightless' labor of prayer on behalf of all persons."[36] This movement modeled its lifestyle on a conception of the idyllic Garden of Eden. Yet once again, such an idea differed markedly from the Biblical Hebrew conceptualization, even on a linguistic level alone. In Genesis 2 God had assigned Adam the *'avodah* ("service-work")[37] of caring for the Garden in a physical way. In dozens of other passages the very same Hebrew concept described public service to God in the Tabernacle; that was, therefore, fundamentally the same type of activity in the BH conception. Moreover, this notion of "serving" God actually extended much further, to a description of one's entire lifestyle: to cease such *'avodah* would mean to cut oneself off from God altogether.[38] However, the Greek Bible had eliminated all these conceptual connections and connotations by selectively translating the latter types of instances by

36. Brown, "Monastic Views of Work," 48. Cf. Brown, *Treasure in Heaven*; Siegal, *Early Christian Monastic Literature*, 161; and literature cited there.

37. Using the verbal form עבד.

38. See, e.g., Josh 24:14–15 (using the verbal form עבד).

leitourgia or related forms, thus completely reshaping the religious discourse of "work."[39]

Interestingly, Byzantine Jews would evidently come to recognize the inherent irrationality of relying for religious purposes on specific translated words when the latter did not align at all with the original concepts. After a long history of familiarity with the LXX and interacting with Christians, in 1547 (already in the Ottoman period) the community printed a new Judeo-Greek translation of the Pentateuch, called the Constantinople Pentateuch (CP). One purpose of this edition was to update the language by incorporating late medieval demotic vocabulary and thus reflecting contemporary Judeo-Greek. Yet—though clearly still strongly influenced by the ancient LXX, as well as other ancient and possibly medieval antecedents[40]—it also followed a different approach, one characterized by Cyril Aslanov as "extreme literalism."[41] Intriguingly, such scrupulous literalness may have stemmed not from naïveté or lack of skill in translation, but rather from an intentional decision to reflect the word choices and intratextual connections built into the original.[42]

---

39. Such as the verbal form λατρεύω (*latreuō*).

40. Other post-LXX ancient Jewish Greek translations existed: the versions of Akylas (Aquila), Theodotion, and Symmachos are known but survive only in fragments. It is very possible that other translations or partial translations were made in the intervening medieval period before the appearance of the CP. Byzantine Jewish communities may have predominantly used the translation of Akylas. See Lange, "Greek Bible Translations."

41. Aslanov, "Judeo-Greek and Ladino Columns," 391. The 1547 CP, printed by Eliezer Soncino, actually encompasses five parallel texts: the Hebrew original, the Judeo-Greek translation, a Ladino (Judeo-Spanish) translation, the Aramaic Targum Onkelos, and the commentary of Rashi. For more, see Krivoruchko, "Constantinople Pentateuch," and the literature cited there.

42. In his edition of the CP Dirk Hesseling remarked about the translator(s): "C'était un homme qui savait très bien le grec. Il a une grande facilité à former des mots qui répondent bien au génie de la langue grecque. S'il viole presqu'à chaque instant les lois de la syntaxe, c'est seulement parce qu'il suit mot à mot, j'allais dire syllabe à syllabe, le texte hébreu, moins soucieux d'être intelligible que d'être exact. C'est au point que les lecteurs non hébraïsants comprendront difficilement le texte sans l'aide d'une traduction moins littérale. Ces hébraïsmes sont tellement nombreux que j'ai dû renoncer à signaler en note: les notes explicatives auraient démesurément grossi le volume." (Hesseling, *Les cinq livres*, vii.) Note that in the twentieth century André LaCocque's friend André Chouraqui adopted a very similar approach to biblical translation, rendering the language in an almost grating form of Judeo-French intended more to reflect the word choices of the original with consistency and some kind of etymological precision than to read fluidly and intelligibly for the target audience (Chouraqui, *La Bible*).

If the LXX had shuffled and reconfigured the Hebrew concepts beyond recognition, then, the CP translators instead strove to preserve the original linkages—even with respect to such mundane matters as "work." Except for rare special cases, they rendered every instance of *mel'akhah* as δουλεία (*douleia*) and every instance of '*avodah* as δούλεψη (*doulepsē*).[43] These two closely related but distinct Greek words had different shades of meaning. The first had signified "slavery" in ancient times but by now carried the simple (if dialectical) meaning of "work" or "job." The second had retained more of the earlier meaning of "servitude," and thus could accurately convey the Hebraic notion of "service-work."[44] Such remarkable consistency in translation could not have come about by accident; it evidences a highly conscious choice informed by the desire not to rupture the integrity of the original concepts.

The CP did not influence Rus', which had already adopted the Greek version of Orthodox Christianity with its concomitant literature several centuries earlier. Translation of this LXX-based corpus into Old Slavic or Church Slavonic further scrambled the different meanings connected to "work," to such an extent that it becomes pointless to speak of any correspondence with the original Hebrew on the level of individual concepts. In Kievan and Muscovite times Rus' monastic communities did seemingly benefit from occasional input from Jews and/or other Hebrew speakers;[45]

43. See in the CP (original: *Sefer kulo maḥamadim*; transcription in Greek script: Hesseling, *Les cinq livres*): Gen 2:2, 3; 29:27; 30:26; 33:14; 39:11; Exod 1:14; 2:23; 5:9, 11; 6:6, 9; 12:16, 25, 26; 13:5; 20:9, 10; 22:8, 11; 27:19; 30:16; 31:3, 5, 14, 15; 35:2, 21, 24, 29, 31, 33, 35; 36:1, 2, 3, 4, 5, 6, 7, 8; 38:21, 24; 39:32, 40, 42, 43; 40:33; Lev 7:24; 11:32; 13:48, 51; 16:29; 23:3, 7, 8, 21, 25, 28, 30, 31, 35, 36; 25:39; Num 3:7, 8, 26, 31, 36; 4:3, 4, 19, 23, 24, 26, 27, 28, 30, 31, 32, 33, 35, 39, 43, 47, 49; 7:5, 7, 8, 9; 8:11, 19, 22, 24, 25, 26; 16:9; 18:4, 6, 7, 21, 23, 31; 28:18, 25, 26; 29:1, 7, 12, 35; Deut 5:13, 14; 16:8; 26:6.

44. See Bassea-Bezantakou and Manolessou. "Historical Dictionary," 30–31; *Epitome of the Kriaras Dictionary*, s.v. δουλεία, δούλευσις (δούλεψις).

45. Jews dwelled in some parts of Kyivan Rus' from the tenth to thirteenth centuries; some medieval Slavonic translations may have been made from Hebrew originals; glossaries of transliterated Hebrew words circulated in European Russia from the thirteenth to eighteenth centuries; and by the seventeenth century a Belorussian monastery owned a Hebrew-Aramaic grammar. See (e.g.) Kulik, "Earliest Evidence"; Pereswetoff-Morath, *Grin without a Cat*, vol. 2; Alekseev, "Perevody s evreiskikh originalov"; Pichkhadze, "K istorii chet'ego teksta"; Thomson, "Slavonic Translation"; Taube, *Logika of the Judaizers*; Kovtun, *Russkaia leksikografiia*; Gruber, "Lexical Daring"; Temchin, "Kirillicheskii rukopisnyi uchebnik"; Pereswetoff-Morath, "Khristianskii antiiudaizm," 429, 448–49 n. 19; Gruber, "Russia." The corpus of medieval Hebrew-Russian glossaries includes a couple of curious translations related to the topic of this paper: михѣа (=Micah) as работенъ (="worklike"); афет (=Japheth) as работание (="service, work"). Neither of

however, this did not alter the fact that their libraries of biblical and patristic works derived almost entirely from Greek antecedents. Slavic translations assimilated much of the structure of the Greek LXX and NT, while also adding their own conceptual overlay and local characteristics.[46]

The Ostroh Bible of 1580–1581, though of course differing in some respects from earlier Slavic versions, provides a convenient point of reference for apprehending the concepts embedded in the East Slavic biblical corpus as a whole. Slavic translators tended to follow their Greek archetypes very closely, so the Greek filter introduced in ancient times inevitably played the dominant role in shaping this new rewriting of Scripture. In the overwhelming majority of cases, passages that in Hebrew had either *mel'akhah* or *'avodah* ended up in Old East Slavic as дѣло (*dělo*) or closely related words, following Greek *ergon*, *erga*, etc.[47] The original BH meanings connected to creative and serving work had thus been definitively reduced to simply "deeds, issues, things"—a most generic notion that additionally amalgamated thousands of occurrences of quite different biblical concepts.[48]

Occasionally the East Slavic translators employed forms of работа (*rabota*), which at the time signified primarily "slavery."[49] However, again due to the Greek mediation, other instances of biblical "service-work" lacked any conceptual link to these passages. After Greek *leitourgia* and related words, the Ostroh text uses слоужба (*slouzhba*), слоуженіе (*slouzheniie*), and related forms for contexts perceived as ritualistic, thus effectively reassigning those passages to the category of "liturgy" rather than "work."[50] And naturally a range of exceptions, as well as the unsurprising use of a single Slavic word to translate multiple Greek words, further complicated

---

these corresponds to Philo or Jerome, two usual sources for such purported etymologies (cf. Grabbe, *Etymology*; Hieronymus, "Liber de nominibus hebraicis").

46. For an extremely thorough overview, see Thomson, "Slavonic Translation."

47. See the verses listed in nn. 17 and 19 above. My analysis is based on the edition of Rafail Torkoniak (*Biblia sirech knigy*).

48. Cf. Sreznevskii, *Materialy*, s.v. дѣло. The simple notion of "something done" (or "doing something" as a verb)—Hebrew עשה—itself occurs in more than 2,800 places in the Hebrew Bible but represents a distinct concept from the words for "work" discussed here.

49. E.g., Gen 30:26; Exod 2:23; 6:6, 9; 12:16. Cf. Sreznevskii, *Materialy*, s.v. работа; *Slovar' russkogo iazyka*, 21:105–6, s.v. работа.

50. E.g., Exod 12:25, 26; 13:5; 23:25.

the picture and again reshuffled the conceptual universe that would be presented to East Slavic readers and hearers of the corpus of Scripture.[51]

The fact that Slavic translators generally attempted to follow their Greek versions quite closely in terms of word choice demonstrates that they did want to preserve the integrity of the original concepts.[52] In the constellation of pros and cons attending any translation choices, these transmitters of the biblical tradition valued conceptual consistency across the corpus. Hence, had they been able to work from a CP rather than the LXX, they actually would have succeeded in offering their readers the possibility of grasping the original conceptual connections inherent in the biblical corpus. However, they were circumscribed by the mediation of a Hellenized restatement that had already dismantled those connections.

Why did Slavic Christian and Byzantine Jewish translators pursue similar translation strategies? In the context of full-fledged religions relying on precise verbal formulae to express claimed divine truth, their choice actually made a lot of sense. As even our brief survey clearly demonstrates, adopting a verbatim approach for dogmatic or credal purposes is pointless if based on texts translated according to different principles. Any translation that is not strictly literalist at the level of word choices cannot help but disassemble and disperse the very concepts of the original, thus resulting in forms of thought that are simply different. Today most translators and readers favor fluidity in the target language over conceptual consistency that matches the original; this is because they have different priorities, compared to medieval theologues, and are therefore prepared to sacrifice different aspects or components of meaning.[53]

One word has been conspicuously absent from the discussion so far—the normal Slavic word for "work" or "labor," троудъ (*troud*).[54] In the five books of the Hebrew Torah, the two most common nouns for "work"

---

51. Specific instances would have to be investigated in their own right. One interesting example is the use of a completely different concept—and an absolutely key one in the biblical/religious context—in Exod 5:11, where Slavic завѣт (*zavět*) curiously translates LXX Greek σύνταξις (*syntaxis*), itself an unusual translation of Hebrew עבדה (*'avodah*).

52. The interest of East Slavic bookmen (however modest) in Hebrew antecedents also suggests some level of desire for the original meanings of biblical terms. See n. 45 above.

53. Note that the LXX was created during a period that can be viewed as prior to the development of either "Judaism" or "Christianity" as *religions* per se (see esp. Boyarin, "Rethinking Jewish Christianity").

54. See Sreznevskii, *Materialy*, s.v. троудъ.

appear no fewer than 149 times.⁵⁵ *In not a single one of these instances did the East Slavic translation use the simple word "troud."* This remarkable fact highlights the extreme modifications introduced largely by the mediation of the LXX, even with regard to one of the most basic of human concepts. The Ostroh Pentateuch did employ *troud* or related forms thirteen times to translate other words, and these cases are quite instructive. Six times Slavonic *troud* stood for Greek μόχθος (*mochthos*), meaning "toil," "hardship," or "distress."⁵⁶ In an additional three instances, *troud* translated the above-mentioned *kopos*—"toil, trouble, suffering, fatigue"—or a related verbal form.⁵⁷ The other four cases rendered similar Greek concepts of "fatigue," "suffering," or "heavy toil."⁵⁸

This brings us back to the ancient Jewish-Greek dependence on *kopos* to express a particular concept of difficult labor. The noun form appears nineteen times in the NT, spread out over eleven different books.⁵⁹ In every single case, without exception, the Ostroh Bible translated *kopos* by means of the Slavonic concept *troud*.⁶⁰ This remarkable correspondence once again underscores the mindset of the East Slavic translators, who wanted to preserve conceptual continuity with their Greek original. Had their exposure been instead to the earlier Hebrew concepts, they almost certainly would have tried to reflect those consistently as well. Yet the combination of LXX mediation and local conceptualizations made it impossible for the key Hebrew notions of work—as craftsmanship and proper service to the one God of Israel—to transfer into their language. In Slavonic the notion of *troud* was connected at root to hardship and difficulty, as seen from the adjectival form троудьныи (*troudnyi*), meaning "difficult." The Slavic conceptualization thus regarded labor as suffering, much like the ancient

---

55. Gen 2:2, 3; 29:27; 30:26; 33:14; 39:11; Exod 1:14; 2:23; 5:9, 11; 6:6, 9; 12:16, 25, 26; 13:5; 20:9, 10; 22:8, 11; 27:19; 30:16; 31:3, 5, 14, 15; 35:2, 21, 24, 29, 31, 33, 35; 36:1, 2, 3, 4, 5, 6, 7, 8; 38:21, 24; 39:32, 40, 42, 43; 40:33; Lev 7:24; 11:32; 13:48, 51; 16:29; 23:3, 7, 8, 21, 25, 28, 30, 31, 35, 36; 25:39; Num 3:7, 8, 26, 31, 36; 4:3, 4, 19, 23, 24, 26, 27, 28, 30, 31, 32, 33, 35, 39, 43, 47, 49; 7:5, 7, 8, 9; 8:11, 19, 22, 24, 25, 26; 16:9; 18:4, 6, 7, 21, 23, 31; 28:18, 25, 26; 29:1, 7, 12, 35; Deut 5:13, 14; 16:8; 26:6.

56. Exod 18:8; Lev 25:43, 46, 53; Num 20:14; Deut 26:7. Cf. LSJ, s.v. μόχθος.

57. Gen 31:42; Deut 1:12; 25:18.

58. Gen 25:29; 29:15 (where LXX has δουλεύω, "to serve as a slave," for Hebrew עָבַד, the verbal form connected to עֲבֹדָה); Exod 18:22.

59. Matt 26:10; Mark 14:6; Luke 11:7; 18:5; John 4:38; 1 Cor 3:8; 15:58; 2 Cor 6:5; 10:15; 11:23, 27; Gal 6:17; 1 Thess 1:3; 2:9; 3:5; 2 Thess 3:8; Heb 6:10; Rev 2:2; 14:13.

60. In one case a related verb form was used (троужаете in Matt 26:10); all other passages have the noun form *troud* in singular or plural.

Manichean view; and simple linguistic realities prevented the alternative biblical notions of work from reaching them via translation.

Thus, East Slavic translations completed a process begun unintentionally by the LXX more than a millennium earlier. The main Hebrew understandings of creative work (*mel'akhah*) and of service-work (*'avodah*)—both of which, if directed toward the right ends, implied connection to God—had dissipated completely and been replaced by unrecognizably different conceptions: *děla*, "deeds," or "doing" things generally; and *slouzhenie*, which could mean "service"—as in servile labor—but often meant just "liturgy." Meanwhile, the main Slavonic word for "work," *troud*, translated completely different passages and thus did not connect at all to the original Biblical Hebrew presentation of human labor.

All this was encoded into the language itself on the very basic level of words, even in literalistic translations. We have not even touched on other potential distortions due to the biases of translators, let alone the influence of theology. Yet the fundamental linguistic reality clearly did have theological and practical implications. Hard labor and suffering became monastic virtues. The reason to work was to suffer and *thereby* draw closer to God. Scripture promised a reward for the suffering of *troud*; the dominant biblical conceptions of labor—which were more positive and joyful—had vanished from the transmitted text.

The vita of the monastic founder Pafnutii of Borovsk (ca. 1500) describes the proper life of a monk as one of strict self-discipline: difficult fasts had to be observed while "always laboring in difficult deeds" (повсегда тружаяся тяжкимъ дѣломъ).[61] The Life of Iosif Volotskii (1546) relates how the monks voluntarily tortured themselves, suffering as much as they were able in order to show their devotion to God. In the same context of enduring as much misery as possible, the text remarks, "In the same way they labored in all services, each as he was able" (такожде и во всѣхъ службахъ тружаяся, елико кто можаше).[62] Such ideas had been inherited from Greek-speaking Byzantium and further entrenched by the nature of the Slavic languages. They did not correspond to (original) biblical ideas of human work or service to God; but they *seemed* to, because of the linguistic peculiarities that had molded sacred translations.

Finally, if suffering was good for me, then it could be good for you, too. The leading monasteries developed into massive feudal landowners

---

61. Kadlubovskii, "Zhitie prepodobnago Pafnutiia," 141.
62. "Zhitie i prebyvanie," 467.

commanding the forced labor of myriads of serfs. Alongside humble hermitages, the large commercial centers like Solovki carried on extensive businesses, engaging "in all deeds both divine and human," to borrow another phrase from Pafnutii's vita (искусенъ во всякомъ дѣле божественемъ же и человѣческомъ).[63] I will leave it to others to address questions of how monks and nuns employed the concepts available to them in rhetoric and in practice. My goal has been simply to point out the extent to which *translation* had already filtered the concepts that were even available to them in the first place. The translators themselves sought to be as conservative and conventional as possible in preserving the meanings of the original. Nonetheless, they transgressed. At least they could rely on a ready excuse: *The language made me do it.*

ON THE MEANING OF WORK AND LIFE

The nature of work—of craftsmanship and labor—is of relevance for human life in all times and places. Biblical texts have provided rich inspiration for reflection and action in this area; yet different versions of those texts—or the many streams branching off from an all-but-lost river—lead us in very different directions. Jewish-Christian understanding can be advanced through mutual investigation of such curious vagaries of the history of translation, conceptual evolution, and resultant thoughts, theologies, and practices. The life and work of Prof. LaCocque remind us that our understandings and convictions regarding all such matters must be challenged and refined if we are to learn how to "serve" (work for) the Creator, be of benefit to our fellow humanity, and live meaningful and worthwhile lives in a fractured world.

Along the way, we must somehow strive to reclaim the Biblical Hebrew notion of creative, serving, sometimes sacrificial work (physical, mental, spiritual) from the destructive and oppressive variant forms of labor that ever and always seek to overwhelm it. Moreover, we should be just as willing to rediscover the conceptual history of all other biblical and religious terms and assumptions, which likely suffer no less from the ravages of history and translation. For Who has reckoned us among the human race after all, and for what purpose?

---

63. Kadlubovskii, "Zhitie prepodobnago Pafnutiia," 141. Cf. Gruber, *Orthodox Russia in Crisis*, 51–74, 143–51.

BIBLIOGRAPHY

Alekseev, Anatolii. "Perevody s evreiskikh originalov v Drevnei Rusi." *Russian Linguistics* 11 (1987) 1–20.
Bassea-Bezantakou, Christina, and Io Manolessou. "The Historical Dictionary of Modern Greek: Dialectological Issues." *Dialectologia* special issue 4 (2013) 25–48.
Boon, Dom Amand, ed. *Pachomiana Latina: Règle et épitres de S. Pachome.* Brussels: Nauwelaerts, 1932.
Boyarin, Daniel. "Rethinking Jewish Christianity: An Argument for Dismantling a Dubious Category (to which is Appended a Correction of my *Border Lines*)." *Jewish Quarterly Review* 99 (2009) 7–36.
Brenton, Lancelot C. L., ed., trans. *The Septuagint Version of the Old Testament, with an English Translation.* London: Bagster, 1851.
Brodskii, Iurii. *Solovki: Labirint preobrazhenii.* Moscow: Novaia gazeta, 2017.
Brown, Peter. "Monastic Views of Work." *Biblical Archaeology Review* 42.1 (2016) 42–49.
———. *Treasure in Heaven: The Holy Poor in Early Christianity.* Charlottesville: University of Virginia Press, 2016.
Chouraqui, André, trans. *La Bible.* Paris: Desclée de Brouwer, 1989.
Dmitrieva, Zoia V. *Bytnye i opisnye knigi Kirillo-Belozerskogo monastyria XVI–XVII vv.* St. Petersburg: Bulanin, 2003.
Epitome of the Kriaras Dictionary. Portal for the Greek Language and Language Education. https://www.greek-language.gr/greekLang/medieval_greek/kriaras/index.html.
Dykstra, Tom E. *Russian Monastic Culture: "Josephism" and the Iosifo-Volokolamsk Monastery, 1479–1607.* Munich: Sagner, 2006.
Goldfrank, David, ed., trans. *The Monastic Rule of Iosif Volotsky.* 2nd ed. Kalamazoo, MI: Cistercian, 2000.
———, ed., trans. *Nil Sorsky: The Authentic Writings.* Kalamazoo, MI: Cistercian, 2008.
Grabbe, Lester. *Etymology in Early Jewish Interpretation: The Hebrew Names in Philo.* Brown Judaic Studies 115. Atlanta: Scholars, 1988.
Graham, William Albert. *Islamic and Comparative Religious Studies: Selected Writings.* Ashgate Contemporary Thinkers on Religion. Farnham, VT: Ashgate, 2010.
Gruber, Isaiah. "Conventions and Transgressions: Concepts of Work in the Monastic Tradition." Paper presented at the Association for Slavic, East European, and Eurasian Studies. Chicago, 12 Nov. 2017.
———. "Lexical Daring: Muscovite Russian Experimentation with Greek Language as a Reflection of Underlying Civilizational Rivalry." In *Slavoi kai Ellēnikos Kosmos*, edited by O. Alexandropoulou and P. Sophoulis, 131–47. Athens: Pelekanos, 2015.
———. *Orthodox Russia in Crisis: Church and Nation in the Time of Troubles.* DeKalb, IL: Northern Illinois University Press, 2012.
———. "Russia." In *Encyclopedia of Hebrew Language and Linguistics*, edited by Geoffrey Khan et al., 3:434–41. Leiden: Brill, 2013.
Hatch, Edwin, and Henry A. Redpath. *A Concordance to the Septuagint and the Other Greek Versions of the Old Testament (Including the Apocryphal Books).* 2nd ed. Grand Rapids: Baker, 1998.
Hesseling, D. C., ed. *Les cinq livres de la loi (le Pentateuque): Traduction en néo-grec publiée en caractères hébraïques a Constantinople en 1547.* Leipzig: Harrasowitz, 1897.
Hieronymus [=Jerome of Stridon]. "Liber de nominibus hebraicis." In *Patrologia latina*, edited by Jacques-Paul Migne, 23:771–858. Paris: Garniere, 1845.

Jassen, Alex P. *Scripture and Law in the Dead Sea Scrolls*. Cambridge: Cambridge University Press, 2014.
Kadlubovskii, A. P., ed. "Zhitie prepodobnago Pafnutiia Borovskago, pisannoe Vassianom Saninym." *Sbornik istoriko-filologicheskogo obshchestva pri Institute kn. Bezborodko v Nezhine* 2.2 (1899) 98–149.
Kovtun, Liudmila. *Russkaia leksikografiia epokhi Srednevekov'ia*. Leningrad: Akademiia nauk, 1963.
Krivoruchko, Julia G. "The Constantinople Pentateuch within the Context of Septuagint Studies." In *XIII Congress of the International Organization for Septuagint and Cognate Studies. Ljubljana, 2007*, edited by Melvin K. H. Peters, 255–76. Septuagint and Cognate Studies 55. Atlanta: Society of Biblical Literature, 2007.
Kulik, Alexander. "The Earliest Evidence of the Jewish Presence in Western Rus." *Harvard Ukrainian Studies* 27 (2004–2005) 13–24.
LaCocque, André. "Creative Life and Crushing Toil." *IBC Roundtables*. 2021. https://israelbiblecenter.com/interviews/perspectives-on-the-bible/life-and-work.
———. *Work and Creativity: A Philosophical Study from Creation to Postmodernity*. Lanham, MD: Fortress Academic, 2020.
Lange, Nicholas de. "The Greek Bible Translations of the Byzantine Jews." In *The Old Testament in Byzantium*, edited by Paul Magdalino and Robert Nelson, 39–54. Washington, DC: Dumbarton Oaks Research Library and Collection, 2010.
Liddell, Henry George, and Robert Scott. *A Greek-English Lexicon*. Revised by Henry Stuart Jones with the assistance of Roderick McKenzie. Oxford: Clarendon, 1940.
Muraoka, Takamitsu. *Hebrew/Aramaic Index to the Septuagint, Keyed to the Hatch-Redpath Concordance*. Grand Rapids: Baker Academic, 1998.
Naidenova, L. P. "Vnutrenniaia zhizn' monastyria i monastyrskii byt (po materialam Solovetskogo monastyria)." In *Monashestvo i monastyri v Rossii, XI–XX veka: Istoricheskie ocherki*, edited by N. V. Sinitsyna et al., 285–301. Moscow: Nauka, 2002.
Oxford English Dictionary. 3rd ed. Oxford: Oxford University Press, 2017. www.oed.com.
Pereswetoff-Morath, Alexander. *A Grin without a Cat*. 2 vols. Lund: Lund University, 2002.
———. "Khristianskii antiiudaizm i iudeisko-pravoslavnye otnosheniia v Vostochnoi Slavii v Srednie veka i rannee Novoe vremia (do 1570 g.)." In *Istoriia evreiskogo naroda v Rossii*, edited by Alexander Kulik, 1:418–52. Jerusalem: Gesharim, 2010.
Pichkhadze, Anna. "K istorii chet'ego teksta slavianskogo Vos'miknizhiia." *Trudy Otdela Drevnerusskoi Literatury* 49 (1996) 10–21.
Pliguzov, Andrei I. *Polemika v russkoi tserkvi pervoi treti XVI stoletiia*. Moscow; Indrik, 2002.
Runia, David T. *Philo in Early Christian Literature: A Survey*. Compendia rerum Iudaicarum ad Novum Testamentum. Section 3: Jewish Traditions in Early Christian Literature 3. Assen: Van Gorcum, 1993.
———. "Philo of Alexandria and the Beginnings of Christian Thought." *Studia Philonica Annual* 7 (1995) 143–60.
Ruzer, Serge. "Hebrew Bible or Septuagint: Later Preferences and the Stance of Nascent Christianity." In *The Bible in Slavic Tradition*, edited by Alexander Kulik et al., 1–20. Studia Judaeoslavica 9. Leiden: Brill, 2016.
Sefer kulo maḥamadim ḥamishah ḥumshe torah . . . bo targum ha-miḳra' be-lashon yevani ve-lashon lo'ez . . . Constantinople [Istanbul]: Soncino, 1547 [1 Tamuz 5307]. Online version: https://www.hebrewbooks.org/11658.

Semiachko, S. A., ed. *Knizhnye tsentry Drevnei Rusi: Severnorusskie monastyri*. St. Petersburg: Bulanin, 2001.
Siegal, Michal Bar-Asher. *Early Christian Monastic Literature and the Babylonian Talmud*. Cambridge: Cambridge University Press, 2016.
Sinitsyna, Nina V. "Tipy monastyrei i russkii asketicheskii ideal (XV–XVI vv.)." In *Monashestvo i monastyri v Rossii, XI–XX veka: Istoricheskie ocherki*, edited by N. V. Sinitsyna et al., 116–49. Moscow: Nauka, 2002.
Slovar' russkogo iazyka XI–XVII vv. 30+1 vols. to date. Moscow: Nauka, 1975–.
Spock, Jennifer. "The Solovki Monastery, 1460–1645: Piety and Patronage in the Early Modern Russian North." 2 vols. PhD diss., Yale University, 1999.
Sreznevskii, I. I. *Materialy dlia slovaria drevne-russkago iazyka po pis'mennym pamiatnikam*. 3 vols. St. Petersburg: Imp. akademiia nauk, 1893–1912.
Taube, Moshe, ed., trans. *The Logika of the Judaizers: A Fifteenth-Century Ruthenian Translation from Hebrew*. Jerusalem: Israel Academy of Sciences and Humanities, 2016.
Temchin, Sergei. "Kirillicheskii rukopisnyi uchebnik drevneevreiskogo iazyka (XVI v.) i vilenskii vetkhozavetnyi svod." *Knygotyra* 57 (2011) 86–99.
Thomson, Francis. "The Slavonic Translation of the Old Testament." In *Interpretation of the Bible*, edited by Jože Krašovec, 605–920. Ljubljana: Slovenska akademija znanosti in umetnosti, 1998.
Torkoniak, Rafail, ed. *Biblia sirech knigy vetkhago i novago zaveta, po iazyku slovensku [1581]*. 77 vols. Lviv: Ukrains'ke bibliine tovarystvo, 2003–2005.
Tov, Emanuel. *Textual Criticism of the Hebrew Bible*. 4th ed. Minneapolis: Fortress, 2022.
Weckman, George. "Bible Interpretation." In *Encyclopedia of Monasticism*, edited by William M. Johnston, 1:151–53. 2 vols. Chicago: Fitzroy Dearborn, 2000.
Wittgenstein, Ludwig. *Philosophical Investigations*. Translated by G. E. M. Anscombe. Oxford: Blackwell, 1953.
"Zhitie i prebyvanie v"krattse prepodobnago ottsa nashego Igumena Iosifa, grada Voloka Lamskago." In *Velikie minei chetii, sobrannyia vserossiiskim mitropolitom Makariem*. Vol. 1: *Sentiabr', dni 1–13*. St. Petersburg: Imp. Akademiia nauk, 1868.

10

Wedded to Power
Two Biblical Women Married to Kings

DOREEN M. McFARLANE

ANDRÉ LaCOCQUE, SCHOLAR PAR *excellence*, in whose honor this Festschrift is dedicated, is remembered for his superb work in forwarding Jewish–Christian relations and founding the Department of Jewish/Christian Studies at the Chicago Theological Seminary. He also became well known for his work in interdisciplinary studies: from his book with Paul Ricoeur, *Thinking Biblically* to his final book, *Work and Creativity: A Philosophical Study from Creation to Postmodernity*. Although highly accomplished in these areas, LaCocque is also especially respected (and beloved) for his scholarship on biblical women. A number of his books address the character and behavior of women in Hebrew scripture. When many feminist biblical scholars were (rightly) addressing issues related to the oppression of women in biblical times and narratives, LaCocque chose to write about them from a unique perspective. He fully acknowledges women's secondary position in many of the stories, and points out, of course that many of these were likely written by men. At the same time, he recognizes that, in spite of their secondary positions, many biblical women rise to the occasion when needed, using what powers they do possess to move the narratives forward and to push for and reach their goals for good. In his 1998 *Romance She Wrote: A Hermeneutical Essay on Song of Songs*, LaCocque goes so far as to say, as the title of his book implies, that the author is a woman.[1] In his 2004 *Ruth: A Continental Commentary*, LaCocque again claims "the author is probably a woman."[2] In *Esther Regina*,[3] he points out that the Hebrew Bible contains many stories in which women get what they want by means of taking advantage of their sexual attraction, their wit, or even their cooking! But, this is by no means a putdown. He, importantly, says "It is worth our while to reflect on the intrinsic subversiveness of women's interventions in the story; a feature so constant in the Bible as to become a principle; one need only think of Sarah, Rachel, Rebecca, Tamar, Deborah, Jael, Ruth, Noadiah, Esther, and so many others ... Such feminine unconventionality is a highly powerful counterbalance to the patriarchalism prevalent in some biblical literary genres."[4]

Power has many faces. Power can often be engaged to gain increase in land, money, and influence. Many Hebrew Bible stories show how power can be used to bring about good or, at least, change, or to bring increase to the wielder of that power, harm to the victims, or both. In this study, I will consider the actions of two women in particular: Bathsheba (in 2 Samuel and 1 Kings) who marries King David and becomes the mother of Solomon, and Esther (in the book of Esther) who marries King Ahaseurus, and saves her people, the Jews, from annihilation. At the outset of the narratives, both women are virtually powerless. Although initially relatively without agency, each woman uses whatever resources are available to her to gain power. Then, employing that power, they successfully influence the kings they have married and, thereby, move the narratives toward positive outcomes. These outcomes are for the good of the people and not specifically for these women themselves, although they do gain more influential positions for themselves in the process.

To begin, it may be noted what these two women had in common. Both Esther and Bathsheba, in time, found themselves (or, to some degree, placed themselves) in positions in which they held some sway in the decision-making of their spouse, the king. Both were said to be beautiful (Bathsheba at 2 Sam 11:2, Esther at Esth 2:7). And both seem to get what they wanted, at least in part because of their physical appeal or attractiveness. It may seem obvious, at first reading, that both employed their sexuality to

1. LaCocque, *Romance She Wrote*, xii.
2. LaCocque, *Ruth*, 13.
3. LaCocque, *Esther Regina*, 124.
4. LaCocque, *Esther Regina*, 124.

turn things in the direction they desired, but this will be considered further on in the essay.

These two women appear also to be very different. When Esther's story begins, she is known as Hadassah. She is Jewish, unmarried, and the ward of her kinsman, Mordecai (Esth 2:7). In two different passages, we are told about the relationship between Hadassah who is Esther and Mordecai of whom she is a ward. Esther 2:7 says "Mordecai had brought up Hadassah, that is, Esther, his cousin, for she had neither father nor mother; the girl was fair and beautiful, and when her father and mother died, Mordecai adopted her as his own daughter." Soon after, in the same chapter (2:15), it says "When the turn came for Esther, daughter of Abihail the uncle of Mordecai, who had adopted her as his own daughter, to go in to the king, she asked for nothing . . ." So, Mordecai's father or mother was a sibling to Esther's deceased father. Bathsheba, as the narrative begins, on the other hand, was a married woman. She was the wife of Uriah the Hittite who fought in David's forces (2 Sam 11:3). Bathsheba was also the daughter of Eliam, one of David's faithful fighters (2 Sam 11:3 and 23:34). This would seem to indicate that Bathsheba was Jewish, because both her husband and her father were fighters for David, but this may or may not be the case. We are told that her father is Eliam (2 Sam 11:3) and (2 Sam 23) that her grandfather is Ahithopel, a Gilonite. All three names are Hebrew, Bathsheba meaning "daughter of an oath." In addition, Bathsheba's bathing appears to have taken place to follow Jewish purification laws, which suggests that she was a practicing Jew, living according to the laws of Moses (2 Sam 11:4).

In the case of Bathsheba, the story of how she comes to be David's wife is not forthcoming regarding any personal involvement on her part. We only learn that, while David was walking around on the roof of the king's house, "he saw from the roof a woman bathing" (2 Sam 11:2). The rest is left to the reader's imagination. Was she naked? The text does not even say that Bathsheba was on the roof; only that David was, and that he saw her bathing from there (2 Sam 11:2). Scholars have recently suggested that Bathsheba could have been completely innocent or that she may have known the king walked on the roof of his own house around that time of day and, from there, he might have been able to see her bathing. Was she at least partly responsible for David's having seen her there? George G. Nicol and others place the burden of seduction on Bathsheba. Nicol argues that "bathing in such close proximity to the royal palace was deliberately provocative."[5] One reason we do not know is, of course, that this text is written from a male perspective. The action is taken by David and he is the king so can have her if he wants her. The story is always about David. Bathsheba is an adjunct though necessary element of the story. The narrative is about David's power, David's sin in taking what is not his (the wife of another man), and about David's fathering Solomon who would later become a great king. It is also related to the continuing story of David in the Second book of Samuel, as David ages and his power wanes.

At the outset of the narrative with relation to Bathsheba, David sends an inquiry about this woman and is told first that she is the daughter of Eliam (so we might assume this information is of primary importance or it would not be in the text) and then, secondly, that she is the wife of Uriah the Hittite (2 Sam 11:3) who is one of his soldiers. This information does not in any way seem to affect David's response. The text says directly "So David sent messengers to get her, and she came to him, and he lay with her" (2 Sam 11:4.) We can assume that the woman had no choice in this activity. Much later, when Bathsheba does possess some power as David's wife and the mother of Solomon, she will be the one to wield that power, but at this early point of the story, she appears to be a pawn. Her position at the outset is tantamount to that of a slave. The king held supreme power. Bathsheba, at this point, possessed no control.

Bathsheba becomes pregnant. Now, we might assume she has the choice to say nothing and let everyone assume her husband Uriah is the father (at least if he would return home and sleep with her before going to war). We may presume that everyone would assume the child was sired by Uriah. But, instead, we are told "The woman sent and told David 'I am pregnant'" (2 Sam 11:5). It is of note that her name is not spoken here by the writer. She is simply (and very intentionally) described as "the woman." Even though it may come to mind that Bathsheba may not have been an innocent victim of rape, once she knew she was pregnant, Bathsheba seems to have become aware of power she now held as the mother of David's child!

It is not uncommon in biblical narratives for trickery to be employed in order to move the narrative in what are seen as good directions. For example, Jacob and his mother, Rebecca, fool her husband Isaac into giving the blessing to Jacob instead of his older twin, Esau (Gen 27). Naomi trains Ruth in how to put herself in a position to make Boaz presume he has taken advantage of her, sexually, so that he will marry her (Ruth 3). Tamar tricks

---

5. Nicol, "The Alleged Rape of Bathsheba"; and Bailey, *David in Love and War*, 88.

her father-in-law, Judah, into thinking she is a prostitute so that he will make her pregnant (Gen 38) in order to produce progeny for this particular family because her husband has died and his brother has refused to impregnate her as was his responsibility. In the biblical texts, there is no shortage of the kind of subterfuge that today's cultures might look upon askance. Yet, in them, circumstances make it such that good comes out of deception.

In the case of Esther, it is made clear that Esther's kinsman, Mordecai has taken note of the opportunity for her to become the wife of the king, and he instructs her in how to go about being chosen by the king and, thereby, acquiring the position as queen in which she will soon hold power. Here, again, as a female, she appears to be virtually powerless at the outset. It is Mordecai who decides what she is to do. And she obeys him. Throughout the text here, Hadassah/Esther is moved into and out of harem groups and through a variety of cosmetic regimens to prepare her to look her best when her turn comes to be presented to the king. He will choose the most appealing young woman to be his wife. Here, she is spoken of not by name, but as "the girl" (2:7 and 9). Her behavior in accepting the various beauty treatments in preparation for attracting the king does not represent any aggressive or intentional acts on her own behalf; as they reflect only her total obedience to the directions of Mordecai, and then of the eunuchs and harem leaders.

Another issue of female/male relationships in the Bible is the question of which one of the couple holds the real power at various times. It is obvious that, during the entire timeline in which any of these stories is written, men certainly held all the obvious and official power. Women, whether queens or slaves, remained without agency. Women's very existence depended on their spouse. If the spouse was deceased, then they were dependent on fathers or brothers. Women's value was seen mainly in the producing of progeny. Consequently, a so-called "barren" woman was shunned and seen as worthless. For this reason, women who did have sons often worked toward building up the power of that male child over the children of other wives or concubines (e.g., Gen 21).

Still, in each of these two narratives, it is the courageous moves on the part of the woman that make things happen. In the case of Esther, once she has been accepted as wife of King Ahaseurus, she shifts into action. Even though it has been made clear to her that she still has no right whatsoever to present herself before the king and is supposed to wait for him to call her into his presence, at the danger of her life, it is said that she "put on her royal robes and stood in the inner court . . . opposite the king's hall" (5:1). The king allows her to approach and asks what she wants. Instead of asking for anything, she wisely offers to give something: a banquet for the king and her kinsman Mordecai's archenemy, Haman (5:8). This banquet is followed by a second banquet, also hosted by Esther. At the second banquet, she requests her life and the life of her people, endangered by the wicked Haman. As a result of Esther's cunning and courage, Haman is hanged, and the Jewish people are saved. Esther has used, in this narrative, the only powers to which she had access: her attractiveness to the king and, apparently, also her skill in throwing a great party. Yes, we can attribute her success to feminine wiles. Still, there was too much at stake to consider not using the attributes she did possess. This is a story of profound female courage and expeditiousness.

Bathsheba, although powerless as the narrative begins, makes at least two profound decisions and related moves. At the beginning of her story, whether or not she has had any choice in becoming pregnant, she does courageously choose to tell David "I am pregnant" (2 Sam 11:5). Surely, she had the choice of waiting it out, hoping her husband Uriah would come home and lay with her, and assume he was the father. In telling David she was pregnant, Bathsheba opened up the choice for him to take her in as a concubine, marry her, or possibly even have her killed. He chose to marry her. Then, toward the end of her story, in 1 Kings, Bathsheba has the courage to remind David that it is the son they had together, Solomon, whom he had promised her would become the next king. David stands by his promises. Solomon becomes king while David is still alive. It is said of Bathsheba that he "rose to meet her and bowed down to her, and then he sat on his throne and had a throne brought *for the king's mother* and she sat on his right" (1 Kgs 2:19). Note that, here, she is described not by name but this time as "the king's mother." In all of this, the writer is making it clear that Bathsheba has gained and now holds great respect and considerable power. We were given few details of the years between her being brought to David at that first sexual encounter and the late encounter with David, except that David did make her his wife (2 Sam 11:27), they lost the child that resulted from their first sexual encounter (2 Sam 12:18), and she became the mother of David's son, Solomon (2 Sam 12:24).

As both the narratives of Esther and Bathsheba move toward a close, each of these women has acquired a substantial amount of power and each employs that power for good. In the case of Esther, it is said that "The king held out the golden scepter to Esther and Esther rose and stood before the king" (8:4). As mentioned above, she accomplished no less than the saving of her people, the Jews, from complete annihilation! And, Esther's kinsman, Mordecai also rises to the top and becomes next in rank to King Ahasuerus himself.

Both women, Esther and Bathsheba, now queens, have come a long way. In addition to gaining great power, each appears also to have accomplished her mission. Bathsheba has her son Solomon firmly established as King of Israel. And Esther has saved her people, along with getting her kinsman Mordecai placed into the position of most powerful person next to King Ahasuerus.

LaCocque was right when he wrote, as mentioned earlier, "It is worth our while to reflect on the intrinsic subversiveness of women's interventions in the story; a feature so constant in the Bible as to become a principle; one need only think of Sarah, Rachel, Rebecca, Tamar, Deborah, Jael, Ruth, Noadiah (Ezra 8:33), Esther, and so many others . . . Such feminine unconventionality is a powerful counterbalance to the patriarchalism prevalent in some biblical literary genres."[6] Feminist scholar Tikva Frymer-Kensky agreed. Importantly, she points out that "there is no "woman-speech" in the Bible; the form of women's argumentation, the nature of their logic and rhetoric are the same as men's."[7] She notes correctly that women without power to achieve their goals on their own, proceeded to work directly or indirectly, by means of men with power, convincing and influencing them to do their bidding.[8] She continues, "There is nothing distinctively "female" about the way women are portrayed in the Bible, nothing particularly feminine about either their goals or their strategies." They are the same goals as those 'held by the biblical male characters."[9] She points out that "female solidarity and rage are completely absent from the biblical record. Women pursue their goals as actively as men, and use the same techniques and strategies that men in their situation could be expected to use . . . Most conspicuously, beauty is never portrayed as a woman's weapon. The beauty of women is a mark of divine favor, as is the beauty of men . . . There are no stories of sexual enticement, no femmes fatales . . . There is no women's toolkit. There are only the strategies . . . used along the various axes of power."[10]

6. LaCocque, *Esther Regina*, 124.
7. Frymer-Kensky, *In the Wake of the Goddess*, 146.
8. Frymer-Kensky, *In the Wake of the Goddess*, 146–48.
9. Frymer-Kensy, *In the Wake of the Goddess*, 140.
10. Frymer-Kensky, *In the Wake of the Goddess*, 140–41.

It is commonly proclaimed that, in Biblical times, women were voiceless and powerless, and completely under the power of men in their lives. This appears to be the case in certain aspects of life. Women were generally relegated to the duties of home; cooking, cleaning, and mothering. Their financial and physical security was the general responsibility of the men in their lives: a husband and, if there was no husband, then the father or brother. Still, surprisingly perhaps, we can see that, in story after story of the biblical narrative, women find ways to break through this barrier and, time after time, accomplish the goals they set out to gain, for the good of others, for the sake of the family, and sometimes even, as in the case of Esther, to save the entire Jewish people from complete annihilation! In Bathsheba's story, this happens as well. She makes it possible that Solomon becomes king. Solomon later builds the first Temple in Jerusalem! In both the cases of Esther and of Bathsheba, their missions were accomplished by way of the powers held by the men, but in both cases, made possible through the courage, work, and wisdom of the women!

It is vital for the future of feminist studies that, while keeping in mind that many restrictions did exist for women in biblical times, the above points made by Frymer-Kensky and LaCocque need to be considered seriously and, at times, moved to the forefront of biblical scholarship. It is especially important that we take seriously LaCocque's profound words that "the consistently subversive nature of their (women's) interventions reveal a different and profound conception of femininity; a core concept that must deeply qualify the often-denounced patriarchy of ancient Israel."[11] LaCocque explains in his book *The Feminine Unconventional* that such women as Esther "confront the enemy face to face . . . tap all the resources of their femininity . . . the feminine stereotype is left behind, but these women are not transformed into men. They show the way to men without themselves losing their congenital graciousness."[12]

BIBLIOGRAPHY

Bailey, Randall C. *David in Love and War*. JSOTSup 75, Sheffield, 1990, 88.

Frymer-Kensky, Tikva, *In the Wake of the Goddess: Women, Culture, and the Biblical Transformation of Pagan Myth*, New York: Fawcett Columbine, 1992.

LaCocque, André, *Esther Regina: A Bakhtinian Reading*. Rethinking Theory. Evanston, IL: Northwestern University Press, 2008.

11. LaCocque, *Esther Regina*.
12. LaCocque, *The Feminine Unconventional*.

———. *Feminine Unconventional: Four Subversive Figures in Israel's Tradition*. Overtures to Biblical Theology. 1990. Reprint, Eugene, OR: Wipf & Stock, 2005.

———. *Romance, She Wrote: A Hermeneutical Essay on Song of Songs*. Harrisburg, PA: Trinity, 1998.

———. *Ruth: A Continental Commentary*. Translated by K. C. Hanson. Continental Commentaries. Minneapolis: Fortress, 2004.

———. *Work and Creativity: A Philosophical Study from Creation to Postmodernity*. Lanham, MD: Lexington, 2020.

LaCocque, André, and Paul Ricoeur. *Thinking Biblically: Exegetical and Hermeneutical Studies*. Translated by David Pellauer, Chicago: University of Chicago Press, 1998.

Nicol, George G. "The Alleged Rape of Bathsheba: Some Observations on Ambiguity in Biblical Narrative." *JSOT* 22 (1997) 43–54.

11

Nonrefoulement

Responding to Asylum-seekers through the Prism of Subversive Stories: A Study of Three Trials of Innocence

CRAIG B. MOUSIN

ANDRÉ LACOCQUE INFORMS US that life is a trial of innocence—a constant struggle to choose to either do well or not do well in the face of evil.[1] The Prime Testament teaches that the trial is both an individual one and one each society or culture must face. LaCocque examined subversive stories that, despite their contrarian messages, nonetheless, were accepted into the canon. This chapter explores how LaCocque's exegesis of biblical subversive stories such as Esther, Ruth, and Job provide insight into those engaged in contemporary trials of innocence—asylum-seekers fearing religious persecution. It examines three related, but distinct trials—past, present, and future—in light of LaCocque's description of the human response to evil in the world.

Part I recalls the legal response to the first trial in which many, if not all, of the nation-states failed by not responding to Nazi Germany and its deliberate attempt to extinguish a people. Subsequently, the Refugee Convention of 1951 (Convention) offered one response to their failure to recognize and protect those refugees. It provided a pathway of asylum and nonrefoulement (nonreturn) for those forced to flee from persecution in

---

1. LaCocque, *Onslaught*, 1, 14; LaCocque, *Trial*, 16, 30.

their native lands.² Those fearing death, or a loss of freedom could be assured of nonrefoulement to homelands that sought their death or detention. The Convention provided evidence that the nation-states intended to do well and not return *bona fide* refugees to persecution. Since its inception, millions of individuals have obtained refugee status, but some governments have since banned many asylum-seekers while other refugees wait outside borders hopeful that formal procedures may commence.

Part II addresses some of the obstacles within the asylum adjudication process. Determining the asylum-seekers' eligibility constitutes this second Trial of Innocence, specifically for this chapter, resolving whether those seeking haven have been persecuted or have a well-founded fear of persecution on account of religion. Asylum-seekers, those forced to leave their nations because their beliefs and actions were deemed incompatible with the dominant culture, will always tell subversive stories. This section examines the legal requirements under refugee law within the prism of the trials of many of the subversives highlighted in the scholarship of LaCocque. Biblical exegesis provides evidence that subversive stories exist within a dominant narrative and pose an alternative vision of a covenantal response to God.

The challenges that the biblical protagonists faced and their responses guide those whose faithful lives challenged contemporary governments that do not welcome diversity of beliefs but rather suppress them.

Finally, Part III addresses a contemporary Trial of Innocence that nation-states now confront. Authoritarian and totalitarian governments, polarization, theocracies, and nations without stable governments condone violence, often based on religious beliefs, that force many to flee. The Convention, itself, and the promise made by its signers face a Trial to determine whether its principles still serve a world that has changed dramatically since 1951. As nations retreat from refugee protection, this section offers a

---

2. United States law offers several potential legal routes to become an admitted refugee including resettlement of refugees based on an overseas process (8 U.S.C. §207), asylum (8 U.S.C.§208), and/or restriction on removal (based on the principle of nonrefoulement) (8 U.S.C. § 241(b)(3). This chapter focuses on asylum and restriction on removal based on claims of persecution on account of religion. Case law has established certain distinctions between asylum and restriction regarding the necessary burden of proof for eligibility, but this chapter focuses on the principle of nonrefoulement that undergirds both asylum and restriction on removal. For a primer on asylum law *see*, TRAC Immigration, "Asylum Law," and non-refoulement, *see*, UNHCR, "Non-refoulement." For more specifics on the alternative ways and additional difficulties those seeking relief face, *see* Mousin, "Standing," 545–48.

thought experiment, envisioning LaCocque's scholarship as the representative of the vulnerable in this Third Trial of Innocence, offering counter-testimony to the powers and principalities, that under the name of Christian nationalism, employ Scripture to deny, detain, and deport the innocent. LaCocque's work adduces evidence of a counter-testimony in support of providing a haven for those who witness the power of love to overcome persecution that ignores or denies their voices. His writings serve to defend the vision of the Convention that nation-states protect asylum-seekers in response to xenophobic and nationalistic forces that abandon the promise of nonrefoulement.[3] The world community awaits the verdict in this third Trial of Innocence as the powers and principalities construct walls.

PART I. THE FIRST TRIAL OF INNOCENCE: WORLD WAR II AND THE HOLOCAUST

The Trial of Innocence the world faced in the mid-twentieth century revealed the failure of many nations to do well. Promises of protection had been violated in unimaginable ways. Although those who crafted the concept of the nation-state proposed that sovereign nations would protect their citizens, Germany failed to protect Jews within its borders eviscerating a key principle of that promise of peace. Moreover, as the Nazis advanced over Europe, the Allies failed to protect the victims in each of the conquered nations. This failure revealed an unexpected weakness of the nation-state's ability to ensure tranquility and justice.

Historically, persons within a state possessed the right to leave a nation, but given the sovereign's prerogative, no state was required to accept and protect any specific person appearing at one's borders. Both World Wars demonstrated that, once the number of refugees seeking protection overwhelmed the legal procedures, nation-states abdicated their responsibility. Hannah Arendt wrote: "the moment human beings lacked their own government and had to fall back upon their minimum rights, no authority was left to protect them, and no institution was willing to guarantee

---

3. Although United States courts have spelled the word nonrefoulement, the introduction summary of the Convention spells it as non-refoulement. French scholar Pascale Anne Brault explained that classical French would traditionally employ the hyphen, but it has been deleted in contemporary usage. She suggests ironically that the hyphen may send the wrong message. Instead of the promise of protection, a refugee reading the word more likely sees: No (you cannot enter)—refoulement (you will be returned)! (email correspondence with the author).

them."[4] Once named outlaws—whether a Jewish German national or a person fleeing from another state, few states intervened or offered haven. Although particularly devastating at that time, the government's designation of humans as the Other had biblical precedent. The Book of Esther recounted that the king's command turned "the Jews [into] outlaws[and] excludes them from the empire and, certainly, from royal protection. They become nonentities, nonexistent. Even before they are physically exterminated, they are without rights of any kind. They may be abused and plundered with impunity."[5]

Germany was not alone, however, as the response of the Allies also failed, betraying their law's promise of protection. Although United States law permitted almost 190,000 European Jews to immigrate, discriminatory practices limited entrance to only about 21,000.[6] This represented a failure of will as well as a failure of law. In wartime, fears of German saboteurs disguised as refugees certainly clouded governmental judgments.[7] Anti-Semitism combined with bureaucratic procrastination, however, demonstrated the promises' hollowness. United States religious voices remained remarkably silent in the face of the slaughter. According to David Wyman, "none of the great American Protestant denominations took a stand during these critical months—or later in the war, for that matter. The American Roman Catholic church also was virtually silent."[8] Therefore, the world needed to guarantee human dignity for all humans, not just those a nation-state chose to protect.

In response, many of the nations adopted the Convention setting forth protections against persecution on account of five enumerated grounds: race, religion, political opinion, nationality, or membership in a particular social group. The nations acknowledged that each sovereign nation could retain its own immigration laws establishing eligibility for admission as immigrants and who might be deported or excluded, but should a person seek asylum, the nations promised nonrefoulement. They would not return persons to their native land unless it was determined that the applicant's life or freedom would not be threatened. In 1980, the United States enacted the Refugee Act (Act) thus finally acknowledging its duty to not return

---

4. Arendt, *Totalitarianism*, 293.
5. LaCocque, *Feminine Unconventional*, 54.
6. Wyman, *Abandonment*, 136.
7. Gross, "Spies," 5.
8. Wyman, *Abandonment*, 101.

refugees, stating that "any alien who is physically present in the United States or who arrives in the United States . . . irrespective of such alien's status, may apply for asylum . . ."[9] The U.N. emphasized the broad meaning of irrespective in the Convention which stipulated "that, subject to specific exceptions, refugees should not be penalized for their illegal entry or stay. This recognizes that the seeking of asylum can require refugees to breach immigration rules."[10] The Convention's principal promise made to the world and to ourselves defines our duty of nonrefoulement—we will not return bona fide refugees to places of persecution and we will promise them a procedure to determine eligibility.[11] This recognition of universal human dignity underscored Emanuel Lévinas's assertion of God's call "Thou Shall Not Kill Me," but added this new command: thou shall not return refugees to a land of persecution where they may be killed.[12] LaCocque concurred as "anyone on earth is a potential victim, in need of being protected."[13] The Convention's adoption suggested a promising beginning, corroborated by LaCocque's assertion that, "the only thing that is undeniably new, after Dachau, is that nothing is the same as before" with the hope that the world would do well in the face of evil and thereafter protect the refugee.[14]

PART II. THE SECOND TRIAL OF INNOCENCE: THE ASYLUM ADJUDICATION

History rendered a guilty verdict to the first Trial, but the Convention promises of change inaugurated this second Trial of Innocence. Significantly, the Convention did not focus on a blanket recognition of groups based on nationality, ethnic, or religious identity, but emphasized the necessity of individuals proving their eligibility for asylum and nonrefoulement. The Convention's focus on individual harm confirmed Leni Yahil's lesson of the Holocaust: "We may, therefore, conclude that at a time of great moral crisis

---

9. 8 U.S.C. § 1158(a)(1).

10. Introduction to the 1951 Refugee Convention, 3.

11. Article 33 of the Convention, 30: "1. No Contracting State shall expel or return ("refouler") a refugee in any manner whatsoever to the frontiers of territories where his life or freedom would be threatened on account of his race, religion, nationality, membership of a particular social group or political opinion."

12. LaCocque, *Work*, 39.

13. LaCocque, *Work*, 39.

14. LaCocque, "Auschwitz," 6.

arising from political turmoil, the initiative of individuals who dare to follow the dictates of their conscience is of great significance."[15] Subsequently, Congress designed the Act to protect that voice and initiative. In seeking asylum, the applicant enters an individual Trial of Innocence to determine eligibility. This trial, especially one seeking asylum based on persecution or threats of persecution, is fraught with difficulties, confusion, and a broken legal system.

For purposes of comparison to the biblical narrative, this chapter focuses on persecution or well-founded fear of persecution on account of religion. Although the courts tend to look at all five enumerated grounds of protection equally, religion presents both different challenges as well as distinctive approaches. All asylum seekers tell subversive stories. Living in a nation that respects diversity of beliefs and practices, one's faith may not challenge a dominant culture to the extent that it puts the individual at risk. But when governments, their agents, or those it empowers by permitting violence with impunity against those individuals, their faith or conscience increases risk. Their beliefs or practices trigger threats to life or liberty, prohibitions on worship, undergo detention, punishment, or torture, thus demonstrating their incompatibility with the nation or dominant culture. Given that lesson of the Holocaust and the great significance of the individual conscience in addressing moral crisis in tragic times, the individual seeking asylum, acting out of belief or conscience, becomes an important witness to protect human rights and diverse views of how to do well.

International law emphasizes "that freedom of conscience, religion, and belief is intended to be thought of as among the most sacred or most fundamental of the universally recognized human rights."[16] Under asylum law, religion is the only enumerated ground that requires the nation to protect the applicant at least as well as nationals of the nation."[17] Although the United States has boasted that the Constitution's protection of religious liberty guarantees the most vigorous protection ever provided by a nation, that claim wilts before the historical record. Over two centuries of litigation over religious liberty has revealed the sharp divide in public perception of assuring what James Madison called "the full and free exercise of religion" by the nation's secular laws.[18] Current First Amendment jurisprudence has

15. Yahil, *Holocaust*, 657.
16. Little, "Conscience," 604.
17. Weis, "Travaux," 37.
18. Gaffney, "Exercise," 796–804.

become unsettled as some see "religious free exercise today is our most powerful and effective means of civil disobedience."[19] Others disagree, finding that the First Amendment has been interpreted "to oppress conservative Christians."[20] Secular judges, in following the Constitution's requirement that they not establish a religion, have long struggled with ensuring liberty, while also refraining from letting their own perceptions of religion enter into their decision-making.[21] Asylum adjudicators have demonstrated the same proclivity in deciding asylum cases. Thus, instead of even providing the minimum protection offered by the First Amendment of the Constitution as required by the Convention, asylum adjudicators have often failed to protect survivors of religious persecution. In 1998, Congress, enacted the International Religious Freedom Act, (IRFA) in part, because asylum adjudicators, immigration judges, and federal judges, either through "ignorance or improper bias" neglected their duty to grant *bona fide* refugees asylum.[22] No other ground for asylum has received such congressional scrutiny. Despite that criticism, adjudicators and judges still fail to understand the full import of IRFA.

In addition, most asylum-seekers arrive with few, if any resources. Asylum cases can be expensive to litigate. Although many good *pro bono* programs provide free or low-cost representation, many applicants must appear without legal representation. One study suggested over two-thirds of asylum applicants appear with the assistance of an attorney.[23] Navigating the complexity of asylum law without legal assistance often leads to removal as the nuances and specific burdens of proof that must be met are unknown to the applicant. When one combines complexity with the reluctance to speak by PTSD survivors, cases based on religious persecution face extreme difficulty. The distinct challenge of religious persecution or exclusion in these biblical stories both share some impediments found in contemporary religious persecution cases, while also offering guidance and resources needed to prevail.[24]

19. Wang, "Disobedience," 1001.
20. Koppelman, "Dangerous," 2288.
21. Gaffney, "Exercise," 807.
22. Mousin, "Bias," 71.
23. TRAC, "Attorneys."

24. In earlier works, I listed several additional problems with the adjudication of religious asylum cases. *See,* Mousin, "Standing," 548–86; Mousin, "Bias," 75–84.

1. Overcoming the Stigma of Being Subversive

For many, the Bible is a source of Western law, even more important than the United States Constitution.[25] The Convention acknowledges that many asylum seekers may appear to have broken the law, but for the system to truly protect those who flee persecution, the label of illegality should not undermine their claims, either before the public or the adjudicator who must decide their case. Indeed, the asylum seeker is often labeled subversive on dual grounds—those that made her incompatible with her native nation's dominant culture and for flight across the U.S. border leading to the charge of being an illegal alien.

Their very claim—they did something; they believed something; or they joined others in community ritual that made them suspect, named them subversive, or resulted in an incompatibility with a nation or a dominant culture. They fled their nation, breaking, perhaps its immigration laws, and possibly breaking other nation's immigration laws in transit, and allegedly breaking United States immigration laws if they cross in flight without proper inspection or admission. The very *raison d'etre* of the Refugee Convention acknowledges that a process must be established to permit that person to tell their story, even if they entered improperly. Otherwise, we would regress to the time of the Holocaust when many deserving people were repelled from safety and returned to persecution and death. Despite the essence of the Convention, human adjudicators underscore what Rabbi Sacks asserts as the way of the world, "The stranger is always potentially a threat."[26] When one can add the appellation "illegal" or "lawbreaker" the conclusion undermines equality under law and makes it easier to doubt the credibility of the applicant.

Moreover, the harm they have escaped leads society to assume they deserve the punishment. As with Ruth and Naomi, if "the populace says there is suffering, there is therefore guilt."[27] That adjudication becomes a second Trial of Innocence within the larger legal system that is based on retributive justice that discerns whether one breaks a law and therefore earns a punishment, or whether, one has not broken the law and demonstrates their innocence. The theory of asylum adjudication poses a contrast where the applicant commences by admitting they have broken at least one law if not

---

25. Jeffress, "Christian Nation."
26. Sacks, *God's Name*, 181.
27. LaCocque, *Ruth*, 58.

many, but seek not punishment, but asylum. The applicant must plead that they have left their homeland and are removable under immigration law, but now seek the decision and discretion of the court to earn the remedy of asylum. Under the law, negative credibility decisions on any testimony, not just elements at the heart of the case, are sufficient to deny a case. Thus, if an adjudicator already retains suspicious doubts about the subversive asylum applicant, a finding of adverse credibility dooms an applicant's case, regardless of the harm suffered. Combining that suspicion with the difficulties of obtaining corroborating proof in the face of political pressures to expedite cases, further enhances the likelihood of denying the claim.[28]

In a time of great polarization over a nation's duty to admit refugees, political rhetoric frequently paints the one seeking haven as an illegal immigrant, at best, or a terrorist.[29] Burdened by epithets and fearmongering, asylum applicants succumb to a media narrative that suggests a pseudo-military invasion or a crisis to democracy. To begin a case, having already been called an illegal immigrant, the perception shifts to a negative conclusion that they are trying to get something for nothing and do not deserve even minimum legal protections. The French etymology for refoulement stresses: "*Chase, repel. Pushing back the enemy, invaders, fugitives, barbarians, immigrants, refugees; they were turned back at the border*" recognizes, by the choice of this word, the critical significance of the duty to not send back refugees even when they might be perceived as a threat.[30] To label them as illegal without any formal adjudication, solidifies the fear. Certainly, Ruth and Naomi were seen as threats. Bethlehem was "astir" upon their arrival as they caused a sensation when the community became defensive and did not even recognize Naomi upon her return.[31] (Ruth 1:19). In the eyes of those at the gate, these two women represented the most dangerous threat to their society—the foreigner.[32] For those that seek to diminish the human rights of asylum seekers, these biblical stories, often initially remembered as narratives of love, provide a new ground of understanding. They reveal to those afraid of the stranger a message of welcome to the newcomer that can transform an asylum adjudicator's perception of the applicant.

---

28. Schrag et al, "Adjudication," 573.
29. See generally, Jones-Correa and Graauw, "Illegality."
30. States as one of its definitions: "II. B. 1. [The suj. denotes an anime] Move backwards.
31. LaCocque, *Ruth*, 56, 71.
32. LaCocque, *Ruth*, 56, 71.

Refugees learn that adjudicators in receiving nations develop their own understandings of why refugees flee or what conditions in native lands might be, regardless of the truth of what actually forces flight. In dealing with hundreds of cases from specific nationalities, adjudicators' views tend to concretize stereotypes. As refugee author Dina Nayeri writes about Dutch asylum officers, "They've already decided what is true. If you offer a different story, you are lying. If you confirm their preferred story too often, you are lying."[33] She adds, "Refugees will spend the rest of their lives battling to be believed. Not because they are liars but because they're forced to make their facts fit narrow conceptions of truth."[34] Even Hannah Arendt confessed that one never escapes the stigma once branded with refugee status, writing, "In daylight, of course, we become only "technically" enemy aliens—all refugees know this."[35] Esther teaches how to live that uncertainty.

Even to use the word refugee reinforces a sense that they are the other, different than ones claiming a link to a land. As Liisa Malkk observes, "identity that can only be whole and well when rooted in a territorial homeland . . . reinforces the assumption that state sovereignty as we know it at the close of the twentieth century is part of a natural or necessary order of things"[36] The refugee is the Other, always different arousing distrust. Yet the Prime Testament is steeped in the concept of accepting and welcoming the foreigner because "the Israelites themselves are 'foreigners' in their own country (Lev 25:23) as they were in Egypt (Exod 2:22; 22:21), as they were in Babylon and in the Diaspora."[37] Subversive Bible stories that undercut presumptions of a natural order empower the newcomer. Esther and Ruth demonstrate resiliency and perseverance and rebut the domination system's adverse perception of the asylum-seeker.

2. The Particularity of Religion in a Context of Well-founded Fear

Nayeri exposes a particular problem of religious asylum applicants who seek a remedy based on a well-founded fear of persecution. Her mother, an Iranian who converted to Christianity and worshipped in a house church,

33. Nayeri, *Ungrateful*, 233.
34. Nayeri, *Ungrateful*, 243.
35. Arrendt, "We Refugees," 4.
36. Malkk, "Exile" 511.
37. LaCocque, *Ruth*, 70.

had great difficulty claiming she had a well-founded fear of persecution. She asks, "what is faith when it's so mired in fear? What is devotion? Or desire? Terror can conjure or stifle any emotion. Fear can render it true in the moment, convincing in some, false in others."[38] Faith may call a person to deny fear. But to deny fear dooms an asylum case. When combined with post-traumatic stress, which any refugee can suffer from, faith may turn to silence. Psychiatric social worker Holbrook Teter highlights the complexity an applicant faces, "'The client is required to tell 'his' story, which is what he most wants not to do. The natural desire is to deny, avoid, repress the feelings engendered by the experience," or to robotically tell the story on the witness stand without emotion, leading an Immigration Judge (IJ) to deny it because he doubted credibility based on the lack of emotion.[39]

But silence also offers the applicant and those of us who will determine the verdict of this trial a choice. Ruth decides not to offer a defense of why she came to Bethlehem. She simply tells Boaz that she is a foreigner. (Ruth 2:10). It is up to Boaz to make the ethical decision to follow the law of the land or the law of God.[40] Like Boaz, asylum adjudicators must show more sensitivity to the claims of those persecuted on account of religion.

3. Failure of Adjudicators to Understand Religion

Supreme Court Justice Robert Jackson predicted that "When one comes to trial which turns on any aspect of religious belief or representation, unbelievers among his judges are likely not to understand and are almost certain not to believe him."[41] Congress enacted IRFA, in part, because adjudicators, through ignorance or improper bias failed to properly decide asylum cases.[42] Although both the First Amendment and precedent in some circuits preclude a judge from deciding whether a believer is a true believer, judges have denied cases based on such judgments. In denying one applicant, an IJ (immigration judge) found a convert not a true Christian, in part, because he could not name the 12 Apostles, finding,

---

38. Nayeri, *Ungrateful*, 222.
39. Rovern, "Torture."
40. LaCocque, *Ruth*, 70.
41. *United States v. Ballard*, 322 U.S. 78, 93, (1944) (Jackson, J., dissenting).
42. Mousin, "Bias," 71.

> The respondent, however, apparently knows very little about the 'Bible' that he studied. The respondent cannot even name the 12 apostles of Jesus Christ. With the Court's understanding that Christianity begins with the life and teaching of Jesus Christ in the New Testament, the 12 apostles have some of the most important if not the most important writings of Christianity.[43]

Another reviewing court noted that an IJ critiqued an applicant for "testifying that Christmas celebrates the arrival of Santa Claus and for not knowing who Jesus Christ was. Piao clearly testified that Christmas also celebrates the birth of Jesus Christ, who she said was the Son of God—two statements completely overlooked by the IJ."[44] In holding an unreasoned decision denying asylum to a practitioner of Falun Gong was improper, Judge Richard Posner pointed to several "disturbing features of handling of this case that bulk large in the immigration cases we are seeing" including "a lack of familiarity with relevant foreign cultures, an exaggerated notion of how much religious people know about their religion."[45] In another case, the IJ doubted the credibility of a young Christian woman from Ghana who fled the sexual assaults of her father, a Trokosi priest. The IJ decided "it has a lot to do with idiolatry (sic) and voodoo and fears and just a lot of nonsense."[46] He then "rejected the evidence that Trokosi was a form of religion, holding that "it does not appear to the Court that this is a religion, it is rather a cult."[47] It is hard to discern what is more troubling; the apparent violation of the First Amendment's establishment clause prohibition or the mistaken understandings of religion by these IJs.

4. Defining Persecution

Subversive stories concur with the Convention that the mere prohibition against the practice of one's religion constitutes persecution. Asylum adjudicators have strayed far from that conclusion. Congress did not define

---

43. *Tougighi v. Mukasey,* 510 F.3d 1059, 1061 (9th Cir. 20070). In another case, the appellate court critiqued an IJ for not determining whether the applicant prayed the wrong words of the Lord's Prayer or whether he instead described a personal prayer he made to the Lord. *Ren v. Holder,* 648 F.3d 1079, 1087 (9th Cir. 2011)

44. *Piao v. Lynch,* 647 Fed. Appx. 727, 728–29. (9th Cir. 2016).

45. *Iao v. Gonzales,* 400 F.3d 530, 533 (7th Cir. 2005)

46. *Fiadjoe v. Att'y Gen.,* 411 F.3d 135, 145 (3d Cir. 2005).

47. *Fiadjoe,* 146.

persecution in the Act, leaving it to the courts to define persecution on a case-case basis. That decision has proven to be especially grim regarding cases of alleged religious persecution. Initially, the Convention's drafters, while acknowledging the lack of a definition, stated it "may be inferred that a threat to life or freedom on account of . . . religion . . . is always persecution."[48] Initial intent seemed favorable. When Congress amended the law for nonrefoulement to eliminate the requirement that the persecution only be understood as physical harm, one Congressman had argued, "techniques of persecution are not limited to bodily violence alone, tyranny over the mind and spirit of a person has been demonstrated as more fearsome than the ancient methods of torture . . ."[49] Nonetheless, courts soon distinguished between physical harm and mental harm. Rebecca Sharpless and Kristi Wintermeyer found, "Although mental harm can qualify as persecution, courts have rarely found persecution based solely on mental mistreatment in a published decision. Furthermore, courts routinely fail to consider the longstanding mental effects of physical mistreatment."[50] Sharpless and Wintermeyer conclude: "The judicial ratcheting up of the pain and suffering required for persecution runs contrary to our current medical understanding of the human body and mind."[51] A few courts have recognized that spiritual denial may constitute religious persecution. Judge Posner explained, "nonphysical harm of equal gravity—that last qualification is important because refusing to allow a person to practice his religion is a common form of persecution even though the only harm it causes is psychological."[52] Few courts follow his admonition. The denial of access to community worship or prohibitions on participation in religious rituals still falls short of constituting persecution for many.

Consider the case of a 16-year-old Chinese Christian woman who was arrested for five days, beaten, and sexually assaulted. The Court of Appeals on review found that "Despite crediting her testimony that the beatings left her with "a lot of contusions" and that she was sexually threatened, the IJ found that this treatment did not seriously bruise or harm her."[53] On review,

---

48. UNHCR, Handbook, Par. 51, p. 9:

49. Musalo, *Refugee*, citing Kovac v. Immigr. & Naturalization Serv., 407 F.2d 102, 106, n. 9 (9th Cir. 1969).

50. Sharpless & Wintermeyer, "Human "Frailty," 730.

51. Sharpless & Wintermeyer, "Human Frailty," 764.

52. *Stanojkova v. Holder* 645 F.3d 943, 948 (7th Cir. 2011)

53. Weiwei Chen v. Holder, 549 Fed. Appx. 567, 568–69 (7th Cir. 2013) To emphasize

the Board of Immigration Appeals (BIA) stated, "It ruled that her detention was too short and her mistreatment too minor to qualify as persecution, and that her fear of future persecution was not objectively reasonable."[54] Significantly, neither IJ nor the BIA (Board of Immigration Appeals) ever addressed whether forced abandonment of worship could constitute persecution. The Seventh Circuit disagreed and remanded the case to the BIA. Such success, however, necessitates ongoing proceedings, further traumatizing her, thus revealing the inability of the law to adequately address harm.

The burden has become even more difficult. After reviewing almost 200 asylum cases, Sharpless and Wintermeyer concluded that judges, "moved from citing physical violence as the archetype of persecution to finding that only high levels of physical violence met the 'extreme concept' test."[55] One appellate court examining a woman who was arrested several times because she failed to follow Iran's laws regarding her hair, denied her claim, stating in part, "Persecution is an extreme concept, which ordinarily does not include discrimination on the basis of race or religion, as morally reprehensive as it may be."[56] Reprehensible, yes, but eligible for asylum, no. Although that case was decided in 1996, Iran continued its relentless oppression of women displaying their hair. In 2022, the death of Ms.

---

the difficulty, I quote from the case: "Chen was interrogated, beaten, and traumatized over the next five days at the station. When she arrived at the station she was tied down, and two officers interrogated her for half an hour. During her first session of questioning, they threatened to send her to a labor camp and accused her church of associating with foreign "reactionary religious influence[s]" and plotting to overthrow the Chinese government. When she refused to reveal information about her church or confess to a crime, the interrogators pinched her, slapped her face, kicked her with their heavy boots, and punched her until she fell to the floor. She received "a lot of contusions" and was "black and blue." The police beat and interrogated Chen three more times before releasing her from custody. During one of these sessions, an officer attempted to sexually assault her. Chen explains that the officer "came close to me, and he tried to touch my body in many different places. And, he even went so far as to try to, you know take my clothes off. But, I was, I was fighting. I said that if you do that, then, I will scream for help." The officer backed off and sent her to her cell. After Chen's five-day detention, the police discharged her. To secure her release her parents paid a 2,000-yuan bond, and she signed a statement prepared by the police promising not to participate in illegal religious gatherings or contact other churchgoers.

As required by the police, she reported to them weekly. She returned to school, but the past abuse, her suspended worship, and weekly visits to the police left her depressed and unable to focus on her studies."

54. Chen, 569.
55. Sharpless & Wintermeyer, "Human Frailty," 742.
56. Fischer v. I.N.S., 79 F.3d 955, 961 (9th Cir. 1996 (en banc).

Mahsa Amini sparked protests against Iran's "morality police."[57] Although the grant of one asylum application might not change Iran's laws, the denial discourages others who might seek safe haven here. Moreover, as Nobel laureate Mohammadi alleged, failure to respond to human rights violations may bring violators to our doors instead of those seeking haven.[58] Courts have also failed to fully comprehend the long-term medical consequences of violence against religious claimants.

5. The Asylum Applicant's Test of Innocence

Biblical exegesis offers the opportunity to rehear the applicant's story in a more familiar resonance while also suggesting that not all subversive stories undermine the common good, but rather, sustain it. Biblical criticism reinforces the value of the subversive element in seeking the common good. LaCocque writes, "Esther is a metaphor for exiles."[59] The asylum-seeker, the contemporary exile, can find solidarity in other biblical stories as well. The book of Ruth, written in a time of great polarization, specifically examines the foreign presence of the exile in the community in violation of the law. But the turmoil in Ruth's narrative is, "resolved, not by the expulsion but by the marriage of the Moabitess with Boaz . . ."[60] As refugee and immigration issues foster greater and greater polarization, Ruth and Esther remind persons of faith that their witness can overcome obstacles and give courage to the asylum-seeker and their legal representative. Those who found ways, not just to confront powerful adversaries in the Bible, but even to find a way to be included in the canon, suggest possibilities for those asylum seekers bringing a distinct voice of faith in response to persecution in other lands. LaCocque reminds us that, "Ever since the death camps, life and particularly human life has become a cheap commodity. In the twentieth century alone, some 100,000,000 humans have been destroyed so far by other humans. It is indeed within that context that the Jewish-Christian testimony to the world must be proclaimed . . ." The person fleeing violence on account of religion continues that proclamation, Jewish, Christian, or other faith that attempted to live a life of faith that challenged existing regimes or

---

57. Chappell and Hernandez, "Iranian,"
58. Bubola, "Children,"
59. LaCocque, *Esther Regina*, 126.
60. LaCocque, *Feminine Unconventional*, 100.

the chaos within broken national states."⁶¹ Those seeking asylum based on religious persecution defy dehumanization.

Esther's witness before the king vanquishes the court intrigue that sought to extinguish a people by designating them as illegal. Esther alerts the king:

> that he had been about to kill none other than his beloved wife and her community . . . the king had been poised to saw off the very branch on which he was sitting. Suddenly, he realizes that the Other is kin so close as to be inseparable from the self—a potent lesson to the haters of foreigners of all times.⁶²

Substitute today, the body politic or Congress for the word king and realize that the witness today pleads do not return me, for although I am the Other, I am kin, not enemy. While the echo chambers of the contemporary polarized world silence the voice of the newcomer, the asylum-seeker's voice, if it is encouraged, revives Esther's message to protect life. Her witness would not have been possible but for her disobedience to the dominant culture's rules. Indeed, "the Book of Esther is a subversive piece of literature."⁶³ LaCocque asserts, "In the crucible of life, disobedience is more often than not the true obedience."⁶⁴ LaCocque adds, "For Paul and his followers, Torah is dynamic, it is the life of authentic Israel, i.e. the history both lived and to be lived by those who *choose* to find their identity in that divine revelation (cf. Ps. 37:31; Isa. 51:7). . . . To 'go by the rule' as if history were a game is perhaps safe, but it always converts life into a technique."⁶⁵ Those fleeing persecution today did not play it safe, but witness to the world much like Esther and Ruth. In emulating the courage of Esther and Ruth, they teach faithful persons to offer hospitality and protection by returning to the roots of the Convention's principles.

Recognizing those principles, Sharpless and Wintermeyer argue, "persecution should be defined as the violation of a human right rather than as extreme harm."⁶⁶ As nations throughout the world renege on

---

61. LaCocque, "Auschwitz," 157.
62. LaCocque, *Esther Regina*, 60.
63. LaCocque, *Esther Regina*. See also, LaCocque, *Romance*: "The Canticle belongs with other pieces of literature—including the Gospels—to a literary genre whose purpose is to subvert the world," 206.
64. LaCocque, *Election* 103.
65. LaCocque, *Election*, 104. (emphasis in original).
66. Sharpless, *Unbreakable*, 77.

the promises made to those fleeing persecution after the Holocaust, the testament of the asylum-seeker rebuts the claims of fear and restriction. Initially, exhibiting courage and faith in native lands, they now face a powerful judicial system backed up by a formidable enforcement regime of border patrol, detention, and judicial proceedings. Yet, the subversive voices revealed by ongoing biblical studies offer confidence. LaCocque again maintains, "weakness is no congenital flaw but a deliberate choice, a tremendous courage to deny the aphorism, 'The powerful is always right.' The biblical trajectory is consistently subversive."[67] Indeed, given the evidence of the deadly journey many undertake to be that witness, the choice takes courage and may sometimes fail. "From the outset of biblical literature, the human choice amounts to an existential option between life and death (see Deut. 30: 15-20). Siding with God ('if you do well') brings about life; not siding with God ('If you do not do well') brings about death."[68] Nonetheless, he concludes, in naming our call to not forget the lessons of Auschwitz, "To be fully human implies the choice to be on the 'wrong' side of the barbed wires."[69]

These individual cases matter. Martin Marty points out that within our nation's history, it is often the individual or the minority faith that the dominant culture perceives as lawless, who through their witness, and at times persecution, transformed the dominant culture to recognize rights and establish full freedom for all within society.[70] Echoing Yahil Lenil's observation about the critical significance of the individual's moral conscience, the individual trial of the person of faith often not only offers freedom to the individual but is a voice of freedom for society and offers a diverse understanding of the world. Whether it is the trial of Jesus of Nazareth, who faced both the religious trial and the political trial,[71] St. Paul arguing for this right to be tried in a Roman court of law, or the asylum-seeker before an asylum adjudicator, this second Trial of Innocence calls society to be just. Today, it may be the Ahmadi seeking the freedom to pursue their faith in a strictly Muslim nation, a Falun Gong member seeking the space to practice, a member of the Church of the Latter-Day Saints, a Jehovah's Witness, a Roman Catholic, or an evangelical speaking out against the violence

67. LaCocque, *Genesis*, 56.
68. LaCocque, *Onslaught*, 56.
69. LaCocque, "Auschwitz," 9.
70. Marty, "Gyres," 670–71.
71. LaCocque, *Central*, 227.

of gangs, each testifies to a human drive to love and be free. To restrict or prohibit that testimony through deportation or erecting legal and physical barriers at the border risks a verdict of a failure to do well in the second Trial of Innocence. But for the acceptance of Ruth and Naomi upon their return, Israel would have forfeited an essential link to its future.[72] But for the courage of Esther, a people may have been extinguished. Esther and Ruth become models for faithful persons in all generations.

PART III: THE THIRD TRIAL OF INNOCENCE: HOW WILL THE NATION-STATE RESPOND?

LaCocque asserts that societies and nations face the same question posed by the Trial of Innocence to do well or not do well.[73] The biblical subversive stories remind asylum applicants that one's vision can matter for the greater good. According to LaCocque, God invites humans to be freethinking partners in the covenantal promise to do well and seek justice.[74] Indeed, each society and individual undergoes a Trial of Innocence every day. Advocates must be prepared to respond and adduce evidence in support of their position because, "The negative side of the universe is in need of both divine and human healing intervention.[75] This section proposes a thought experiment that LaCocque's scholarship advocates for the vulnerable in this third Trial of Innocence. As nations retreat from the protections devised in the wake of the Holocaust, his exegesis presents a defense for a verdict enjoining further retreat and restriction from the post-Holocaust promises. The Trial contains three parts, first, it critiques the nation-state's reliance on the Ezra-Nehemiah narrative to influence public policy and law, second, it proposes one example of how biblical criticism might inspire a more just legal process, and third, it seeks to render a verdict on the future of nonrefoulement.

---

72. LaCocque, *Ruth*, 27.
73. LaCocque, *Onslaught* 84, 97, 143.
74. LaCocque, "Justice," 22.
75. LaCocque, "Deconstruction," 87.

1. A Critique of Efforts to Fuse Political Power with Biblical Exegesis to Deny Asylum-Seekers

Despite the post-World War II promise of nonrefoulement to secure the safety of asylum-seekers, many nations have subsequently reneged on those promises, hardened their borders, and returned asylum-seekers to the sea, deserts, or third nations to persecution or death without any opportunity to testify. Today, barbed wire ensnares or repels refugees from the Rio Grande at the same time it prevents the federal officers from accessing the river to save families in distress or drowning.[76] Refugee camps, already straining under inadequate food and medical care, are bombed in the name of national security or experience devastating fires. Boats overloaded with refugees sink while Coast Guards abdicate their responsibility. Billions of dollars provide profits to contractors and private prisons in the name of border security, while government budgets starve courts from responding to those deserving legal remedies.[77]

Presidents and authoritarian leaders have implemented policies to deny asylum-seekers.[78] Specific bans against a particular religion such as the 2017 Muslim ban or preventing entry of asylum-seekers undermine the protections born in response to the Holocaust. Prospectively, Donald Trump, announced that come 2025 "he'd turn away those who 'don't like our religion. We don't want you in our country'"[79] adding the racist claim that "immigrants are poisoning our blood."[80] His advisors have revealed their plans to further restrict immigration and end asylum.[81] Steven Miller, having learned the lessons from their failure to scuttle asylum protections after 2016, boasted that, if reelected, "Trump will unleash the vast arsenal of federal powers to implement the most spectacular migration crackdown."[82]

The fear of the Other—the immigrant, the refugee, the one coming to our gates seeking safety—propels much of the current polarization. Conflating racism with national pride has made immigration reform

---

76. Montoya-Galvez, "Texas."

77. Mousin, "Constantine," 381–83.

78. Trump's policies implemented over 1,000 changes to immigration practice. Stillman, "Race;" see also Tracking Project.

79. Owens, Tess, "Religion'"

80. Gabriel, "Rhetoric."

81. Savage et al., "Sweeping,"

82. Savage, et al., "Sweeping."

impossible over the last three decades while fueling proposals to eviscerate the protections of the Convention. One commentator seemingly brushed off any sensibility of the tragic genesis of those protections by calling for a review of the "decades old international commitments [that] bind us . . ."[83]

Political positions regarding immigration have promoted the national divide. Mr. Trump's "strategy of polarization—identifying out-groups, especially immigrants . . . as enemies of the people" both "vilifies and ridicules his critics with the government, the society, or his party."[84] These anti-immigrant claims have found willing followers. Barbara Walter observed that Trump's 2016 election campaign "emphasized the downgrading of the former white majority—America's own sons of the soil" as they saw immigrants, "whose first language wasn't English, whose religion was not Christianity—get lucrative tech jobs and live an American dream that no longer existed for them."[85] Alan Abramowitz and Jennifer McCoy show that "racial/ethnic resentment" has led to a growing alignment of partisanship with race, religion, and ideology, resulting in "affective polarization, ethnocentrism (predisposition to divide society into Us vs. Them groups), social intolerance of out-groups, and unwillingness to cooperate and compromise."[86] Spewing hatred has become an all too frequent election ploy as "the psychology of polarization becomes fundamental as mechanisms of dehumanization, depersonalization, and stereotyping all contribute to the emotional loathing, fear, and distrust of the out-partisans."[87]

This anti-immigrant perspective stems, in part, from the scriptural claims of white Christian nationalists that rely upon Ezra-Nehemiah's account in support of reclaiming that mythical America fueling a resentment that mourns a lost age of homogeneity. Martin Marty described how private beliefs were transformed into public policy by some on the Christian Right, to exacerbate a "politics of resentment" by people who were or who felt themselves to have been demeaned, overlooked, or inhibited."[88] White Christian nationalism generally combines "nationalist and Christian fundamentalist ideologies" including "anti-immigrant prejudice" and

---

83. Ratner and White, "How to Fix."
84. Abramowitz and McCoy, "Resentment," 150.
85. Walter, *Wars*, 150.
86. Walter, *Wars*, 140.
87. McCoy, et al, "Polarization," 23.
88. Marty, "Gyres," 663.

"dehumanization of immigrants."[89] It includes "assumptions of nativism and white supremacy."[90] Rachel Mikva points out that although Christian nationalists often claim that they subscribe to "traditional Judeo-Christian religious values and beliefs," they instead engage in a "perverse appropriation of Judaism, deployed as a cover for Christian exclusivism."[91]

Significantly, some evangelicals attempt to distinguish themselves from Christian nationalists, refusing to advocate for a theocracy, but still seeking for a Christian influence in governance and legislation.[92] Ralph Drollinger, who has substantial ties to elected leaders, argues that he knows no Christian nationalists in government. In contrast, Mikva points to men like Senators Hawley and Cruz as purveyors of the same goals as white Christian nationalists, under the guise of code words.[93]

For purposes of responding to refugees at our border, however, even if Drollinger correctly distinguishes evangelicals from Christian nationalists, he spoke for many evangelicals when he asserted that the Bible provided permission to build a border wall that would repel asylum-seekers from entry, branding them "illegals."[94] Attorney General Jeff Sessions defended enforcement decisions based, in part, on Nehemiah's return to Jerusalem "to build a wall."[95] In analogizing that building a wall was approved by God with Nehemiah, First Baptist of Dallas minister Robert Jeffress announced, "The Bible says even heaven itself is gonna (sic) have a wall around it." He added, "not everyone is gonna (sic) be allowed in."[96] Speaker of the House Mike Johnson defends the state of Texas' decision to straddle the Texas-Mexico border with miles of razor wire.[97] Drollinger, Sessions, Jeffress, Johnson, and Miller, among others, resemble those palace courtesans that name religion as their value, but in the end, dehumanize the vulnerable ones. The Book of Esther warns, however, to be vigilant because "the

---

89. Al-Kire, et al., "Nationalism," 354.
90. Mikva, "Threat" citing Whitehead Perry, "Taking America Back."
91. Mikva, *"Threat."* See also, Gedicks and Hendrix, "Uncivil Religion," "conservative Christians seeking to narrow the meaning of Judeo-Christian symbols and practices" 287.
92. See, e.g., Jeffress, "Christian America." Founders "designed our brilliant system of government not on enlightenment principles but upon precepts gleaned from the Bible."
93. Mikva, "Threat."
94. Drollinger, "Letter."
95. Blair, "Sessions."
96. Mooney, "Trump's Apostle."
97. Brownstein, "Johnson."

danger coming from those 'who do not know what they are doing' is great and even lethal because even the king is easily misled by court intrigues and power games."[98]

To rebut these nationalist claims, LaCocque presents two arguments. First, the biblical narrative discounts human yearning for belief in any nationalism, Christian or otherwise. Second, the subversive stories recognize the necessity of following a God of justice and mercy, not domination or judgment that leads to exclusion of the foreigner.

a) The Biblical Narrative Critiques Nationalism

History teaches us that when communities declare certain writings Scripture, they enter a dangerous territory.[99] Some may use it as a weapon, others ignore the voices that have been silenced and not given prominence within the canon.[100] Nonetheless, any reading of Scripture invites an interpretation, or else it is meaningless.[101] To advocate that Scripture contains but one meaning to justify a border wall places a thumb on the scale of justice, undermining the very purpose of the trial.

In this Trial of Innocence determining how to implement policies responding to those seeking safety, LaCocque's scholarship adduces evidence to counter those who argue a Christian nation must build walls and exclude. They remind us that the biblical message found in the Prime Testament, although formed in a particular time and place, offers a vision by God of a universal call for justice and mercy. J, one of the authors of Genesis, taught that "by making Adam a human without nationality, J has readily sort-circuited all attempts at Israelite exclusivism."[102] LaCocque adds, "Thus, to universalism, J adds a dimension of egalitarianism: the fruits of the Garden are equally for all to eat, they are given to the 'human one' (*'adam*). The idea is doubtlessly at the root of Israel's sense of social justice."[103] "National isolationism is defeated by J's worldview. The Yahwist's understanding of 'chosen people' is not static but dynamic."[104] Anne Roiphe reminds us:

98. LaCocque, *Regina*, 128.
99. Mikva, *Dangerous*, 17.
100. LaCocque, *Regina*, 7; LaCocque, *Romance*, 58.
101. LaCocque, *Onslaught*, 83.
102. LaCocque, *Trial*, 34.
103. LaCocque, *Trial*, 34.
104. LaCocque, *Onslaught*, 10.

We live private lives, and each death and each life casts its own light. But simultaneously we belong to a larger group that can suffer and inflict suffering without regard to individual need or worth. Our contemporary story has made us painfully certain that we need collective strength. But we also understand that human beings can become figur, 'stuff,' and states can become monsters whose religion has turned malignant.[105]

To rely upon Nehemiah to banish "illegals" in the name of national security dehumanizes the stranger and misses Israel's covenantal response to social justice.

b) From the Universal Claims of Genesis, the Subversive Stories of Esther, Ruth, Zechariah, and Job Rebut the National Needs to Build a Wall against the Foreigner

Those who seek to build a wall to keep immigrants out rely on that metaphor of the wall of Ezra and Nehemiah. They build a wall and operate a legal system of detention, and deportation based on a legal system that fails to offer fundamental fairness or due process. It must be recognized that this debate is not new. Rachel Mikva compares the Book of Ruth with Ezra and Nehemiah providing competing visions within Israel.[106] The book of Esther, as subversive literature, critiques "the Jerusalem establishment, especially after the reforms of Ezra and Nehemiah."[107] Ezra and Nehemiah feared the loss of identity as a community. They responded in fear and built "a fence around the Torah," transforming it into "a code, a legal constitution of the nation . . ."[108] Appointed by the Persian King, Ezra and Nehemiah engage on a mission of statecraft: "They come to Jerusalem to give to Torah the authority of a state law, something the 'law of Moses' had never been before."[109] Nationalism becomes paramount. In this Trial, nationalism necessitates responding to Esther's dilemma: "The choice is clear. Either share the power with the hierocrats or be rejected by them. The second choice

---

105. Roiphe, "Nehemiah," 477.
106. Mikva, *Dangerous*, 105–06.
107. LaCocque, *Esther Regina*, 127.
108. LaCocque, *Election*, 101.
109. LaCocque, *Feminine Unconventional*, 71.

certainly seems to be the least good, but it is in fact God's choice, for God himself is rejected by the powerful."[110]

A similar fusion of Scripture with national identity invigorates modern efforts to follow the Ezra-Nehemiah model. "Nationalism has become blind obedience, even to absurd or inhuman orders; heroism means deafness to the victims' cries for elementary compassion . . ."[111] LaCocque concludes that too frequently even after the promise of a resurrected Christ, "Christians have not only returned to business as usual, but they have also more gravely taken advantage of the vision of Truth to improve the credibility of their lie and have used the vision of Justice to increase the efficiency of their injustice."[112] Business as usual also blinds us to our responsibility to address the harms that our greed has caused in the asylum-seekers home countries, whether through military intervention or environmental destruction.[113] In addition to the legal responsibilities the Convention and the Act establish, Karen Musalo writes, "even if a country has the sovereign right to close borders, and exclude non-citizens, it may not be the moral or ethical thing to do" because our nation possess responsibility for how "US policies and interventions were major contributors to the root causes of refugee flight . . ."[114] To those who seek to exclude, the biblical narrative of Job reveals that the legal system needs to be challenged to ensure justice: "God as destroyer of a fundamentalist and closed-minded worldview. The friends' arguments are exposed as a vain exercise because, in truth, they are revealed as merely a sophisticated way to escape the necessary commitment to fight evil."[115]

White Christian nationals' reliance on Scripture reveals the critical importance of the biblical subversive stories that challenge the priority of national law. Esther, Susana, Judith, and Ruth share a "sharp criticism of an ideology incapable of generosity and of real sensitivity, as it understands its task as one of compartmentalizing and categorizing the ethical rules of an exclusivist community."[116] They provide a counter-testimony on how the fear of the stranger can be mitigated by understanding that they proclaim a welcome to the other regardless of national law. Power linked to a

---

110. LaCocque, "II Zacharie," 145.
111. LaCocque, "Auschwitz," 2.
112. LaCocque, "Auschwitz," 6.
113. Mousin, "Hospitality," text between footnotes 161–66.
114. Musalo, "Responsibility," 763; see also, Lustgarten, "Climate Migration."
115. LaCocque, "Deconstruction," 96.
116. LaCocque, *Feminine Unconventional*, 117.

dangerous weapon can be used to silence, exclude, or return those deemed most vulnerable. These stories provide the counterargument in this third Trial of Innocence determining our nation's response to asylum-seekers for those seeking to follow the biblical call to welcome the stranger.

Ruth's witness reveals the failure of national law to offer justice. Ruth's pleas to Boaz that she is a foreigner pose similar challenges to contemporary law. As the Ruth narrative unfolds, we first meet Boaz as a conservative resident of Bethlehem and a strict follower of the law.[117] The law gives a "pretext" to reject Ruth and send her back to Moab. But again, the narrative tells us that the "Torah loves to break barriers."[118] In the context of the laws against marriage to foreign women of Ezra and Nehemiah, Boaz must discern that "the inherent suffering due to change is not recognized by the governors of Judah in the fifth century."[119] Boaz has a choice, as all face, for the "'letter' would kill Ruth, 'the spirit' give her life—literally (see 2 Cor. 3:6)"[120] Ruth forces Boaz to choose between Nehemiah and Abraham." Boaz chose the former by choosing Ruth. Boaz lives, as we live, in the tension between "two fronts—judicial systems and welcoming the foreigner."[121] Similarly, Joyce Baldwin argues that the author of Esther teaches that "loyalty both to temporal rule and to eternal principles is possible in an alien state, though it may involve conflict" and certainly gives credence that what appears to be disloyal may instead serve the best interests of society.[122] Although the Book of Ruth identifies this dual challenge, it, nonetheless, critiques both religious and secular law for the failure to ensure justice.[123] Likewise, the asylum-seeker today adduces evidence in this third Trial of Innocence calling us to be like Boaz and transform the nation-state's law.

2. The Need for an Independent Immigration Court

Like all the protagonists of the subversive stories, citizens who claim faith or personal convictions live in a world with dual loyalties to sovereigns. For those who suggest that these subversive stories are too utopian, too

117. LaCocque, *Ruth*, 65.
118. LaCocque, *Ruth*, 71.
119. LaCocque, *Ruth*, 71.
120. LaCocque, *Ruth*, 70.
121. LaCocque, *Ruth*, 154.
122. Baldwin, "Introduction," 28; LaCocque, *Feminine Unconventional*, 60.
123. LaCocque, *Ruth*, 154.

hopeful for love to eliminate the need for law, these protagonists also teach ways to address the concerns of law. For example, one can look to Esther, which LaCocque calls the most modern biblical book, especially after Auschwitz.[124] As we each decide how to respond to our daily trials of innocence, we can similarly, much like Esther, seek to urge our nation to do well. Given the difficulties asylum seekers experience and given the forces that seek to exclude refugees from our land, we can also seek to live up to our nation's commitment to equality under law by ensuring that adjudications of asylum eligibility are independent and free from political influence.

Under immigration law, the first two levels of court—the IJs and the BIA—are administrative courts and not fully independent. They work under the supervision of the United States Attorney General (AG) who has the power to reverse decisions and write a precedential decision without the typical adversary trial that includes arguments from any opposing view. IJs are employees of the Department of Justice (DOJ) as are the government attorneys who appear before them. Critics have long maintained that the absence of independence has led to a bias against asylum applicants. The American Bar Association calls for an independent court "as the ongoing politicization" of the immigration court "demonstrates how important it is to fully sever the judicial function of immigration decision-making from the DOJ.[125] After extensive study, the Appleseed Foundation recommended eliminating the supervision responsibility by establishing a new process to ensure both independence and impartiality.[126] Similarly, former IJ Dana Leigh Marks exhorts, "To end the distortion and chaos at the immigration courts, let the judges be judges."[127] Judges must not only be impartial but also avoid the appearance of impartiality, but that joint demand is impossible if an adjudicator's supervisor also supervises the very lawyers who appear before them arguing that the AG's theory of the case must prevail. Jeffrey Chase, also a former IJ, critiques this dual responsibility and asks, "shouldn't judges who make such important decisions that sometimes involve life and death be 'only judges?'"[128] Retired IJ Paul Wickham Schmidt concludes that "racial justice and harmony will continue to elude us as a nation unless and until we come to grips with the ongoing abuses in the

---

124. LaCocque, *Esther Regina*, 41.
125. American Bar Association, "Promise," 2021,
126. Appleseed, "Assembly Line Injustice," 35.
127. Marks, "Independent," Prospect.
128. Jeffrey Chase, "Immigration Court."

Immigration Courts."[129] The semblance of fairness and aspirations of due process lead Kathleen Arnold to observe,

> The highly bureaucratized and policed sphere of immigration policy has the appearance of liberal order, but legally suspends the law, acting in a highly discretionary way as 'reason of state' and 'rational domination' on behalf of the common good, thus conforming to liberal norms while being deployed undemocratically.[130]

Although the immigration courts have been established democratically, the juxtaposition of their power to deport and separate families with the absence of independence undermines the liberal norms they allegedly represent.[131] Steven Miller's predictions, moreover, eviscerate any semblance of independence.

Miller's defense that he simply enforces the law that exists recalls other lawyers such as those 1930 bureaucrats whose dedication to the letter of the law condemned many to die in the camps of Europe. Moreover, the lawyer who challenged Jesus in the Good Samaritan parable believed he could rely on the law. Jesus taught him that compliance with the law without compassion kills.[132] Miller's policies such as banning Muslims and forcing applicants to remain in Mexico led to many innocent deaths and injuries. LaCocque reminds us that "Obedience to the Law always must be continually reinvented. I know how to hate evil—murder, theft, adultery, coveting. But the problem always remains of knowing how to love."[133]

Subversive stories confirm that the law can strangle compassion. The letter of the law can kill, but the spirit gives life."[134] The subversive story found in Job demonstrates that society's law is not the final answer. For as the friends try to convince Job to repent, the friends have come with the 'best' theology seems to offer and defend the law. It is the all-too-common seductive and damaging ideological construct repeated throughout history.

---

129. Schmidt, "Heights," 3.

130. Arnold, "Sanctuary," 1180.

131. The trend now swerves away from a more just process as the February 4, 2024 proposed Senate border bill eliminated current judicial review for asylum-seekers. See: NIJC, "Analysis," 2–3.

132. LaCocque, *Central Jew*, 127, n. 189.

133. LaCocque, *Ruth*, 152.

134. LaCocque, Ruth, 70.

It attempts to justify evil and victimizes others by being judgmental and condemnatory.¹³⁵ Gustavo Gutierrez notes that Job's

> faith prompts him to inquire into the possibility of finding the appropriate language about God that does justice to the situation of suffering. Not to make the effort is to risk succumbing to impotent resignation, a religion of calculated self-interest, a cynical outlook that forgets the suffering of others, and even despair.¹³⁶

A verdict in this Third Trial will answer whether, in despair or neglect, we repeat the mistakes marked by the silence of the religious denominations that failed to speak out or adequately respond to the cries of the vulnerable in Europe.¹³⁷

Today, we are told by the media that we face a crisis at our borders. Dina Nayeri writes, "And here is the biggest lie in the refugee crisis. It isn't the individual stories. It is the language of disaster often used to describe incoming refugees—*deluge,* or *flood* or *swarm*. These words are lies."¹³⁸ Our nation has previously responded to higher numbers of people fleeing persecution. In the first year of the Act, the United States resettled 200,000 refugees.¹³⁹ The United States has shown the capacity to welcome far more refugees than we have since 1980. Instead, when individuals are lumped together, dehumanizing them as hordes, we risk that the dominant culture will commit murder. We know there are millions of refugee children, but when we characterize them as a dehumanized enemy at our gate, we risk making the wrong choice by failing to do well.¹⁴⁰ If we recapture the spirit that led to the Convention's response to the fires of Auschwitz, we too can offer a verdict to do well and preserve the promise of nonrefoulement. In LaCocque's words,

> Do we side with Cain or side with Abel? "By siding with him [Abel], 'by his wound we are healed'(Is. 53:5) because with him we have chosen innocence... The choice is costly; it may be paid with our life. But, siding with Abel is also siding with J's God.¹⁴¹

---

135. LaCocque, "Fundamentalism," 95
136. Gutierrez, *Job*, 93.
137. Wyman, *Abandonment*, 141.
138. Nayeri *Ungrateful Refugee*, 262
139. Migration, "Refugee Admissions."
140. LaCocque, *Onslaught*, 143.
141. LaCocque, *Onslaught*, 143.

3. The Verdict to Do Well

Christian realists may argue that the subversive stories of Ruth and Esther offer utopian visions of how to love in a world filled with pain. Certainly, the Bible provides multiple stories of convictions and faith. The canon accepted subversive stories because they included calls to the Prime Testament's fundamental call to social justice. These subversive stories exist within a dominant culture that seeks to exclude and deport. The verdict demands we choose which text to interpret and follow. The text's presence becomes key evidence in this Trial for not only do we interpret the text, but the text interprets us and our choices.[142] God calls us as a free people to interpret the word and respond to the covenantal relationship. Care must be given, however, when faith fuses with national power as in the case of Ezra-Nehemiah. But in our freedom, we can also observe a different covenantal relationship proposed by the subversive stories that survived and were included in the canon.

The politics of polarization seek to persuade that the Other is less than human, out to steal national resources, pouring oil on the embers of resentment, further dividing the nation. History also teaches, however, the miscarriage of pragmatic realism. LaCocque reminds that, "ever since the death camps, life and particularly human life has become a cheap commodity."[143] In the twenty-first century, thousands drown in the Mediterranean, the South Asian Sea, and the Caribbean. Others die in the desert or the jungles of the Darian Gap or fall prey to gangs who rob them on their pilgrimage. Billions in enforcement dollars have made Customs and Border Protection the largest police force in the United States while enriching private detention corporations and many in the prison-industrial complex.[144] A focus on a more just legal system—more judges and lawyers to assist applicants, a return to the promises of the drafters of the Convention, could provide an alternative pragmatic solution. Many have proposed solutions in establishing an independent immigration court.[145]

But to change that requires a collective voice for a realignment of funding to a more compassionate response. Recalling these subversive stories, moreover, encourages emulation of Ruth, Boaz, Esther, or Job. Ruth could

---

142. LaCocque, *Ruth*, 154.
143. LaCocque, "Auschwitz," 10.
144. Jones, *Protected*.
145. Tsankov, "Article I," 124–25.

have been banned at the gate—the foreigner from Moab—but individuals, Naomi and Boaz questioned the dominant culture and Ruth's powerful witness changed Israel, indeed, gave Israel a missing piece in its genealogy, and a reminder that the foreigner can provide a gift.[146] Esther gave courage to untold thousands. Job could have abdicated his faith to the pragmatic arguments of his friends. None retreated. Theodore Jennings recalls that "Steve Biko in South Africa saying that it is not a matter of organizing a movement to bring about liberation but preparing people for the liberation that is coming" and therefore, we should be engaged with "communities of generous welcome that exhibit a new sort of justice outside of the law."[147] Kathleen Arnold celebrates the faithful voices of those who seek justice as a counterweight to liberal democracies that have violated due process to secure national security. She argues that the birth of religious sanctuaries for refugees in opposition to the law occurred "precisely to combat this undemocratic and yet legal sphere of the law."[148] Today, communities have responded to new arrivals offering shelter, food, and clothing to rebut the claim that we live in an unsolvable crisis.[149]

Recognizing that "[c]ompassion is the essence of religion and morality" and that our selfishness leads us astray, Karen Armstrong argues that the presence of the vulnerable "[r]equires us to regard others as equal to ourselves, refuse to put ourselves into a privileged category, and deem the needs, desires, and ambitions of our fellow human beings to be as valuable as our own."[150] Instead of listening to Nehemiah, our task may be "to heal not the wall but the hurt of human beings" and recognize human dignity.[151] Acknowledging that dignity when the asylum-seekers request aid, we should pause before we return them. Let us heed Lévinas' call to see the claim in the other's face, telling us do not kill.[152] If we take the lessons of the Holocaust seriously, that admonition includes the promise of nonrefoulement: do not send me back to death or persecution. Let the compassion

---

146. Lacocque, *Ruth*, 39.

147. Jennings, *Outlaw*" 218.

148. Kathleen R. Arnold, "Sanctuary" 1177. See also, *American Baptist Churches v. Thornburgh*, 760 F. Supp. 796 (N.D. Ca. 1991) (Settlement agreement reopening a decade of denied Guatemalan and El Salvadoran asylum cases. The author's congregation, Wellington Avenue United Church of Christ was one of the plaintiffs in this case.)

149. Brown, "Healing."

150. Karen Armstrong, Sacred Nature, 119.

151. Roiphe, "Nehemiah," 484.

152. LaCocque, Work, 39.

of subversive stories provide sustenance to make that choice to do well in these tempestuous times.

CONCLUSION

Three Trials of Innocence—one in the past whose guilty verdict of failing to do well led to hopes of a second Trial of Innocence which has only partly been fulfilled. Over time, however, promises are forgotten, a fusion of power and a loss of memory has often led to a failure to do well. The subversive stories reject a single unified power, but instead, celebrate a universalism and egalitarianism that welcomes the foreigner. Indeed, they look to foreigners to contribute to a history that is incomplete without their presence. As Texas Governor Abbot uncurls concertina barbed wire on the banks of the Rio Grande and wraps buoys with barbed wire in international waters of the river, each of us is called to decide on which side of the barbed wire we stand.[153] Ruth and Esther, Job, and Jesus provide one choice; Ezra Nehemiah another.

Professor Mikva correctly notes that this debate is not new, but it is also correct that it has not finished. LaCocque's assertion that each of us faces a trial of innocence to do well or to not do well requires that we engage biblical criticism and the text to decide. The dominant culture does not cede its power easily. It threatens anarchy should we grant too many exceptions and accommodations to religious liberty[154] and fuels fear of an alleged invasion of dehumanized migrants that must be repelled. It relies, in part, on its reading of Ezra-Nehemiah's concern for law and exclusion. But as LaCocque argues, the text interprets us even as we seek understanding.[155] The dominant culture included subversive stories in the canon as evidence of an inbreaking of God's promise of justice for all. Esther, Ruth, Job, and Jesus break through the barriers of the nation-states' promise of security at the expense of the Other and reveal a call to a justice of inclusion. With the barbed wire at the border, we must decide on what side we

---

153. Goodman, "Texas."

154. Justice Antonin Scalia wrote, "Fearing rule permitting relatively easy exception to a nation's laws based on requests for religious accommodation "would be courting anarchy, but that danger increases in direct proportion to the society's diversity of religious beliefs..." *Emp. Div., Dep't of Hum. Res. of Oregon v. Smith*, 494 U.S. 872, 888, 110 S. Ct. 1595, 1605, 108 L. Ed. 2d 876 (1990). See also, Marty, Gyres, 663.

155. LaCocque, *Ruth*, 154.

will find ourselves standing, "each must stand before the divine tribunal, and there we know that there is justice. It is a justice, however, that does not condemn but welcomes."[156]

If we seek to live the justice of Ruth, Esther, and Jesus and seek God's peace and justice, we will fulfill nonrefoulement. Indeed, if we reach out and further seek ways to reduce the many factors that force people to flee their lands, to avoid the destruction of the environment that turns fertile land into deserts and lakes into dry beds, if we "give others a chance to live with dignity in a land and place of their own"[157] we may eliminate the very need of the promise of nonrefoulement. When combined with a more just legal system, we will hear the biblical promise reiterated by André LaCocque, "The end is not tragic for, according to an insight of the ancient rabbis and backed up by all the biblical tradition, the last divine word they heard in Eden (3:19), *tasub ('you shall return!')* is still ringing in the ears of Adam and Eve."[158]

BIBLIOGRAPHY

Abramowitz, Alan, and Jennifer McCoy. "United States: Racial Resentment, Negative Partisanship, and Polarization in Trump's America." *The Annals of the American Academy of Political and Social Science* 681.1 (2019) 137–56. https://doi.org/10.1177/0002716218811309.

Al-Kire, R. et al. "Protecting America's Borders: Christian Nationalism, Threat, and Attitudes toward Immigrants in the United States." *Group Processes & Intergroup Relations* 25 (2022) 354–78. https://doi.org/10.1177/1368430220978291.

American Bar Association. "Achieving America's Immigration Promise." (2021) 1–49. https://www.americanbar.org/content/dam/aba/administrative/immigration/achieving_americas_immigration_promise.pdf.

Appleseed Foundation. "Assembly Line Injustice." (May 2009) 1–36. http://www.chicagoappleseed.org/wp-content/uploads/2015/10/Assembly-Line-Injustice-2009.pdf.

Arendt, Hannah. "We Refugees." *Menorah Journal* 31 (1943) 69–77 in *Amro Ali*, (April 2017). https://amroali.com/tag/arendt/.

———. *The Origins of Totalitarianism*. New ed. with added prefaces. San Diego: Harvest, 1968.

Arnold, Kathleen R. "Sanctuary in a Trumpist Context: Creating Spaces of Democratic Exception." *Political Research Quarterly* 75 (2022) 1173–85. https://journals.sagepub.com/doi/epub/10.1177/10659129211052493/.

Bailey, Sarah Pulliam. "'God Is not against Building Walls!' The Sermon Trump Heard from Robert Jeffress before His Inauguration." *Washington Post*, January 20, 2017.

---

156. Jennings, *Outlaw*, 206.
157. Roiphe, "Nehemiah," 484.
158. LaCocque, *Innocence*, 31.

https://www.washingtonpost.com/news/acts-of-faith/wp/2017/01/20/god-is-not-against-building-walls-the-sermon-donald-trump-heard-before-his-inauguration/.

Baldwin, Joyce, G. *Esther: An Introduction and Commentary*. Downers Grove, IL: InterVarsity, 1984.

Blair, Leonardo. "Jeff Sessions, Sanders Cite Bible in Defense of Border Policy Separating Children from Families." *The Christian Post* (June 15, 2018). https://www.christianpost.com/news/jeff-sessions-sanders-cite-bible-defense-border-policy-separating-children-families.html/.

Brown, Rev. Dr. Beth. "Keynote: Healing, Hope and Humanity," Community Renewal Society Annual Meeting (November 9, 2023). https://www.communityrenewalsociety.org/videos/v/2023ama (at 30:20).

Bubola, Emma. "Children of Jailed Narges Mohammadi Accept Her Nobel Peace Prize." *New York Times*, December 10, 2023. https://www.nytimes.com/2023/12/10/world/middleeast/narges-mohammadi-nobel-peace-prize-ceremony.html/.

Centre National de Ressources Textuelles et Lexicales, refouler. I.B.1. https://www.cnrtl.fr/definition/refouler.

Chappell, Bill, and Hernandez, Joe. "Why Iranian women are burning their hijabs after the death of Mahsa Amini." *The New York Times*, September 21, 2022. https://www.npr.org/2022/09/21/1124237272/mahsa-amini-iran-women-protest-hijab-morality-police/.

Chase, Jeffrey S. "The Immigration Court: Issues and Solutions." (March 28, 2019). https://www.jeffreyschase.com/blog/2019/3/28/i6el1do6l5p443u1nkf8vwr28dv9qi/.

Convention Relating to the Status of Refugees, July 28, 1951, 189 U.N.T.S. 150. https://www.unhcr.org/media/convention-and-protocol-relating-status-refugees/.

Drollinger, Ralph. "Better Understanding of the Fallacy of Christian Nationalism." *Capitol Ministries* (September 18, 2023). https://capmin.org/better-understanding-fallacy-christian-nationalism-ralph-drollinger/.

———. "Letter to the Cabinet, Senate, and House Bible Studies," (January 26, 2019). https://capmin.org/wp-content/uploads/2019/01/The-Bible-and-The-Wall-by-Ralph-Drollinger-2019.pdf.

Gabriel, Trip. "Trump Escalates Anti-Immigrant Rhetoric With 'Poisoning the Blood' Comment." *The New York Times*, October 5, 2023. https://www.nytimes.com/2023/10/05/us/politics/trump-immigration-rhetoric.html/.

Gaffney, Edward McGlynn, Jr. "Full and Free Exercise of Religion." In *Religious Organization in the United States, A Study of Identity, Liberty, and the Law*, edited by James A. Serritella et al., 773–810. Durham, NC: Carolina Academic 2006.

Gedicks, Frederick Mark, and Roger Hendrix. "Uncivil Religion: Judeo-Christianity and the Ten Commandments." *West Virginia Law Review* 110 (2007) 275ff. https://digitalcommons.law.byu.edu/faculty_scholarship/316/.

Goodman, J. David. "Texas Will Expand Effort to Control Land along Mexican Border, Abbott Says." *The New York Times*, February 4, 2024. https://www.nytimes.com/2024/02/04/us/texas-border-abbott-governors.html/.

Gross, Daniel A. "The U.S. Government Turned Away Thousands of Jewish Refugees, Fearing That They Were Nazi Spies." *Smithsonian* (November 18, 2015) 1–8. https://www.smithsonianmag.com/history/us-government-turned-away-thousands-jewish-refugees-fearing-they-were-nazi-spies-180957324/.

Hoiphe, Anne. "Nehemiah." In *Congregation, Contemporary Writers Read the Jewish Bible*, edited by David Rosenberg, 473–88. San Diego: Harcourt Brace Jovanovich, 1987.

Immigration Policy Tracking Project. https://immpolicytracking.org/home/.
Jennings, Theodore W., Jr. *Outlaw Justice, The Messianic Politics of Paul*. Stanford: Stanford University Press 2013.
Jeffress, Dr. Robert P. "America Is a Christian Nation." https://firstdallas.org/america-is-a-christian-nation/.
Johnson, Mike. "Speaker Johnson and House Republicans Visit Southern Border to Highlight Biden Administration and Senate Democrat Refusal to Address Crisis." U.S. Congressman Mike Johnson Press Release. (January 3, 2024). https://mikejohnson.house.gov/news/documentsingle.aspx?DocumentID=1353.
Jones, Reece. *Nobody Is Protected: How the Border Patrol Became the Most Dangerous Police Force in the United States*. Berkeley: Counterpoint, 2022.
Jones-Correa, Michael and de Graauw, Els, "The Illegality Trap: The Politics of Immigration & the Lens of Illegality." *Daedalus* 142 (2013) 185–98. https://www.jstor.org/stable/4329725/.
Kerwin, D. and Kerwin, B. "What Will It Take to Eliminate the Immigration Court Backlog? Assessing 'Judge Team' Hiring Needs Based on Changed Conditions and the Need for Broader Reform." *Journal on Migration and Human Security* (January 29, 2024). https://doi.org/10.1177/23315024241226645.
Koppelman, Andrew, "The Increasingly Dangerous Variants of the 'Most-Favored-Nation' Theory of Religious Liberty." *Iowa Law Review* 108 (2023) 2237ff. https://ilr.law.uiowa.edu/volume-108-issue-5/2023/07/increasingly-dangerous-variants-most-favored-nation-theory-religious-liberty/.
LaCocque, André. *But as for Me: The Question of Election for God's People*. Atlanta: John Knox, 1979.
———. "The Deconstruction of Job's Fundamentalism." *JBL* 126 (2007) 83–97. https://doi.org/10.2307/27638421.
———. *Esther Regina: A Bakhtinian Reading*. Evanston, IL: Northwestern University Press, 2008.
———. *The Feminine Unconventional: Four Subversive Figures in Israel's Tradition*. Overtures to Biblical Theology. 1990. Reprint, Eugene, OR: Wipf & Stock, 2005.
———. "God after Auschwitz: A Contribution to Contemporary Theology." *JES* 33 (1996) 1–2. https://web-p-ebscohost-com.ezproxy.depaul.edu/ehost/detail/detail?vid=2&sid=c127f47b-5e91-41b2-bd63-b5f30f07b698%40redis&bdata=JnNpdGU9ZWhvc3QtbGl2ZSZzY29wZT1zaXRl#AN=107457&db=a9h.
———. *Jesus the Central Jew: His Times and his People*. Early Christianity and Its Literature 15. Atlanta: SBL, 2015.
———. "Justice for the Innocent Job!" *BibInt* 19 (2011) 19–32.
———. *Onslaught against Innocence: Cain, Abel, and the Yahwist*. Eugene, OR: Cascade Books, 2008.
———. *Ruth: A Continental Commentary*. Translated by K.C. Hanson. Continental Commentaries. Minneapolis: Fortress, 2004.
———. *Romance, She Wrote: A Hermeneutical Essay on Song of Songs*. Harrisburg, PA: Trinity, 1998.
———. *The Trial of Innocence: Adam, Eve, and the Yahwist*. Eugene, OR: Cascade Books, 2006.
———. *Work and Creativity: A Philosophical Study from Creation to Postmodernity*. Lanham, MD: Lexington, 2020.

———. II Zacharie. In *Aggée, Zacharie, Malachie*. Commentaires de l'Ancien Testament XIc. Neuchâtel-Paris: Delachaux et Niestlé, 1981.

Little, David. "Does the Human Right to Freedom of Conscience, Religion, and Belief Have Special Status?" 2001 B.Y.U. L. Rev. 603 (2001). https://digitalcommons.law.byu.edu/lawreview/vol2001/iss2/8/.

Lustgarten, Abram, "The Great Climate Migration Has Begun." *The New York Times*, July 7, 2020. https://www.nytimes.com/interactive/2020/07/23/magazine/climate-migration.html/.

Malkki, Liisa H. "Refugees and Exile: From 'Refugee Studies' to the National Order of Things." *Annual Review Anthropology* 24 (1995) 495–523. https://www-annualreviews-org.ezproxy.depaul.edu/doi/pdf/10.1146/annurev.an.24.100195.002431/.

Marks, Danna Leigh. "Immigrant Courts Should Be Independent—Not an Arm of the Administration." *Prospect* (April 24, 2017). https://prospect.org/justice/immigrant-courts-independent-arm-administration/.

Marty, Martin E. "The Widening Gyres of Religion and Law." *DePaul Law Review* 45 (1996) 651–75. https://via.library.depaul.edu/law-review/vol45/iss3/4/.

McCoy, J. et al. "Polarization and the Global Crisis of Democracy: Common Patterns, Dynamics, and Pernicious Consequences for Democratic Polities." *American Behavioral Scientist* 62 (2018) 16–42. https://doi-org.ezproxy.depaul.edu/10.1177/0002764218759576/.

Migration Policy Institute. "U.S. Annual Refugee Resettlement Ceilings and Number of Refugees Admitted, 1980–Present." 2023. https://www.migrationpolicy.org/programs/data-hub/charts/us-refugee-resettlement/.

Mikva, Rachel S. "Christian Nationalism Is a Threat, and not Just from Capitol Attackers Invoking Jesus." *USA Today*, January 31, 2021. https://www.usatoday.com/story/opinion/2021/01/31/christian-nationalism-josh-hawley-ted-cruz-capitol-attack-column/4292193001/.

———. *Dangerous Religious Ideas: The Deep Roots of Self-Critical Faith in Judaism, Christianity, and Islam*. Boston: Beacon, 2020.

Miller, Todd. "More Than a Wall: Corporate Profiteering and the Militarization of US Borders. *Transnational Institute* (September 2019). file:///Users/cmousin/Downloads/more-than-a-wall-report.pdf/.

Montoya-Galvez, Camilo. "Texas Defies Federal Demand That It Abandon Border Area, Setting up Legal Showdown." *CBS News*, January 18, 2024. https://www.cbsnews.com/news/texas-border-us-mexico-ken-paxton-attorney-general/?hsmi=29072423 1&hsenc=p2ANqtz-887x3gEkKvRtRXexGY34v_QvxF3fdxqJ2FrQSp_16Rk9lnps1 NoyfXvPi63bRD66py673wAEeRYiC3CPFgDvIT_xMD8w/.

Mooney, Michael J. "Trump's Apostle." *Texas Monthly* (August 2019). https://www.texasmonthly.com/news-politics/donald-trump-defender-dallas-pastor-robert-jeffress/.

Mousin, Craig B., "Can One Still Call It Ignorance or Improper Bias?" In *Migration and Religious Freedom: Essays on the Interaction Between Religious Duty and Immigration Law*, edited by Carolus Grütters and Dario Dzananovic, 71–100. Nijmegen: Wolf Legal, 2018. https://papers.ssrn.com/sol3/papers.cfm?abstract_id=3329604/.

———. "Constantine's Legacy: Preserving Empire While Undermining International Law." In *Christianity and International Law: An Introduction*, edited by P. Slotte and J. Haskell, 366–94. Cambridge studies in Law and christianity. Cambridge: Cambridge

University Press, 2021. https://papers.ssrn.com/sol3/papers.cfm?abstract_id=3960335.

———. "Standing with the Persecuted: Adjudicating Religious Asylum Claims after the Enactment of the International Religious Freedom Act of 1968." *BYU Law Review* (2003) 541. https://digitalcommons.law.byu.edu/lawreview/vol2003/iss2/5/.

———. "You Were Told to Love the Immigrant, but What If the Story Never Happened? Hospitality and United States Immigration Law." *Vincentian Heritage* 33 (2016) art. 8. https://papers.ssrn.com/sol3/papers.cfm?abstract_id=2784951/.

Musalo, Karen, "The Legal and Moral Responsibility to Protect." *Fordham International Law Journal* 45 (2022) 751–79. https://repository.uclawsf.edu/cgi/viewcontent.cgi?article=2877&context=faculty_scholarship/.

Musalo, Karen et al. *Refugee Law and Policy: A Comparative and International Approach*. 5th ed. Durham, NC: Carolina Academic (2018).

National Immigrant Justice Center. "Analysis: Senate Supplemental Funding Bill Is an Affront to Refugee Protection." 2–3 (February 5, 2024). https://immigrantjustice.org/ssites/default/files/content-type/press-release/documents/2024-02/NIJC-Analysis-Border-Provisions-2024%20Supplemental_February-5-2024.pdf?eType=EmailBlastContent&eId=23921fa2-2c41-4b5a-8614-348c30a59087/.

Nayeri, Dina, *The Ungrateful Refugee: What Immigrants Never Tell You*. New York: Catapult, 2019.

Office of the High Commissioner for Human Rights. "The Principle of Non-refoulment under International Human Rights Law." https://www.ohchr.org/sites/default/files/Documents/Issues/Migration/GlobalCompactMigration/ThePrincipleNon-RefoulementUnderInternationalHumanRightsLaw.pdf/.

Office of the United Nations Commissioner for Refugees. "Convention and Protocol Relating to the Status of Refugees." Geneva (December 2010). https://www.unhcr.org/media/convention-and-protocol-relating-status-refugees/.

Owens, Tess. "Trump Vows to Block Immigrants Who 'Don't Like Our Religion.'" *Vice News*, October 24, 2023. https://www.vice.com/en/article/bvjpv8/trump-immigration-christian-nationalism/.

Rabey, Steve, "With FlashPoint Live: Roster of Pentecostal 'Prophets' Hits the Road for Trump." *RNS*, February 2, 2024. https://religionnews.com/2024/02/02/with-flashpoint-live-familiar-roster-of-pentecostal-preachers-hits-the-road-for-trump/.

Savage, Charlie et al "Sweeping Raids, Giant Camps and Mass Deportations: Inside Trump's 2025 Immigration Plans." *New York Times*, November 11, 2023. https://www.nytimes.com/2023/11/11/us/politics/trump-2025-immigration-agenda.html/.

Schmidt, Paul Wickham. "From the Heights of Kasinga to the Depths of America's Deadly Star Chambers: Will the Biden Administration Tap the New Due Process Army to Fix EOIR & Save Our Nation?" (November 12, 2020). https://immigrationcourtside.com/2020/11/12/from-the-heights-of-kasinga-to-the-depths-of-americas-deadly-star-chambers-will-the-biden-administration-tap-the-new-due-process-army-to-fix-eoir-save-our-nation/.

Schrag, Philip G., et al., "The New Border Asylum Adjudication System: Speed, Fairness, and the Representation Problem." *Howard Law Journal* 66.3 (2023) 571ff. https://papers.ssrn.com/sol3/papers.cfm?abstract_id=4233655/.

Sharpless, Rebecca, and Kristi E. Wintermeyer, M.D. "Human Frailty, Unbreakable Victims, and Asylum." *Columbia Human Rights Law Review* 54 (2023) 726–79. https://hrlr.law.columbia.edu/files/2023/05/Sharpless-Finalized-5.23.23.pdf.

Stillman, Sarah, "The Race to Dismantle Trump's Immigration Policies." *The New Yorker*, February 1, 2021. http://www.newyorkercom/magazine/2021/02/08/.

TRAC Immigration. "Asylum Decisions Vary Widely Across Judges and Courts –Latest Results." (January 30, 2020). https://trac.syr.edu/immigration/reports/590/.

TRAC Immigration. "Asylum Law, Asylum Seekers and Refugees: A Primer." (August 7, 2006). https://trac.syr.edu/immigration/reports/161/.

TRAC Immigration. "Judge-by-Judge Asylum Decisions in Immigration Courts FY 2018–2023" (October 19, 2023). https://trac.syr.edu/immigration/reports/judgereports/.

TRAC Immigration. "Too Few Immigration Attorneys: Average Representation Rates Fall from 65% To 30%." (January 24, 2024). https://trac.syr.edu/reports/736/.

Tsankov, Mini. "An Article I Immigration Court." *AILA Law Journal* (Full Court, Fastcase, Inc.) 5.2 (2023) 121–36. https://www.aila.org/library/aila-law-journal-an-article-i-immigration-court/.

UN High Commissioner for Refugees (UNHCR). Handbook on Procedures and Criteria for Determining Refugee Status under the 1951 Convention and the 1967 Protocol Relating to the Status of Refugees. (reissued February 2019). https://www.unhcr.org/media/handbook-procedures-and-criteria-determining-refugee-status-under-1951-convention-and-1967/.

———. *The Refugee Convention, 1951: The Travaux Préparatoires Analysed with a Commentary by Dr. Paul Weis*. 1990. https://www.unhcr.org/us/media/refugee-convention-1951-travaux-preparatoires-analysed-commentary-dr-paul-weis/.

Walter, Barbara F. *How Civil Wars Start and How to Stop Them*. New York: Crown 2022.

Wang, Xia "Religion as Disobedience." 76 Vanderbilt Law Review 76 (2023) 999ff. https://vanderbiltlawreview.org/lawreview/2023/05/religion-as-disobedience/.

Wyman, David S. *Abandonment of the Jews: America and the Holocaust, 1941–1945*. New York: Pantheon, 1984.

Yahil, Leni. *The Holocaust: The Fate of European Jewry, 1932–1945*. Oxford: Oxford University Press, 1987.

Books of André LaCocque[1]

FRENCH

1960 "Israël Moderne et Prophétie." In *Hommage à Wilhelm Vischer: Maqqel Shaqedh, La Branche d'Amandier*, edited by Jean Cadier, 114–26. Montpillier: Causse Graille, Castelman.

1964 *Pérennité d'Israël: Croire, Penser, Espérer*. Geneva: Labor et Fides.

1967 *Le Devenir de Dieu: Commentaire Biblique*. Paris: Delachaux.

1968 *Martin Buber: L'Homme et le Philosophe*. Collaboration of Gabriel Marcel, Emmanuel Levinas, André LaCocque. Collection du Centre national des hautes études juives. Brussels: Éditions de l'Institut de sociologie de l'Université libre de Bruxelle.

1976 *Le Livre de Daniel*. Commentaire de l'Ancien Testament 15b. Paris: Delachaux & Niestlé.

1981 *Malachie* in *Aggée, Zacharie 1–8, Zacharie 9–14, Malachie*. Samuel Amsler, André LaCocque, René Vuilleumier. Paris: Delachaux et Niestlé.

1984 *Daniel et son Temps: Recherches sur le Mouvement Apocalyptique Juif au IIe Siècle avant Jésus-Christ*. Monde de la Bible 8. Geneva: Labor et Fides.

---

1. Courtesy of Elizabeth Brunner, daughter of André LaCocque.

1988   *Malachie* in *Aggée, Zachary 1–8, Zachary 9–14, Malachie*. S. Ampler, A. LaCocque, R. Vuilleumier. 2nd ed. Geneva: Labor et Fides.

1989   *Le Complexe de Jonas: Une Étude Psycho-Religieuse du Prophète*. With Pierre-Emmanuel LaCocque. Paris: Cerf.

1992   *Subversives, ou un Pentateuque de Femmes*. Lectio Divina 148. Paris: Cerf.

1998   *Penser la Bible*. With Paul Ricoeur. La Couleur des Idées. Paris: Seuil.

2004   *Le Livre de Ruth*. Commentaire de l'Ancien Testament. Geneva: Labor et Fides.

2005   Editor. *Guide des nouvelles lectures de la Bible*. Paris: Bayard.

2023   *Travail et créativité*. Paris: Cerf.

ENGLISH

1975   *Pentecost 1*. With Morris J. Niedenthal. Philadelphia: Fortress.

1979   *The Book of Daniel*. Translated by David Pellauer. Atlanta: John Knox.

1979   *But as for Me: The Question of Election in the Life of God's People Today*. Atlanta: John Knox.

1981   *The Jonah Complex*. With Pierre-Emmanuel LaCocque. Atlanta: John Knox.

1988   *Daniel in His Time*. Studies in the Personalities of the Old Testament. Columbia: University of South Carolina Press.

1990   *The Feminine Unconventional: Four Subversive Figures in Israel's Tradition*. Overtures to Biblical Theology. Minneapolis: Fortress.

1990   *Jonah: A Psycho-Religious Approach to the Prophet*. With Pierre-Emmanuel LaCocque. Studies in the Personalities of the Old Testament. Columbia: University of South Carolina Press.

1994   Editor. *Commitment and Commemoration: Jews, Christians, Muslims in Dialogue*. Chicago: Exploration Press.

1998   *Romance, She Wrote: A Hermeneutical Essay on Song of Songs*. Harrisburg, PA: Trinity

2003 *Thinking Biblically: Exegetical and Hermeneutical Studies*. Translated by David Pellauer. Chicago: University of Chicago Press.

2004 *Ruth: A Continental Commentary*. Translated by K. C. Hanson. Continental Commentaries. Minneapolis: Fortress.

2005 *The Feminine Unconventional: Four Subversive Figures in Israel's Tradition*. Reprint, Eugene, OR: Wipf & Stock.

2006 *The Trial of Innocence: Adam, Eve, and the Yahwist*. Eugene, OR: Cascade Books.

2008 *Esther Regina: A Bakhtinian Reading*. Rethinking Theory. Evanston, IL: Northwestern University Press.

2008 *Onslaught Against Innocence: Cain, Abel, and the Yahwist*. Eugene, OR: Cascade Books.

2010 *Captivity of Innocence: Babel and the Yahwist*. Eugene, OR: Cascade Books.

2015 *Jesus the Central Jew: His Times and His People*. Early Christianity and Its Literature 15. Atlanta: SBL Press.

2018 *The Book of Daniel*, 2nd ed. Cascade Books.

2020 *Work and Creativity: A Philosophical Study from Creation to Postmodernity*. Lanham, MD: Lexington.

www.ingramcontent.com/pod-product-compliance
Lightning Source LLC
Chambersburg PA
CBHW051744230426
43670CB00012B/2150